Reason and Explanation

Palgrave Innovations in Philosophy

Series Editors: **Vincent F. Hendricks**, University of Copenhagen and Columbia University in New York and **Duncan Pritchard**, University of Edinburgh.

Titles include:

Mikkel Gerken
EPISTEMIC REASONING AND THE MENTAL

Kevin Meeker
HUME'S RADICAL SCEPTICISM AND THE FATE OF NATURALIZED EPISTEMOLOGY

Ted Poston
REASON AND EXPLANATION: A Defense of Explanatory Coherentism

Forthcoming titles:

J. Adam Carter
THE PROSPECTS FOR RELATIVISM IN EPISTEMOLOGY

E. J. Coffman
LUCK: Its Nature and Significance for Human Knowledge and Agency

Annalisa Coliva
THE VARIETIES OF SELF-KNOWLEDGE

Julian Kiverstein
THE SIGNIFICANCE OF PHENOMENOLOGY

Jonathan Matheson
THE EPISTEMIC SIGNIFICANCE OF DISAGREEMENT

Aidan McGlynn
KNOWLEDGE FIRST?

David Pedersen
POLITICAL EPISTEMOLOGY: Epistemic Theories and Knowledge Institutions

Christopher Pincock and Sandra Lapointe (*editors*)
INNOVATIONS IN THE HISTORY OF ANALYTICAL PHILOSOPHY

John Turri
THE KNOWLEDGE ACCOUNT OF ASSERTION

Palgrave Innovations in Philosophy
Series Standing Order ISBN 978–0–230–36085–3 (hardback)
(*outside North America only*)

You can receive future titles in this series as they are published by placing a standing order. Please contact your bookseller or, in case of difficulty, write to us at the address below with your name and address, the title of the series and the ISBN quoted above.

Customer Services Department, Macmillan Distribution Ltd, Houndmills, Basingstoke, Hampshire RG21 6XS, England

Reason and Explanation

A Defense of Explanatory Coherentism

Ted Poston

palgrave
macmillan

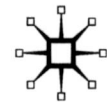

© Ted L. Poston 2014

All rights reserved. No reproduction, copy or transmission of this publication may be made without written permission.

No portion of this publication may be reproduced, copied or transmitted save with written permission or in accordance with the provisions of the Copyright, Designs and Patents Act 1988, or under the terms of any licence permitting limited copying issued by the Copyright Licensing Agency, Saffron House, 6–10 Kirby Street, London EC1N 8TS.

Any person who does any unauthorized act in relation to this publication may be liable to criminal prosecution and civil claims for damages.

The author has asserted his right to be identified as the author of this work in accordance with the Copyright, Designs and Patents Act 1988.

First published 2014 by
PALGRAVE MACMILLAN

Palgrave Macmillan in the UK is an imprint of Macmillan Publishers Limited, registered in England, company number 785998, of Houndmills, Basingstoke, Hampshire RG21 6XS.

Palgrave Macmillan in the US is a division of St Martin's Press LLC, 175 Fifth Avenue, New York, NY 10010.

Palgrave Macmillan is the global academic imprint of the above companies and has companies and representatives throughout the world.

Palgrave® and Macmillan® are registered trademarks in the United States, the United Kingdom, Europe and other countries

ISBN: 978–1–137–01225–8

A catalogue record for this book is available from the British Library.

A catalog record for this book is available from the Library of Congress.

Transferred to Digital Printing in 2014

Contents

Series Editors' Preface   viii

Preface   ix

1 Introduction   1
   1.1 A brief history of coherentism   2
   1.2 Two traditional objections to coherentism   8
      1.2.1 The input objection   8
      1.2.2 Alternative systems objection   10
   1.3 Overview   12

2 Epistemic Conservatism   18
   2.1 The anti-conservative probability argument   21
   2.2 Conservative justification and warranted assertion   28
   2.3 Conservatism and autobiographical epistemology   30
   2.4 The extra boost and conversion objections   34
      2.4.1 The extra boost objection   34
      2.4.2 Conversion objections   36
   2.5 Conservatism and the perspectival character of justification   38
      2.5.1 The argument from perspective   39
      2.5.2 Two challenges   41
   2.6 Conclusion   44

3 Reasons without First Philosophy   45
   3.1 The basic reasons dilemma   46
      3.1.1 The first horn   46
      3.1.2 The second horn   48
   3.2 The argument against first philosophy   49
      3.2.1 The nature of basic reasons   49
      3.2.2 No first philosophy   52
   3.3 Framework reasons   56
   3.4 Weak foundationalism and framework reasons   62
   3.5 Bergmann on foundationalism and epistemic circularity   64
   3.6 Conclusion   68

4 Explanation and Justification   69
   4.1 Explanation and its virtues   70

		4.1.1	Three arguments for primitiveness	73
		4.1.2	The virtues of explanation	80
	4.2	An explanationist theory of justification		85
		4.2.1	The goal	86
		4.2.2	The Ex-J account	87
		4.2.3	Ex-J and mentalism	91
		4.2.4	Ex-J and evidentialism	92
		4.2.5	Ex-J and propositional and doxastic justification	95
	4.3	Supporting cases and putative counterexamples		96
		4.3.1	Case-by-case comparison	96
		4.3.2	Putative counterexamples	102
	4.4	Conclusion		109
5	BonJour and the Myth of the Given			110
	5.1	BonJour's anti-foundationalist argument and the Sellarsian dilemma		111
	5.2	BonJour's new foundationalism		115
		5.2.1	BonJour's nonconceptualism	116
		5.2.2	Nonconceptualism and justification	118
	5.3	The phenomenal concept strategy		121
	5.4	Conclusion		128
6	Is Foundational A Priori Justification Indispensable?			129
	6.1	BonJour's indispensability arguments		130
		6.1.1	Observation-transcendent inference	131
		6.1.2	Putative a priori truths and the parade argument	133
		6.1.3	Reasoning	136
		6.1.4	Taking stock	138
	6.2	BonJour's anti-coherence objection		139
		6.2.1	Explanationism and noncontradiction	140
		6.2.2	Coherence and circularity	140
		6.2.3	Coherence and presupposition	142
	6.3	Coherence and awareness		145
	6.4	Conclusion		148
7	Bayesian Explanationism			149
	7.1	Bayesianism		150
		7.1.1	An introduction to Bayesianism	151
		7.1.2	Arguments for Bayesianism	154
		7.1.3	Examples of Bayesian unification	161

		7.1.4 Summary	166
7.2	Are Bayesianism and IBE compatible?		167
	7.2.1	Van Fraassen's incompatibility argument	168
	7.2.2	The Heuristic view	169
7.3	Bayesian explanationism		174
7.4	Explaining or representing?		179

Bibliography 182

Index 189

Series Editors' Preface

Palgrave Innovations in Philosophy is a series of short monographs. Each book will constitute the 'new wave' of pure or applied philosophy, both in terms of its topic and the research angle, and will be concerned with 'hot' new research areas in philosophy and its neighbouring intellectual disciplines. These monographs will provide an overview of an emerging area while at the same time significantly advancing the debate on this topic and giving the reader a sense of where this debate might be heading next. While the series will devote attention to core topics of philosophy, it will also feature books with an interdisciplinary outlook, as we believe that many of the most exciting developments in our discipline involve a fusion of philosophy with other subjects.

Vincent Hendricks, Copenhagen
Duncan Pritchard, Edinburgh

Preface

The guiding idea of this book is that a person's normative standing in the space of reasons is constituted by her explanatory standing. Thus, the ultimate justification of a person's beliefs is constituted by how well those beliefs fit into a virtuous explanatory system which beats relevant competitors. Epistemic justification is holistic because it depends on the facts about a subject's entire explanatory position. This book presents a case that a belief's epistemic justification is determined by the explanatory virtues of a subject's entire system of beliefs.

Writing a book is a community project. Ideas are presented, debated, refined, debated some more, and refined yet again. The final process combines insights from many philosophers. I am grateful for the outstanding comments I have received on this project from many superb philosophers. I thank audiences at Northwestern University, Vanderbilt University, Rutgers University, the Alabama Philosophical Society, the Orange Beach Epistemology Workshop, the Central States Philosophical Association, the Southeastern Epistemological Conference, and the American Philosophical Association. For helpful and probative comments along the way of developing this project, I am indebted to Selim Berker, David Black, Brit Brogaard, Adam Carter, David Christensen, Trent Dougherty, Mylan Engel, Branden Fitelson, William Fleisher, Richard Fumerton, Alvin Goldman, Ali Hasan, David Henderson, Mike Huemer, Tom Kelly, Peter Klein, Jonathan Kvanvig, Eric Loomis, William Lycan, Jon Matheson, Kevin McCain, Matthew McGrath, Kevin Meeker, Lisa Miracchi, Brad Monton, Andrew Moon, Erik Olsson, Jim Pryor, Bill Roche, Jeff Roland, Daniel Rubio, Bruce Russell, Jonah Schupbach, Jonathan Schaffer, Ernest Sosa, Matthias Steup, Kurt Sylvan, Josh Thurow, Christopher Tucker, John Turri, Michael Williams, and Chase Wrenn. I thank the Chicago Cubs for keeping it real. I owe special thanks to the University of South Alabama who provided funding for a sabbatical leave to finish this project, as well as to Ernest Sosa and Rutgers University for hosting my sabbatical leave. This manuscript improved considerably from the comments I received at Rutgers University. I am especially grateful to fellow Alabama explanationist Kevin McCain who provided tremendously helpful comments on the entire manuscript. Finally, I owe more than I can state to my wife Christine who has been a constant source of love and encouragement. This project would not have been possible without her support.

Several of the following chapters are adapted from previously published work. Chapter 2 is a significantly revised version of Poston (2012b). Chapter 3 is based on Poston (2012a). The arguments of both papers are significant reworked. Chapter 5 "BonJour and the Myth of the Given" is based on Poston (2013a). Chapter 6 "Is A Priori Justification Indispensible?" is based on Poston (2013b, 2014).

1
Introduction

> A coherent Thinker, and a strict Reasoner, is not to be made at once by a Set of Rules.
> I. Watts *Logick* 1725
>
> Be plain and coherent.
> Dickens *Dombey and Son* 1848
>
> It is reason's proper work to provide us with a maximum of explanatory coherence and comprehensiveness
> Sosa *Knowledge in Perspective* 1991

Epistemic coherentism has not merited much attention throughout the history of philosophy. Two explanations for this neglect stand out. First, when a statement is challenged one defends it by citing another statement. This aspect of how to respond to challenges in specific contexts leads to the thought that the structure of epistemic justification corresponds to the structure of responding to challenges in a specific context. Socrates' persistent search for particular reasons or Descartes' method of doubt manifests this natural tendency. Both search for reason's proper ground in some unchallengeable propositions whose epistemic merits is independent of any particular perspective. It is natural to extend this pragmatic feature of the activity of justifying belief to the state of being justified in one's beliefs. This natural search for reason's proper grounding obscures the plausibility of epistemic coherentism.

The second reason coherentism has been neglected lies in the assumptions undergirding the traditional regress argument. The regress problem presented by Aristotle and subsequent philosophers offers three non-skeptical options to the general question *how is any claim justified?*: circles, regresses, or foundations. Do we start with some controversial claim and defend it by reasoning through many propositions which eventually loop back to the original claim? Does reason continue forever? Or do we reason to some claim which provides a reason without itself requiring a reason? Of these non-skeptical options foundationalism seems the most plausible; a claim is justified by being basic or inferred from basic beliefs. But these reasons support a foundationalist epistemology only if they exhaust the plausible options. Yet as many coherentists have pointed out there is a fourth non-skeptical option: holism, the support of any particular claim is a matter of how well the claim is supported by everything else within the relevant system. Justification is not foundational because any specific claim requires a reason. Justification does not require an infinite regress because holistic support does not require an infinite number of non-repeating claims. And justification is not circular because holistic support is different from circular arguments. It is up to the specific holist view to say more precisely how justification works. My task in this book is to defend an explanatory coherentist form of holism. I contend that a subject's propositional justification for any claim is a matter of how that claim fits into a virtuous explanatory system that beats relevant competitors.

1.1 A brief history of coherentism

Holism is a historically curious view. Metaphysical holistic views arose alongside idealism. The idealists resist a dualism of mind and world, insisting that reality is fundamentally mental. Idealists reject the correspondence theory of truth according to which a true statement corresponds to some fact. On idealist views the truth of a statement consists in its coherence with other statements. This metaphysical form of holism, though, has dubious connections with confirmational holism, also known as *epistemic coherentism*. That epistemological view arose within the pragmatist tradition and upon reflection on the revolutions in the formal and physical sciences of the late nineteenth and early twentieth centuries.[1]

Epistemic coherentism is the view that a statement's justification—its acceptability for the purposes of getting at the truth and avoiding error—consists in its overall coherence or fit with the rest of accepted statements. Otto Neurath expresses this by the simile of rebuilding a raft at sea. The process of epistemic improvement is like rebuilding a

---

[1] William Alston (1983, 73) observes that both absolute idealists and the mid-twentieth-century pragmatists argued against immediate awareness.

ship at sea. One can improve parts of the ship only by relying on other parts of the ship; there is no dry dock to rebuild on firm ground. The simile suggests that one can improve one's stock of beliefs only by relying on other beliefs one has; there are no properly basic beliefs whose justification is independent of other justified beliefs. All belief revision takes place within an assumed background of accepted beliefs. Neurath's raft simile contrasts with Moritz Schlick's pyramid metaphor. For Schlick, another member of the Vienna Circle, epistemic justification has a pyramid structure; the justification for some beliefs rests upon the justification for other beliefs whose justification does not depend on the justification of other beliefs. The development of logical empiricism up to Quine and Sellars favored Schlick's foundationalism over Neurath's holism.[2]

W.V.O. Quine and Wilfrid Sellars each forcefully argued against the logical empiricist project and advanced a coherence view of justification. Quine argued that the backbone of the logical empiricist attempted reconstruction of acceptable statements depended on the myth of a sharp distinction between analytic statements and synthetic statements. According to logical empiricism, each statement could be determined to be analytic or synthetic solely in virtue of its form. The analytic statements were justified by themselves and the synthetic statements required experience to be justified. The class of synthetic statements itself was divided into statements which report pure experience (the experiential statements) and those which were logical constructions of the experiential statements. Theoretical statements of science were to be treated as logical constructions of experiential statements. These theoretical statements are then analyzed into analytic equivalences of synthetic statements. Quine's famous paper 'Two Dogmas of Empiricism'

---

[2] Michael Friedman (1999) presents a different view. Friedman argues that the philosophical legacy of logical empiricism, specifically Carnap, has been misunderstood. Friedman observes that the early positivists—Mach, Schlick, and, to some extent, Carnap in the *Aufbau*—held a view similar to the one attributed to the positivists. This is the view that the goal of philosophy is to use the development of modern logic to show how all theoretical statements can be reduced to statements about fleeting subjective experience. Friedman then observes that many of the positivists—chiefly, Carnap—abandoned this view in response to Neurath's early criticism of it. Friedman's overall narrative, though, is that Carnap's project in the *Aufbau* is constitutional theory, one that isn't wedded to a traditional empiricist conception. What's interesting (and surprising) about Friedman's narrative is that it places the development of coherentist themes earlier within the Vienna Circle itself.

forcefully attacked the principled analytic-synthetic distinction presupposed by the logical empiricist program. Quine's contrasting picture was a holistic view in which the justification of any statement depends on its role in the web of belief.

Wilfrid Sellars' famous paper 'Empiricism and the Philosophy of Mind' attacked logical empiricists supposition that there are pure experiential statements directly justified by experience. Logical empiricists claimed that the content of these statements directly match the content of the associated sense experience in such a way that provided a guarantee of their truth. Sellars argued that the existence of these statements is a myth; it is one form of "the myth of the given." Sellars argues that sense experience either has belief content or it does not. Belief content is content that has a truth-value and can be endorsed in belief. If sense experience lacks any belief content then it is a mystery how sense experience can justify any belief that the world is one way rather than another. In this case it would be a complete mystery why an experience could justify a specific belief. Yet if sense experience has belief content then there must be some reason for thinking that that belief content is true. The claim that the content of a belief would require justification and yet the belief content of experience would not is incoherent; for the content to be justified in one case is the same as the content that doesn't need to be justified in the other case. The distinction between the belief mode of hosting a content and the experience mode is artificial. If content requires justification and sense content is belief content then their epistemic fates stand or fall together. Sellars, thus, reasoned that the logical empiricist project of ending the regress of justification in pure experiential statement is a myth.

The fate of epistemic coherentism becomes murky after Quine and Sellars. The influence of these seminal philosophers extended from the early 1950s through much of the twentieth century. Yet epistemology took a curious turn in 1963 with the publication of Edmund Gettier's paper 'Is Justified True Belief Knowledge?' Gettier argued that knowledge is not justified true belief. Knowledge requires some additional property than justified true belief. Gettier's paper led to a flourishing of new approaches to knowledge. At the time epistemologists thought that the relationship between knowledge and true belief must be thought out anew. Hence, epistemologists turned their backs on the methodological issues of science which grew out of reflection on logical empiricism and instead focused on finding a solution to the Gettier problem. One dominant approach was the formulation of epistemic externalism, the idea that knowledge should not be conceived in terms of justification or reasons, but rather as a natural relation that one bears to one's environment. For example, it was proposed that knowledge is the state of believing that p when the belief is caused by the fact that p. The rise of externalist approaches to knowledge led to the vigorous internalist externalist debate in epistemology.

The burst of activity on the Gettier problem shifted attention away from the methodological issues pertaining to theory construction which engaged the logical empiricists and subsequently Quine and Sellars. However, important developments on methodology still occurred. In the mid-1970s epistemologists realized that several prominent arguments against foundationalist views wrongly assumed that the foundational beliefs must be infallible. For example, D.M. Armstrong's 'distinct existence' argument contended that experience is not an adequate ground for belief because experiential states are ontologically distinct from belief states; the one can exist without the other. Consequently, Armstrong reasoned, experience cannot provide an indubitable ground for belief. William Alston and Mark Pastin both independently observed that foundationalist views need not be committed to the thesis that experience is an infallible ground for belief. This defeasible foundationalist view held that basic beliefs are justified but can be undermined by additional information. Even so, Alston and Pastin contended that experience is still a proper stopping point in the regress of reasons.

Such was the current state of play when Laurence BonJour published his well-regarded defense of coherentism in 1985. BonJour's book *The Structure of Empirical Knowledge* defends a coherentist account of empirical knowledge by way of two prominent arguments. First, BonJour argued that epistemic justification required more than simply a reason why the belief is likely to be true; a subject must be in cognitive possession of such a reason. BonJour argued that this requirement conflicts with externalist views of knowledge and justification. Second, BonJour argued via the Sellarsian dilemma that experience is unable to provide such a reason. This argument attacks internalist foundationalist views. The view left standing after BonJour's arguments is a form of epistemic coherentism.[3]

BonJour's arguments for epistemic coherentism are clear and forceful. However, his overall coherentist view is curious for two reasons. First, BonJour restricts his coherentist account to empirical knowledge,

---

[3] These two arguments don't eliminate an infinitist view. BonJour argued that infinitism was implausible since it is impossible for a human being to possess an infinite number of empirical beliefs (BonJour, 1985, 24).

explicitly adopting a traditional rationalist foundationalist view of the a priori. His foundationalism about the a priori is at odds with the arguments he offers for resisting a foundationalist account of empirical knowledge. More recently, BonJour has renounced coherentism because of this problem.[4] Second, related to his bifurcated epistemology, BonJour's development of epistemic coherentism does not fit with the coherentism of Quine, Sellars, Harman, Goodman, and Lycan. In his Appendix B 'A Survey of Coherence Theories' BonJour notes that he will not discuss the views of Quine, Sellars, and Harman because they all ascribe to epistemic conservatism. Conservatism is the thesis that belief is an epistemically relevant factor and, under some conditions, is a sufficient condition for justification. BonJour argues that conservatism is a form of weak foundationalism and thus not a coherentist view. In contrast to BonJour's argument, though, conservatism runs deep in the pragmatist tradition, and the mid-century coherentists were all pragmatists. Thus, BonJour's coherentist view is considerably different from the confirmational holism espoused by philosophers writing in the tradition of Quine and Sellars. BonJour's coherentist view shifted discussion away from the pragmatist coherentist view of the mid-twentieth-century epistemologists.

Even so, excellent work on coherentist themes continued. Keith Lehrer's books *Knowledge*[5] and *A Theory of Knowledge*[6] argued for a novel form of epistemic coherentism based on the idea of a competing system. Lehrer argued that a belief's justification is a matter of its membership in a subject's veritic system of beliefs which beats all competitors. Gilbert Harman's superb books *Thought*[7] and *Change in View*[8] developed the Quinean coherentist project by focusing on justified change in belief. Harman is less concerned with defending an analysis of epistemic justification and more concerned with defending a conservative, non-skeptical epistemic view that gets human inference right. William Lycan's second half of his book *Judgment and Justification*[9] defends a pragmatist explanationist view which is explicitly rooted in a broadly Quinean epistemology. Lycan advances the thesis that a belief's justification consists in its membership in a virtuous explanatory system.

---

[4] See BonJour (1997).
[5] Lehrer (1974).
[6] Lehrer (2000).
[7] Harman (1973).
[8] Harman (1986).
[9] Lycan (1988).

Lastly, Paul Thagard has steadily developed a broadly coherentist epistemology aimed at tying that approach into recent discoveries in cognitive science.[10]

In the last fifteen years two groups of literature on coherentism have breathed new life into the discussion on epistemic coherentism. First, alongside the general emergence of Bayesianism, there has been focused interest on probabilistic measures of coherence. This literature has produced an important impossibility result, according to which there is no probabilistic measure of coherence on which coherence is truth-conducive.[11] More recent discussion has uncovered that the impossibility result may be less significant than initially advertised.[12] The interest in probabilistic measures of coherence is a mixed blessing. Bayesian coherentism provides a model of confirmation, according to which the confirmation of any statement is dependent on an entire probability function. This is one way of making sense of holism. Yet Bayesian coherentism finds its roots in logical empiricism with its sharp distinction between framework considerations and empirical considerations. Contemporary Bayesian views have more affinity to Carnap's project of explication than Quine's naturalism. Carnap held that empirical inquiry could not properly begin until one had selected a language which involved rules for justified and unjustified moves within that language. The choice of one language over another was entirely pragmatic. Quine vigorously opposed this by arguing that the distinction between pure pragmatic choices and proper epistemic choices was not sharp. I consider the role Bayesianism can play with respect to an explanatory coherentist view in the final chapter.

The second group of literature on coherentism focuses on replying to historically prominent objections to the view. After Alston's and Pastin's development of a fallible foundationalism, the tide turned against coherentism. Several standard objections to the view—the input, isolation, and alternative systems objections—were taken to be decisive. Yet recent developments demonstrate that these objections rest on issues that either misrepresent a coherentist view or afflict more than coherentism.[13] The present state of coherentism is that these objections are no longer obstacles to the plausibility of the view.

---

[10] See Thagard (2000).
[11] Olsson (2005).
[12] Huemer (2011); Roche (2012); Wheeler (2012).
[13] For an overview see Kvanvig (2008).

1.2 Two traditional objections to coherentism

Coherentism faces several standing objections: the input objection, the isolation objection, the alternative systems objection, and the objection from the truth connection. These, however, are not four distinct objections. Rather they organize around two common objections. The input and isolation objections center on problems attending to the role of experience within a coherentist account. The alternative systems and truth connection objections focus on an allegedly problematic relationship between coherentist justification and truth. Recent developments show that these objections are not troublesome for a properly formulated coherentist view.[14]

1.2.1 The input objection

The input or isolation objection finds its root in the traditional understanding of coherence as a relation between beliefs. BonJour explains:

> Coherence is purely a matter of the internal relations between the components of the belief system; it depends in no way on any sort of relation between the system of beliefs and anything external to that system. Hence if, as a coherence theory claims, coherence is the sole basis for empirical justification, it follows that a system of empirical beliefs might be adequately justified, indeed might constitute empirical knowledge, in spite of being utterly out of contact with the world that it purports to describe. Nothing about any requirement of coherence dictates that a coherent system of beliefs need receive any sort of input from the world or be in any way causally influenced by the world.[15]

This input objection arises because the traditional understanding of coherence limits the relata of the coherence relation to a subject's beliefs. This understanding of coherence sets no epistemic role for experience. At times it seems that coherentists endorse this implication. Donald Davidson claims that "nothing can count as a reason for holding a belief except another belief."[16] Alvin Plantinga appeals to

---

[14] See Kvanvig and Riggs (1992); Kvanvig (1995a,1995b, 2008).
[15] BonJour (1985, 108).
[16] Davidson (1986, 126).

this standard feature of coherentism to argue that the view is "clearly mistaken."[17] He presents the following colorful counterexample:

> Consider the Case of the Epistemically Inflexible Climber. Ric is climbing Guide's Wall, on Storm Point in the Grand Tetons; having just led the difficult next to last pitch, he is seated on a comfortable ledge, bringing his partner up. He believes that Cascade Canyon is down to his left, that the cliffs of Mount Owen are directly in front of him, that there is a hawk gliding in lazy circles 200 feet below him, that he is wearing his new *Fire* rock shoes, and so on. His beliefs, we may stipulate, are coherent. Now add that Ric is struck by a wayward burst of high-energy cosmic radiation. This induces a cognitive malfunction; his beliefs become fixed, no longer response to changes in experience. No matter what his experience, his beliefs remain the same. At the cost of considerable effort his partner gets him down and, in a desperate last-ditch attempt at therapy, takes him to the opera in nearby Jackson, where the New York Metropolitan Opera on tour is performing *La Traviata*. Ric is appeared to in the same way as everyone else there; he is inundated by wave after wave of golden sound. Sadly enough, the effort at therapy fails; Ric's beliefs remain fixed and wholly unresponsive to his experience; he still believes that he is on the belay ledge at the top of the next to last pitch of Guide's Wall, that Cascade Canyon is down to the left, that there is a hawk sailing in lazy circles 200 feet below him, that he is wearing his new *Fire* rock shoes, and so on. Furthermore, since he believes the very same things he believed when seated on the ledge, his beliefs are coherent. But surely they have little or no warrant for him. . . . Clearly, then, coherence is not sufficient for positive epistemic status.[18]

Plantinga's vivid case assumes coherentism cannot include experience in the elements over which coherence is defined. If the coherence of a subject's informational system includes belief and experience then Plantinga's case easily fits within a coherentist epistemology.[19] There is nothing about the relation of coherence that prevents it from being defined over experiential states. For example, if the coherence relation requires consistency between propositional contents then this relation

---

[17] Plantinga (1993b, 80).
[18] Plantinga (1993b, 82).
[19] Kvanvig and Riggs (1992) make this point.

can be defined over the propositional contents of both beliefs and experiences. The one constraint that does arise within coherentism is that experience is not sufficient on its own to justify belief. But a coherentist may hold that experience is necessary to justify certain kinds of beliefs. A coherentist view of this kind is a non-doxastic coherentism. In fact, the focus on belief in BonJour and Davidson is ambiguous between the state of believing or the content of the state. If we take the emphasis to be on belief content then their remarks do not conflict with non-doxastic coherentism. In any case, if coherence is a relation over propositional content and experience has this kind of content then the input objection to coherentism vanishes. The view I defend is a non-doxastic form of explanatory coherentism. Experience is necessary, but not sufficient, for the justification of certain kinds of beliefs.

1.2.2 Alternative systems objection

The other class of common objections to coherentism concern the allegedly problematic relation to truth. A good work of fiction may be highly coherent but that gives us no reason to believe that it is true. The alternative systems objection raises the specter of multiple incompatible sets of beliefs for which one has good reason to accept. The objection assumes that coherence is an internal relation between a set of propositions. If a subject has a good reason to believe a coherent set of propositions then, given the fact that there are an infinite number of incompatible coherent systems, a subject has justification for believing an infinite number of incompatible sets of propositions. The alleged conclusion is that coherentism is false; epistemic justification require more than internal coherence.

Ernest Sosa provides an engaging and novel example of this objection. Sosa himself is considerably sympathetic to coherentist themes, assigning a prominent role to coherence for reflective knowledge. But he maintains that coherence alone is not sufficient for adequate epistemic justification. He explains:

> Coherentism seems false. Each of us at any given time believes a set of propositions, some of them consciously or explicitly, some subconsciously or implicitly. Many of these will be about the believer as himself and many about the time of belief as the time then present. In English one would express these beliefs respectively by such sentences as those of the form "...I..." or "...me..." and by such sentences as those of the form "...now..." or in the present tense. The self-abstract of such a set is obtained by removing any

self-concept of the believer from every one of its appearances in any proposition in the set. The present-abstract of such a set is similar obtained by removing any concept of the temporary present (as such) from every one of its appearances in any proposition in the set. ... The problem for coherentism is that the self-abstract and present-abstract of one's set of believed propositions at any given time would seem uniformly instantiable with respect to a personal individual concept P and temporal individual concept T in such a way that the result is nearly enough as coherent and comprehensive as the original without being cognitively justified in the sense relevant to knowledge.[20]

Sosa claims that the self and present abstract of one's beliefs will be just (or nearly) as coherent as one's original belief but lacking in justification. Consider instantiating for the personal concept *Donald Trump* and the time *May 1, 2025*. Currently I believe that 'I am now seated'. The operation Sosa envisages changes this belief to 'Donald Trump is seated on May 1, 2025'. Is such a belief justified? Our natural judgment is that it is not. But given the complete transformation Sosa envisions, that belief is incorporated into an allegedly highly coherent story. A coherentist, therefore, may be saddled with this problematic implication.

But is the self and present abstract of one's belief system instantiated for some P and T highly coherent? Two points suggest not. First, I believe that *I am not Donald Trump* and *I am a philosopher but Trump is not*. But Sosa's objection lands me with the following beliefs: *Donald Trump is not Donald Trump* and *Donald Trump is a philosopher but Donald Trump is not a philosopher*. We had coherence before the operation but after it there are massive incoherences of this sort.

A second issue with this operation focuses on the role of *de se* beliefs. De se beliefs are beliefs about oneself as oneself. Consider Sam who, when looking through a mirror, sees a guy whose pants are on fire. Sam believes that *that guy's pants are on fire*. Sam doesn't realize that he is that guy. When the realization hits him, he acquires a new belief 'My pants are on fire!' Sam acquires a de se belief.

De se beliefs place oneself *as oneself* at the center of one's experience. They are crucial for connecting information from experience with personal action. When one sees an oncoming bus, one doesn't simply believe that 'an oncoming bus is seen'; rather one believes of oneself 'I now see an oncoming bus.' When one hears an alarm one believes not

---

[20] Sosa (1991, 202).

simply 'an alarm is heard'; rather one believes that 'I myself hear with my ears that an alarm is near'. It is difficult to imagine a person with no de se beliefs. Such a person would lack proprioceptive awareness, the kind of awareness of one's current bodily position in space. Such awareness (together with justified background assumptions) allows one to come to know things like 'I am now seated' and 'I now see (with my eyes) a cup on the desk.' Proprioceptive awareness is distinct from the kind of awareness we have of other people.

Sosa's self and present abstract instantiated to some P and T is incoherent with proprioceptive awareness. For any property one is proprioceptively aware of, one believes this of oneself at the present time. Yet the self and present abstract requires that one believes this of a distinct individual at a distinct time. To focus on just one sort of incoherence, one would believe the following incoherent propositions: *This is my body, this is Donald Trump's body, my body isn't Donald Trump's body.* The problem for Sosa's thought experiment is that either the self and present abstract removes all proprioceptive awareness in which case the operation significantly reduces the comprehensiveness of one's beliefs, or the operation does not disturb it in which case the operation lands one in massive incoherence.

Sosa takes the upshot of his self and present abstract argument to be that coherentism needs, but evidently can't have, that "the subject who holds that view place himself within it at the time in question with awareness both of his own beliefs at the time and of his possible means of access to himself and the world around him at that time and in the past."[21] I've argued that any coherentism that gives proper place to proprioceptive awareness satisfies this requirement. The input objection showed that coherentism needs to appeal to experiential states; this present objection shows that it should include proprioceptive awareness as well. Again, a non-doxastic coherentism survives traditional objections to the view.

1.3 Overview

The judgment that coherence is an important epistemic factor is widespread and yet the presence of the Gettier problem has stunted the natural development of a full-fledged coherentist view. The common objections to coherentism rely on an impoverished conception of the

---

[21] Sosa (1991, 210).

view. I aim to take several steps to develop an explanatory coherentist view of justification. The first three chapters develop an explanationist view of justification and reasons. The next three chapters examine arguments against the view. In the following I offer a brief summary of the overall argument.

Chapter 2 'Epistemic Conservatism' defends the claim that the attitude of believing can generate some epistemic justification for the content of the belief. Conservatism is a standard explanatory virtue. Goodness in explanation is constrained by how well an explanation fits with accepted beliefs. Epistemic conservatism is widely criticized on the grounds that it conflicts with the main goal of epistemology to believe all and only truths. My primary aim is to argue that conservatism does not conflict with this goal. I argue that the objection to conservatism from the truth goal fails. Next, I examine several forceful challenges to conservatism and argue that these challenges are unsuccessful. The first challenge is that conservatism implies the propriety of assertions like 'I believe p and this is part of my justification for it.' The second challenge argues that conservatism wrongly implies that the identity of an epistemic agent is relevant to the main goal of believing truths and disbelieving falsehoods. The last two challenges are the 'extra boost' objection and the conversion objection. Each of these objections helps to clarify the nature of the conservative thesis. Finally, I consider the extent to which conservatism is supported by argumentation. I argue that conservatism is supported by the perspectival nature of epistemic internalism. The upshot of this chapter is that epistemic conservatism is an important and viable epistemological thesis.

The next chapter 'Reasons without First Philosophy' develops a coherentist account of reasons—the framework theory of reasons—in the context of epistemic conservatism. An ongoing soft spot for coherentist views is the necessity of permitting some noninferential justification while also arguing against foundationalist accounts of basic reasons. I formulate a general dilemma—the basic reasons dilemma—and explain how this afflicts existing coherentism views. I then turn to developing an account of reasons that responds to this dilemma. The framework account of reasons avoids the Scylla and Charybdis of arbitrariness and circularity. On this view a reason for another proposition requires a body of justified commitments. These commitments may be justified in part by conservatism, but crucially no single commitment can provide a reason for another distinct belief. Only by working together can justified beliefs provide reasons. Epistemic conservatism coupled with explanatory coherence turns propositions into reasons.

Chapter 4 'Explanation and Justification' addresses the nature and role of explanation and its virtues in an account of epistemic justification. Explanatory coherence is a valuable cognitive goal. Human beings desire not simply to know, but to possess knowledge that produces understanding. The epistemological tradition coming from Quine, Sellars, and Harman stresses the centrality of explanation and coherence to valuable human cognition. My goal in this chapter is to turn the plausible idea that one's normative standing in the space of reasons is determined by one's explanatory position into a specific theory of epistemic justification, *Ex-J*. I begin by discussing the nature of explanation and its virtues. I argue that the nature of explanation lacks an informative analysis into necessary and sufficient conditions. The nature of explanation is simple and it is grasped early on in cognitive development by way of 'because' answers. I then briefly discuss the main epistemic virtues of explanation: conservativeness, explanatory power, and simplicity. In the second section I formulate a specific explanationist view, arguing that it is an instance of a mentalist, evidentialist theory of justification. In the final section I consider supporting cases for my view and putative counterexamples. Explanatory coherentism is often misunderstood. My discussion of the putative counterexamples clarifies the role of explanation in an explanatory coherentist view. The upshot of this chapter is that explanationism is a feasible theory of epistemic justification. It provides a natural home for the valuable cognitive goal of explanatory coherence; it is an instance of a plausible, general evidentialist view; and it is supported by natural judgments and it survives putative counterexamples.

Chapter 5 'BonJour and the Myth of the Given' tackles the challenge of phenomenal beliefs. These beliefs are about one's immediate experience. It is easy to think that our justification for phenomenal beliefs is direct and not based at all on coherence considerations. I argue against this by examining BonJour's careful discussions on the Sellarsian dilemma. BonJour once defended the soundness of this dilemma as part of a larger argument for epistemic coherentism. BonJour has now renounced his earlier conclusions about the dilemma and has offered an account of internalistic foundationalism aimed, in part, at showing the errors of his former ways. I contend that BonJour's early concerns about the Sellarsian dilemma are correct, and that his latest position does not adequately handle the dilemma. I focus my attention on BonJour's claim that a nonconceptual experiential state can provide a subject with a reason to believe some proposition. It is crucial for the viability of internalistic foundationalism to evaluate whether this claim is true. I argue it is false. The requirement that the states that provide justification give reasons to a subject conflicts with the idea that these states are nonconceptual. In the final section I consider David Chalmers' attempt to defend a view closely similar to BonJour's. Chalmers' useful theory of phenomenal concepts provides a helpful framework for identifying a crucial problem with attempts to end the regress of reasons in pure experiential states.

Chapter 6 'Is Foundational A Priori Justification Indispensable?' tackles the challenge to coherentism from the *a priori*. BonJour's (1985) coherence theory of empirical knowledge relies heavily on a traditional foundationalist theory of a priori knowledge. He argues that a foundationalist, rationalist theory of a priori justification is indispensable for a coherence theory. BonJour's more recent book *In Defense of Pure Reason* (1998) continues this theme, arguing that a traditional account of a priori justification is indispensable for the justification of putative a priori truths, the justification of any non-observational belief, and the justification of reasoning itself. While BonJour's indispensability arguments have received some critical discussion,[22] no one has investigated the indispensability arguments from a coherentist perspective. This perspective offers a fruitful take on BonJour's arguments because he does not appreciate the depth of the coherentist alternative to the traditional empiricist-rationalist debate. This is surprising on account of BonJour's previous defense of coherentism. Two significant conclusions emerge: first, BonJour's indispensability arguments beg central questions against an explanationist form of coherentism; second, BonJour's original defense of coherentism took on board certain assumptions that inevitably led to the demise of his form of coherentism. The positive conclusion of this chapter is that explanatory coherentism is more coherent than BonJour's indispensability arguments assume and more coherent than BonJour's earlier coherentist epistemology.

Chapter 7 'Bayesian Explanationism' argues that Bayesianism and explanationism are compatible. It would be incredibly surprising if it turned out that first-order predicate logic was inconsistent with a substantive epistemological theory. Similarly, I confess, it would be astonishing if the mathematical theory of probability applied to degrees of belief turned out to be inconsistent with substantive views in epistemology. I argue for a new form of compatibilism according to which explanatory reasoning is not simply a heuristic to realizing good

---

[22] Gendler (2001); Harman (2001); Beebe (2008).

probabilistic reasoning. Rather, explanatory reasoning undergirds and is required for inductive projection. I begin this chapter by explaining the nature of the Bayesian framework and arguments for it, all with an eye to illustrating its compatibility with explanationism. Second, I argue that inductive confirmation requires explanatory information. This constraint-based compatibilism makes for a powerful merger of Bayesianism and explanationism.

The view I defend in this book is thoroughly explanationist. The justification of a subject's beliefs consist in the simplicity, conservativeness, and explanatory power of the system of propositions she accepts in comparison with other relevant systems. This is a form of a mentalist evidentialism, but it does not rely on the epistemic priority of either sense experience or a priori intuition. To the extent that my view relies on any epistemic priority, it is the priority of our background beliefs, where they are evaluated by explanatory considerations. This view provides an internalist, non-skeptical epistemology. Justification, reasons, and knowledge are possible. Yet this possibility comes with the cost of explanation. If one is justified in believing an entire body of information that information needs to do explanatory work for the subject.

One of the main themes running throughout this book is that there is a neglected dimension of positive epistemic normativity in which a proper epistemic evaluation of a subject's beliefs depends on the theoretical virtues of the subject's beliefs. Putative cases of immediately justified beliefs depend for an important normative status on broader theoretical dimensions. Bertrand Russell claimed that common sense is "a piece of audacious metaphysical theorizing."[23] Common sense holds that there is a public, multi-dimensional world of permanent objects and others minds existing beyond the specious present. Much current epistemology helps itself to substantive metaphysical assumptions undergirding common sense. Part of my goal in defending explanationism is to provide a framework in which we can see how we have good reason for thinking that these assumptions are true. I also aim to highlight the broader role of the theoretical dimension in our normative evaluation, a dimension that is underappreciated by the ascendancy of defeasible foundationalist views of epistemic justification. This conclusion holds not just for epistemic justification but also for knowledge. Knowledge-first approaches are a welcome relief to the somewhat tiresome justification debates. Yet there is a dimension in which knowledge-first approaches neglect the

---

[23] Russell (1993, 107).

broader theoretical evaluations that fill out our understanding of the role of self-knowledge, perception, testimony, and inference. My hope is that this book manages to highlight the important dimension in which the proper epistemic evaluation of our beliefs must take into account a broader theoretical perspective. Explanationism is a plausible way of developing the important role of this theoretical perspective.

2
Epistemic Conservatism

Does the attitude of belief confer some positive epistemic merit on the content of belief? Epistemic conservatism is the doctrine that belief—the state of a subject who is disposed to assert a proposition and use that proposition in theoretical and practical reason—confers some positive merit on the proposition. Conservatism is deeply controversial. While it is recognized as an explanatory virtue, it is widely relegated to a noncognitive, pragmatic virtue. On that approach, conservatism is a good heuristic for selecting among alternative explanations but it provides no reason for thinking that the more conservative theory is more likely to be true. My goal in this chapter is to defend a substantive conservative doctrine.

Conservatism lays at the heart of any feasible explanatory coherentist view. To the extent that anyone is justified in believing anything it is because of a host of background beliefs. Background beliefs together with the other explanatory virtues provide the ultimate material for justification. I do not see any way to resist a thoroughgoing skepticism without these background beliefs having some level of justification simply in virtue of being believed. I defend a conservative doctrine by showing that the objections to the view rest on mistaken assumptions. At the close of the chapter I offer a positive argument for conservatism which relies on epistemic internalism. The upshot of this chapter is that background beliefs have some level of justification in virtue of being believed.

The benefits of epistemic conservatism are numerous. It embodies cognitive efficiency;[1] it helps to handle radical skepticism and skeptical worries about induction; it helps with the justification of beliefs based

---
[1] Sklar (1975).

on memory and the phenomenon of forgotten evidence;[2] it can help with the problem of easy knowledge;[3] it helps to make sense of the role of particularism in epistemology and the role of intuition in philosophy;[4] it can help to understand rational belief in the face of peer disagreement; and it can make sense of how perception, construed as a species of intentional states, is a source of reasons.[5] This last benefit is a neglected virtue of conservatism. If reason-giving states must have content that stand in logical relations to belief content then, arguably, conservatism lies at the heart of trusting the deliverances of any reason-giving source. Conservatism provides the crucial background perspective for underwriting the intentional contents of perceptual states.

With benefits like these one might expect conservatism to be a popular doctrine. However, the core conservative thesis that belief confers some positive epistemic merit on the content of belief is widely panned. Richard Foley says that "conservatism must be dismissed as implausible."[6] David Christensen writes, "[T]here is something intuitively suspect in the basic conservative idea. How could the mere fact that an agent happens to believe something justify her, to any extent at all, in continuing to believe that same thing in the future?"[7] Hamid Vahid complains that "one cannot help feeling that there must be something unsatisfactory about a thesis that takes the mere holding of a belief to endow it with epistemic worth."[8] Even those who defend a version of conservatism quickly modify the view to avoid the implication that they will defend the core conservative thesis. Lawrence Sklar, for instance, defends a "more modest" principle of conservatism, complaining against the core idea that "surely not only is believing p not sufficient grounds for believing p. [But] believing p is no grounds at all for believing p."[9] In short, the core conservative thesis appears to be

---

[2] Harman (1986); McGrath (2007).
[3] McCain (2008).
[4] Fumerton (2008).
[5] Fumerton (2008).
[6] Foley (1983, 179).
[7] Christensen (1994, 70).
[8] Vahid (2004, 98).
[9] Sklar (1975, 377). Similar remarks can be found in Kvanvig (1989). Kvanvig writes, "The [conservative] doctrine in its starkest, and most implausible form claims that a belief has some presumption of rationality simply because it is held. A more careful formulation of the doctrine is this: some degree of rationality can be generated for a person's belief merely in virtue of the doxastic commitments of that person" (1989, 143).

the one thing in epistemology that everyone agrees about; conservatism makes for bad epistemology.

It is not difficult to see why the core conservative idea meets so much resistance. The goal of epistemic inquiry is to gain true beliefs and avoid false beliefs. Roderick Chisholm expresses the idea thus: "Each person is subject to two requirements in connection with any proposition he considers: (1) he should try his best to bring it about that if that proposition is true then he believe it; and (2) he should try his best to bring it about that if that proposition is false he should not believe it."[10] Epistemic justification is conceived of in terms of this goal. A justified belief is one that is suitably truth apt, one that directly contributes to the goal of gaining true beliefs and avoiding false beliefs.[11] Given the truth goal, the thought that a proposition gains some positive epistemic merit simply by being believed is apt to leave one perplexed. How does the mere fact that one believes p show that p is thereby more likely to be true than not? Apart from Donald Davidson's argument that the nature of assigning meanings to utterances requires that most of one's beliefs are true,[12] it just seems confused to think that the state of believing implies the content of belief is more likely to be true.

This argument from the truth goal to the falsity of conservatism is easy to reconstruct, but it is mistaken. The content of the anti-conservatism intuition is that nothing about the state of belief renders its content likely to be true. One of my goals is to destabilize this intuition. To accomplish that I devote the first section to the anti-conservative probability argument, an argument that takes this intuition to provide a compelling reason to reject conservatism. I show that this argument completely fails to rebut conservatism; its failure undermines the anti-conservative intuition. After the first section, our dialectical position should be one in which conservatism is a live issue. I then devote several sections to undermining additional arguments against conservatism. Conservatism is poorly understood; many objections arise from an inadequate conception of the view. In the final section I explore a positive argument for conservatism from the perspectival character of epistemic justification.

---

[10] Chisholm (1977, 15). See also Goldman (1980, 32). For recent discussion on the nature of the epistemic goal see Kvanvig (2003); David (2007).

[11] Cohen (1984) illustrates the difficulties in trying to unpack this intuition.

[12] See Davidson (1986). For critical discussion see Fumerton and Foley (1985).

2.1 The anti-conservative probability argument

The naive conservative thesis is that the state of believing p confers some positive epistemic merit on p. A more nuanced conservative view adds qualifications to the relevant state of belief. The view I defend holds that in the special evidential situation in which a subject believes p but lacks any relevant evidence for p then a subject has some justification for maintaining her belief that p. I refer to this state as *mere belief*. A subject that merely believes p is in the special evidential situation in which she lacks any evidence for p and any evidence against p. Her evidential situation is symmetrical with respect to p. Cases of symmetrical evidence fall into two classes: first, when a subject possesses evidence both for p and against p but the balance of the evidence doesn't favor either p or not-p; second, when a subject lacks any evidence for or against p. When people talk about 'counterbalanced evidence' I find that they exclusively focus on the case in which there *are* evidential considerations at hand but the evidential considerations are symmetrical. As I argue, epistemic conservatism is properly concerned with the second case of symmetrical evidence. Let us refer to this special case as one of *empty symmetrical evidence*.

The state of empty symmetrical evidence is special. It is one in which there is not evidence relevant for determining a unique prior probability. Take the proposition that *Johnson has won the lottery*. One has no direct evidence that this is true and no direct evidence that this is false. One hasn't been told that Johnson won or that someone else did. Yet, one does possess enough evidence to determine that it is unlikely that Johnson won the lottery. This isn't a case of empty symmetrical evidence. This special state also rules out evidence that one will have positive evidence. Suppose one is about to flip a coin. One knows that one will shortly have positive evidence relevant to whether it landed heads or tails. One's evidence supports that there will be positive evidence in the future but one's present perspective on that future evidence is symmetrical. This isn't a case of empty symmetrical evidence.

Is anyone ever in this state of empty symmetrical evidence? Ludwig Wittgenstein held that people are in this state with respect to "hinge propositions," the propositions upon which the door of inquiry turns. These propositions form the background against which we distinguish between true and false (Wittgenstein, 1969, §94), are affirmed without any evidence (Wittgenstein, 1969, §136 and 138), are groundless (Wittgenstein, 1969, §166), are presupposed whenever we test anything (Wittgenstein, 1969, §163), are the assumed part of the logic of scientific investigation (Wittgenstein, 1969, §§341–3), and form the basis for inquiry (Wittgenstein, 1969, §§472–477). Wittgenstein's thought is that some propositions function as the basis upon which we investigate other propositions without themselves being the kinds of things that are affirmed on the basis of positive evidence. Our evidential situation with respect to hinge propositions is empty symmetrical evidence; there are not positive considerations for them and no positive considerations against them.

Crispin Wright echoes this Wittgensteinian thought. He claims that "all enquiry involves so far untested presuppositions and that the attempt to improve one's epistemic position in this respect is doomed to failure."[13] Many of these propositions concern fundamental assumptions that we take for granted. Consider our basic trust that memory is reliable. It is hard to see how one could have positive evidence for the reliability of memory without assuming that memory is reliable. Similarly, it is hard to see how one could have positive evidence that inference is reliable without relying on some basic patterns of inference as reliable. And certain metaphysical assumptions such as the stability of meaning and object permanence are such that there are no directly relevant evidence considerations to bear on these matters. They form the hinges upon which the door of inquiry turn.[14]

A test for hinge propositions is whether there is at best a rule circular argument for it. Our basic trust in the reliability of memory is one upon which we have at best a rule circular argument for its justification. Any argument for the reliability of memory must depend on the reliability of memory for its justification. Similarly with induction. Any argument for the reliability of induction must depend on the crucial claim that the unobserved cases resemble the observed cases. This holds as well for the claim that we have the ability to track objects and properties across time. Any argument for that requires that there are some objects and properties—for example, the premises of the argument—that we do track through time. These propositions are natural, are believed, and are held in the state of empty symmetrical evidence.

My defense of epistemic conservatism is directed toward beliefs held in the state of empty symmetrical evidence. My view is not committed to belief providing some extra evidence for p or belief in the face of

---

[13] Wright (2011).

[14] See also Harman and Sherman (2004). Harman and Sherman argue that all knowledge rests on assumptions that are taken for granted. See, as well, Alston (1993) in which Alston argues in detail that there are no non-question begging arguments for the reliability of our basic belief-forming mechanisms.

defeaters making it rational to believe p. Rather the view is about a justification-conferring factor in the absence of evidential considerations. I return to these remarks later on but the crucial point is that to evaluate the conservative thesis one should focus on the state of *mere belief*—that is, belief in the state of empty symmetrical evidence—and not distracters such as potential defeaters or the evidential "boost" provided by belief.

The anti-conservative intuition attempts to do just this. It focuses on mere belief and intuits that there's nothing about that state that makes its content likely to be true. One way to form this intuition into an argument against conservatism is to appeal to the instrumental character of epistemic justification, that is, epistemic justification requires likelihood of truth.[15] Laurence BonJour complains that Gilbert Harman's conservative principle of epistemic justification does not uphold the instrumental character of epistemic justification. He writes, "There is no apparent reason to think that the sort of 'justification' offered by general foundationalism [i.e., conservatism] has any bearing at all on the likely truth of the beliefs in question and thereby no reason to regard general foundationalism [i.e., conservatism] as even one of the contenders for an account of epistemic justification."[16] With this notion of justification in place, the argument against conservatism is straightforward.

The anti-conservative probability argument

1. Necessarily, a subject's belief that p is justified only if p is likely to be true.
2. Possibly, a subject merely believes p and p is not likely to be true.

So,

3. Possibly, a subject merely believes p and p is not justified.

On the face of it this argument provides a strong reason to reject conservatism. But on reflection the argument is deeply flawed. To make this argument clearer we need to understand the notion of 'a proposition being likely to be true'. I assume that this is to talk about a proposition's

---

[15] On the instrumental character of justification see White (2007, 117–119).

[16] BonJour (2001b, 692). BonJour, following Harman, uses the term "general foundationalism" in place of conservatism. The difference is merely terminological. Harman notes that his "general foundations theory" went by the name "general conservatism" in earlier articles. See Harman (2001, 657, no. 2) and Harman (1995, 1999).

24 *Reason and Explanation*

probability. Thus, to evaluate the argument we must examine how its premises fare on various interpretations of probability. I argue that on any interpretation of probability the argument either has a false premise or begs the question against epistemic conservatism.

Let us begin by examining frequency and propensity interpretations of probability.[17] On these views probabilities are out there in the world. Probabilities are objective properties of statements. The probability that attaches to the statement that 'This coin lands heads' is identified with either (i) the relative frequency this coin in this particular setup lands heads over all other outcomes or (ii) the propensity of this coin in this setup to produce heads. A serious problem with both interpretations as elucidations of epistemic justification is that they cannot recover a non-zero probability for necessary falsehoods. Consider Frege's belief in the axiom of comprehension, that is, for any meaningful predicate there exist a set of exactly those items which satisfy the predicate. Prior to receiving Russell's letter disclosing the now famous paradox, Frege was justified in believing that the axiom was true. But, on a frequency or propensity interpretation, Frege is justified in believing the comprehension axiom only if it has a positive frequency or propensity of being true. Since the axiom is necessarily false, it lacks either of these properties. The upshot is that a frequency or propensity interpretation of probability cannot make heads or tails of the likelihood of a necessary falsehood.

One might reply that this argument fails once a proper reference class is selected. Any frequency interpretation of probability needs a suitable chosen reference class, and necessarily false propositions can have a positive probability if the reference class includes other claims that aren't necessarily false. The proposition '$2^4 = 32$' is necessarily false, but it may have a positive probability if the reference class is "things one hears from a teacher."

This reply succumbs to the reference class problem that afflicted Hempel's attempt to characterize inductive-statistical explanation.[18] Hempel required that the explanandum, the event to be explained, belonged to a homogeneous reference class, a class that could not be sub-divided into other classes that changes the relevant probability of the event. Hempel needed but couldn't find an objective manner of determining the relevant reference class. In our case with claims that

---

[17] See von Mises (1957); Popper (1959).
[18] Hempel (1965).

are necessarily true or false, the problem is worse. One often knows that the claim is necessarily true, if true at all. Suppose one is considering the Riemann hypothesis that *all non-trivial zeros of the zeta function have real part $\frac{1}{2}$*. One learns the Riemann hypothesis from a reliable informant, a person whom one knows speaks the truth 9 times out of 10. Should one's probability of the Riemann hypothesis be .9? One knows that it is either necessarily false or necessarily true. In this case it does not make good sense to assign the Reimann hypothesis some non-extreme probability, for one knows that it does not have a non-extreme probability and therefore assigning it such a probability knowingly misrepresents what your evidence supports. The basic problem is that one knows one's reference class is not homogeneous. There is a relevant division of it into claims that are necessarily true and claims that are necessarily false. Clearly, whichever class the Reimann hypothesis falls into is directly relevant to its probability.

The problem of justified necessary falsehoods afflicts the logical interpretation of probability as well.[19] This interpretation determines probabilities by an a priori examination of the space of possibilities. However, like the frequency and propensity interpretation, a logical interpretation of probability cannot recover a non-zero probability for necessary falsehoods. After intense and prolonged reflection on the nature of space Euclid believed that *necessarily, the shortest distance between two points is a straight line*. Plausibly, Euclid was justified in believing this; however, it is necessarily false. Non-Euclidean geometries illustrate the possibility that the shortest distance between two lines is a curve. The logical interpretation falsifies the connection with positive epistemic merit and likelihood of truth.

The subjective interpretation of probability can recover a probability for necessary falsehoods but it falsifies the other premise of the anticonservative probability argument.[20] On the subjective interpretation of probability, probabilities are identified with degrees of belief. Because probabilities are identified with degrees of belief, the fact that one believes p implies that p is likely to be true (for a subject). Consequently, the above argument against conservatism fails on this interpretation, that is, premise 2 is false.

---

[19] See Carnap (1950).

[20] For a development of subjective probability see Howson and Urbach (1993). Some philosophers appeal to what an ideally rational agent would believe. The argument I give in the next paragraph about the evidential interpretation applies to this move as well.

The remaining interpretation is the evidential one.[21] This interpretation identifies probabilities with a subject's strength of evidence. An initial problem with this argument is that 'evidence' is an epistemic notion. The evidential interpretation, thus, requires a broader epistemology, one which specifies what is a subject's evidence. For the purposes of the anti-conservative probability argument it will obviously matter whether that broader epistemology is conservative. If so, then the anti-conservative argument won't get off the ground. But if not, then the anti-conservative probability will look good but only because it is interpreted in a broader anti-conservative epistemology.

Consider the relevant premises of the anti-conservative probability argument: when a subject believes that p in empty symmetrical evidence there is no positive evidence for p and no positive evidence against p. Hence the evidential interpretation implies that p is not likely to be true. Why does the evidential interpretation have this result? Precisely because in the broader epistemology which specifies what one's evidence is the fact that one believes p does not count as relevant. But that just pushes the argument back to the broader epistemology.

There is another problem with the evidential interpretation of probability. A probability function requires substantive claims which cannot be modeled within the function. Our evidential situation for these claims is one of empty symmetrical evidence. Consider the problem of determining which predicates are candidates for inductive projection. Carnap provided a framework for understanding the probability of any particular statement[22] but, as Goodman observed, Carnap had to first choose a language with predicates like "green" instead of "grue."[23] Which predicates one allows in the language significantly affects the subsequent probabilities, yet this choice cannot be modeled by a probability function. Similarly, the assumptions that meaning is stable and that objects persist through time lay in the background of any attempt to apply the probability calculus. Consider trying to apply a diachronic Bayesian principle without helping oneself to the assumption that the sentence used for conditionalization expresses the same proposition as it did earlier. The evidential interpretation of probability cannot provide

---

[21] See Achinstein (2001, Ch. 5).
[22] Carnap (1950).
[23] Goodman (1979).

a probability for these statements; the truth of these statements is a precondition for applying the probability calculus. On my view the only recourse is that these propositions believed in the situation of empty symmetrical evidence have some level of justification simply by being believed.

The failure of the anti-conservative probability argument is instructive because epistemic conservatism is perplexing. Inquiry aims at acquiring accurate beliefs. Epistemic justification assesses whether belief thus aimed is appropriate. But there is no feature of the state of believing that renders the content of belief likely to be true. Yet the failure of the anti-conservative probability argument destabilizes this short argument. The argument invokes probability considerations, and we've just seen that any interpretation of probability will imply either that there's no interesting connection between probability and justification (i.e., some non-epistemic interpretation of probability) or that the interpretation of probability invokes epistemic notions (e.g., strength of one's evidence). Neither option supports the anti-conservative intuition. Regarding the first option, if there is no interesting connection between justification and probability then the failure of belief to make its content probable is not epistemically noteworthy. Some necessary falsehoods have zero probability and yet a subject can be justified in believing them. On the other hand, if an interpretation of probability invokes epistemic notions then it is incumbent to consider how good of an epistemic view that interpretation provides. I've argued that the case of empty symmetrical evidence is deeply problematic for epistemic interpretations of probability. Such views require substantive assumptions to set up the probability calculus and yet those assumptions cannot be modeled within the probability calculus.

In the next three sections I explore further objections to epistemic conservatism. I argue that these objections rest on an impoverished conception of the view. Conservatism, as Lawrence Sklar remarks, is a "means of 'last resort' when other [evidential] principles fail to motivate a decision for us."[24] This special feature of conservatism is, on my view, applied only in the special situation of empty symmetrical evidence. Once that is made clear, many of the objections to conservatism evaporate. It remains in the final section to explore to what extent there are any positive arguments for conservatism.

---

[24] Sklar (1975, 375).

2.2 Conservative justification and warranted assertion

Conservative justification seems odd. David Christensen writes:

> The principle of epistemic conservatism takes many forms. But the basic idea behind it is simple: that an agent is in some measure justified in maintaining a belief simply in virtue of the fact that the agent has that belief. Thus an agent may, according to the conservative principle, correctly say "I happen to believe it—and that is part of my justification for continuing to believe it!"[25]

In this section I explain why conservatism does not have this alleged consequence. The key idea is one familiar to recent epistemology—assertion creates certain implicatures that can be misleading. In the case at hand, the assertion "I believe p and that's part of my justification for it" violates the conversational maxim to make one's contribution relevant. In particular, this assertion creates the improper expectation that one's belief is evidentially relevant to the conversation at hand.

Since Grice's influential article 'Logic and Conversation' it is widely recognized that pragmatic aspects of conversational contexts can generate false expectations. If you are interested in understanding the Great Recession and I say "I took an Economics course in college" that creates the (false) expectation that I can help you understand this event. In light of this aspect of conversational contexts, Grice conjectures that conversations are governed by the Cooperative Principle. This principle states: "Make your conversational contribution such as is required, at the stage at which it occurs, by the accepted purpose or direction of the talk exchange in which you are engaged."[26] Among the sub-maxims that flow from the Cooperative Principle is the maxim to make your contribution one that is relevant.[27] My assertion, in the above case, creates the expectation that it is relevant to my interlocutor's concern to understand the recent financial collapse.

Epistemological interest in the cooperative principle lies in its utility in offering a pragmatic explanation of mistaken epistemic intuitions. Consider Dretske's Zebra Case.[28] You go to the zoo and see a pen marked

---

[25] Christensen (1994, 69).
[26] Grice (2001, 167).
[27] Ibid., 168.
[28] Dretske (1970).

"Zebra." You look, and at a close range, in good lighting, and so on, see a striped equine animal. You thus believe that the animal is a zebra. Intuitively you know that it is a zebra. But do you know that the animal is not a cleverly disguised mule? We feel some pressure to say 'no'. One way to explain away this pressure as misleading is to stress that it is improper to assert 'That animal is not a cleverly disguised mule'. The infelicity of this assertion, though, is compatible with knowing its content. The reason is that the assertion creates the false expectation that you have some special evidence that the animal is not a cleverly disguised mule. But you have no special evidence. Rather you rely on general background information about the way zoos work, the difficulty of disguising a mule, the lack of any apparent motivation to engage in such deception, and so on, to knowingly believe that that animal isn't a cleverly disguised mule.

The significance of this is that when one has merely conservative justification for p, one's conservative justification is unassertable. In any context in which the question of whether p is true is a live issue, our adherence to the cooperative principle makes one's belief that p entirely irrelevant to the discussion of whether p is true. In such contexts the assertion that "I believe p" creates the false expectation that one's believing p is relevant for the purposes at hand. This feature of conservatism explains why in challenged underdetermination cases it is wrong to *say* that one is justified in believing p, even though one can remain justified in believing p.

This feature of conservatism is similar to attempts to minimize the strength of conservative justification. Many defenders of conservatism claim that the positive merit a content possesses via the conservative principle is very small. William Lycan, for instance, writes that the justification conferred by conservatism is vanishingly small: "only a credibility value of $.5 + \epsilon$, where ϵ is vanishingly close to zero."[29] This strikes me as the wrong way to explicate conservative epistemic merit. If the positive merit is infinitesimal then conservatism is unlikely to help with any epistemic problems, for example, the justification of memory beliefs or the justification of underdetermined theories. A better way to elucidate the idea that conservative epistemic merit is "small" is that in challenged contexts conservative justification is unassertable.

---

[29] Lycan (1988, 171).

One might object to this line of reasoning that pragmatic implicatures are cancelable, and thus one should be able to assert "I'm not implying that I have any special evidence but I believe that p and that's my justification for it." Yet, it looks as if that's an admission that one lacks any justification for p. The main problem with this objection is that the language of 'justification' is ambiguous between the state of being justified and the activity of justifying. When we give a justification we give an argument. It's natural to read this assertion as offering an argument while saying that one isn't. The correct way to understand this assertion is as offering a justification-conferring condition. Perhaps, there is some oddity in offering a justification conferring condition when one knows that your interlocutor does not meet that condition. But there are other cases in which this makes sense. It is commonplace among mathematicians to maintain beliefs about unproved conjectures. Many mathematicians believed that Fermat's last theorem was provable before Andrew Wiles demonstrated that it's true. Mathematicians now widely regard Goldbach's conjecture as true, even though they explicitly recognize that the inductive evidence for conjectures like Goldbach's is neither here nor there. We can envision mathematicians saying something similar to the speech above: "I maintain this belief even though I don't have any special evidence for it. I find myself believing that Goldbach's conjecture is true." So, in at least some cases, the relevant implicatures can be canceled without revoking one's justification.

2.3 Conservatism and autobiographical epistemology

Conservatism has been subject to multiple alleged counterexamples and more nuanced forms of argument.[30] A reply to each of these arguments and counterexamples is beyond the scope of this chapter. What I aim to accomplish in this section is to uncover the essence of many objections to conservatism. We can accomplish this by examining David Christensen's interesting attempts to undermine conservatism.

---

[30] See Foley (1983); Vogel (1992); Christensen (1994, 2000); Vahid (2004); Fumerton (2008). As mentioned even defenders of conservatism are quick to distance themselves from the simple view that belief confers positive merit of its content. See Sklar (1975); Kvanvig (1989); McGrath (2007); McCain (2008).

Let us begin our discussion with one of Christensen's initial counterexamples to conservatism. Christensen describes the case as follows:

> Suppose that my wife is pregnant, and I form the belief that the child she is carrying is a girl. But it's not that I caught a glimpse of it in the ultrasound picture, or that we have any family history of predominately female children, or that I believe myself to have mystic communion with the baby. I don't consider myself to have any justification for forming this belief; I simply form the belief capriciously, or perhaps on the basis of wishful thinking. In such a case, my belief does not reflect any learning on my part. And, naturally enough, in this case we do not have the intuition that the fact that I currently have the belief gives me reason to maintain it.[31]

Even though Christensen says that this case seems to provide a counterexample to conservatism, he acknowledges that "the force of the example derives from evidence of defect in the agent's initial belief system."[32] In this case one has evidence that one's belief was formed irrationally. Accordingly, the defender of conservatism might include a ceteris paribus clause to the effect that absent reason to think one's belief is defective, belief confers some justification on its content. Christensen admits that the addition of this ceteris paribus clause leaves the conservative thesis motivated and more difficult to undermine by counterexample.[33]

This point is significant. I want to stress this by examining one of Christensen's earlier alleged counterexamples to conservatism. Christensen describes the case of a scientist who holds a theory, T, which states that a certain class of diseases is caused by viruses. A new competing theory is formulated stating that the class of diseases is caused by environmental toxins. The scientist then acknowledges that the two theories are equally supported by the available evidence.[34] Christensen remarks that according to epistemic conservatism the scientist would be justified in giving more credence to T because it is believed. But, Christensen claims, this is wrong.[35]

---

[31] Christensen (2000, 355).
[32] Christensen (2000, 355).
[33] Ibid., 355–356.
[34] See Christensen (1994, 82). This is a standard type of underdetermination case that occurs in the literature (see Vogel (1992). and Feldman (2003, 143–144).
[35] See Christensen (1994, 83).

In reply, this is a case of positive symmetrical evidence, not empty symmetrical evidence. When the new theory comes to light and it's acknowledged to be equally supported by the available evidence this indicates that there are positive yet equally balanced considerations for each theory. Since conservatism is a principle of 'last resort' and evidential considerations are relevant then one should withhold judgment until future evidence decides the case. This feature of my conservative view agrees with Christensen's judgment that undermining evidence by the formulation of a equally supported theory can destroy conservative justification. Yet in cases of empty symmetrical evidence, conservatism is not threatened by these kinds of cases.

As we have seen Christensen acknowledges that conservatism, properly understood, is not subject to straightforward counterexample; yet he continues to resist the core conservative idea. In an effort to locate the core objection to conservatism Christensen designs a case with the following conditions: "(1) coherence considerations aside, an agent has at her disposal an epistemically reasonable option for changing her beliefs, but (2) she does not also have evidence that her current beliefs are defective."[36] Christensen notes that the search for such a case is difficult because "typically, situations in which it is reasonable to change one's beliefs involve having reasons to distrust one's present beliefs."[37] He thinks, though, that by engaging in some science fiction we can construct a case. He constructs the following *downloader case*:

> Suppose that I have a serious lay interest in fish, and have a fairly extensive body of beliefs about them. At a party, I meet a professional ichthyologist. Although I ... believe that she shares the vast majority of my beliefs about fish, I know that she can probably set me straight about some ichthyological matters. However, I don't want to trouble her by asking a lot of work-related questions. Fortunately, I have a belief-downloader, which works as follows. If I turn it on, it scans both of our brains, until it finds some ichthyological proposition about which we disagree. It then replaces my belief with that of the ichthyologist, and turns itself off.[38]

Christensen acknowledges that this case does not pose a threat to conservatism since there is a more reliable means of acquiring

---

[36] Christensen (2000, 357).
[37] Christensen (2000, 357).
[38] Ibid.

information.[39] But he takes this case to be one of a range of cases in which the expertise factor varies. In the present case the downloader would be used on an expert. But in another case one could use the downloader on an epistemic peer. In the peer case Christensen claims you should be indifferent to the downloader's use.[40] He explains:

> My intuition ... in the case where I have positive reason to believe the other agent equally reliable [is] ... that it is a matter of epistemic indifference. Of course, I'm taking a risk in using the downloader: my belief could be true and the stranger's belief could be false, in which case I'll end up with a false belief instead of a true one. But in the imagined case, I have no reason to believe that this is any more likely than the opposite possibility: that my belief is false and the stranger's belief is true. Thus, in declining to use the downloader, I would take an equivalent risk of ending up with the false belief rather than the true one. Given my information in this sort of case, the net epistemic expectation from using the downloader is for neither improvement nor diminishment. Thus, from an epistemic point of view, I have no reason to use, or refrain from using, the downloader.[41]

Christensen's peer case is an interesting case for epistemic conservatism. If he is right that one should be indifferent to the downloader's use then one's beliefs carry no positive epistemic merit whatsoever. But is this right?[42] One might reply that the use of the downloader will bring about synchronic incoherence in one's beliefs.[43] The downloader may replace one's belief that p with a belief that not-p even when p is heavily inferentially integrated within one's corpus of beliefs. This would produce fairly significant incoherence in one's new body of beliefs. Or the downloader's use may result in inscrutable belief change in which one recalls formerly believing p but now believes an incompatible proposition, q. This too is a type of synchronic incoherence. These problems may have more weight than Christensen gives to them, but let us bypass them to move on to Christensen's core objection to conservatism.

---

[39] Ibid., 358.
[40] Ibid., 357.
[41] Christensen (2000, 360).
[42] See McGrath (2007, 14–17) for an extended reply to Christensen.
[43] Christensen (2000, 361–362) considers this reply.

Christensen thinks the "ultimate problem" with conservatism is that "it accords importance to a factor that should be epistemically irrelevant: the identity of the agent having the initial beliefs."[44] He explains, "Diachronic coherence principles [conservative principles] insert autobiographical considerations into an enterprise whose proper concern is limited to the detached pursuit of truth."[45] Moreover, he later complains that conservatism "gives credit for characteristics of belief that are irrelevant to the fundamental aim of accurate representation of the world."[46] This locates Christensen's central concern with conservatism. In light of the key role the truth goal has played in epistemology and the widespread resistance to conservatism, it's not implausible that this worry lays at the center of many objections to conservatism. But, if this is right, a proper stress on the perspectival character of justification removes this obstacle. Rather than providing an argument against conservatism, reflection on the perspectival character of justification provides a natural home for conservatism. Concerns about inserting autobiographical information (i.e., one's beliefs) into an enterprise whose proper concern is a subject's achieving true belief are unmotivated. Achieving true belief isn't something that permits a detached pursuit. Consequently, the identity of the agent is crucial for achieving the truth goal.

2.4 The extra boost and conversion objections

Some philosophers continue to feel a deep dissatisfaction with conservatism. Perhaps these philosophers are drawn to externalism or to skepticism, but in personal conversation two objections stand out. The first objection is that conservatism is suspect because if it were true then belief itself could provide an extra boost of confidence. The other objection is the conversion objection, roughly the idea that a proposition which is unjustified for a subject to accept could become justified merely by the fact that a subject comes to believe it. In the following I address both objections.

2.4.1 The extra boost objection

Suppose your evidence for q is counterbalanced. You then realize that there's a sound argument for q from p and p→q. You appropriately

---

[44] Ibid., 363.
[45] Ibid., 363.
[46] Ibid., 364.

believe q. Your confidence in q should be bumped up to the appropriate level given your confidence in p and p→q. Suppose this confidence level is .8. Now, if conservatism is true, it looks as if you have yet another reason to raise your confidence level in q—you believe q. Suppose it bumps you up to .85. But this extra boost of confidence is inappropriate.

In reply, this objection mistakenly assumes that in the presence of good evidence belief provides some extra evidence for its content. Conservatism is the thesis that mere belief is a source of justification. Mere belief is the state of believing p in the absence of any good evidence for it and in the absence of any good evidence against it. Sklar remarks that conservatism is "applied as a means of 'last resort' when the other principles fail to motivate a decision for us."[47] The key for understanding conservatism is that mere belief itself can generate justification, but this does not require that belief provides extra evidence for some claim.

This "last resort" feature of epistemic conservatism leads to another objection. Granted belief does not provide an extra boost because belief is relevant only in the very special evidential situation in which one lacks evidence for the content of the belief, but it now looks as if one can acquire positive evidence for p but decrease one's overall justification for p. If one is in the state of merely believing p but then one acquires weak evidence for p then it looks like the appropriate response is to believe p to the degree one's evidence now warrants and that may well be less than one's original conservative justification.

Two points undermine this objection. First, the objection requires that there is a number, n, that gives the level of justification one has via conservatism, and another number, m, that gives the positive level of justification one has by the weak evidence, and that $m < n$. For reasons pertaining to Lycan's attempt to explicate conservative justification via a credibility of $.5 + \epsilon$ (where ϵ is infinitesimal), I doubt that one can think of conservative justification as providing some specific level of credence given by some real number. Conservative justification is best explained as a factor that makes continued acceptance rational rather than a strength of evidence factor. Such an evidential factor can be represented by a number reflecting how *much* evidence a person has for a particular proposition. Conservative justification is not a strength of evidence factor.[48]

---

[47] Sklar (1975, 375).

[48] A different response to the present objection adopts Lycan's (1988, 171) claim that conservative merit confers infinitesimal credibility in which case the objection collapses since there is no n between $.5$ and $.5 + \epsilon$.

Second, Bayesianism implies that sometimes acquiring positive evidence for p can decrease one's overall justification for p. Suppose one has good grounds for believing that it is a natural law that 'all Fs are Gs.' One thus has good grounds for believing that all Fs are either Gs or Hs, where G and H are incompatible properties. But then one acquires evidence that some F is an H. This is positively relevant to the proposition that all Fs are either Gs or Hs, but it decreases one's overall justification for that claim. Why? Because one learns that some Fs are not Gs but Hs. And thus one may well think that there can be Fs that are neither Gs or Hs. One acquires positive evidence that the law one previously thought is not a law and thus there's not a lawlike connection between Fs and Gs. Given your evidence now, you no longer have good grounds for supposing that anything that is not a G or H is not an F. Similarly, with conservative justification if one acquires positive evidence then the principle of "last resort" no longer applies and definite evidential considerations come into play. Whereas one had believed in the special situation of empty symmetrical evidence one now learns that there is direct evidence to bear on this issue. Positive evidence may consequently reduce one's overall justification. The present objection fails.

2.4.2 Conversion objections

The conversion objection is that conservatism may improperly change the epistemic situation of a subject. Richard Foley considers two subjects, S and T, in the same sort of epistemic situation except for the difference that S believes h and T withholds on h. In this situation, Foley stipulates, it is just barely more rational for T to withhold on h than for T to believe h. He then asks: is it acceptable for S to believe h?[49] Foley invites us to answer 'no.'

David Christensen offers a case of a scientist whose evidence is counterbalanced apropos theory R and who does not believe theory R.[50] In this situation it would be irrational for the scientist to believe R. The scientist comes across an experimental result that tips the balance of evidence in favor of R and she now rationally believes R. Later, though, the scientist comes to learn that this evidence was fabricated. The scientist, however, continues to believe R, perhaps because she forgot that her sole reason for accepting it had been undermined. Importantly, though, it looks like her epistemic situation is the same as it was before she had the experiential result and thus her belief is irrational.

---

[49] Foley (1983, 176).
[50] Personal conversation.

Both of these putative counterexamples involve cases in which a claim is counterbalanced by the evidence and then by conversion a subject comes to rationally believe the claim.[51] The alleged counterintuitive result is that conservatism implies that belief can change the epistemic situation so that the believed content is now rational to believe whereas formerly it was not. This is a forceful challenge to conservatism because as Foley observes "all conservative positions will imply that simply by being believed a proposition acquires some kind of favorable epistemic status which in some way alters what is required to make that proposition or some other propositional rational for the person to regard as true."[52] Apart from this feature conservatism will be unable to perform the job it is designed to perform: that is, address underdetermination worries, concerns about memorial justification, and so on. So it is incumbent on the conservative to clearly answer this worry.

An initial question about these cases is whether it is a genuine case of empty symmetrical evidence or a case of positive symmetrical evidence? Foley does not indicate which kind of symmetry case he has in mind. Christensen's counterexample involves positive, albeit fabricated, evidence for a claim which is then undermined. The subject then possesses evidence that there is evidence bearing on this claim. This converts the subject's epistemic situation into one of positive symmetrical evidence. Hence, conservatism does not apply here.

Conservatism is a principle of last resort. When there are definite evidential considerations to bring to bear on a proposition then those considerations swamp any other considerations. This agrees with the deep scientific respect for experiential results; yet it also affords a proper place for theoretical virtues. In the following I discuss this and the conversion objections by way of an example from Gilbert Harman.

Harman considers a case to illustrate the difference between a foundations views and a coherence view.[53] The case concerns Karen who receives an aptitude test, which shows that she has considerable abilities in science and music but little ability in history and philosophy. Karen's previous grades do not correlate perfectly with these results. She had scored well in both physics and history but had scored poorly in music and philosophy. But she accepts the results of the aptitude test. She then

---

[51] Christensen's case involves the loop through undermined evidence. The point of Christensen's counterexample, though, is that conversion to theory R is doing the allegedly improper epistemic work after the evidence is undermined.
[52] Foley (1983, 179).
[53] Harman (1986, 34–36).

comes to accept that her poor grade in music was due to a lack of effort on her part, and her high grade in history was due to the ease of the course. Karen takes it that her competence in physics as reported by the test explains her good performance in her physics class and her incompetence in philosophy explains her poor performance in that course. Moreover, she takes it that although she is competent in music her lack of attention explained her poor performance in that course. Similarly, the ease of her history class explains her good performance in that even though she lacks the relevant abilities. In short, Karen accepts the results of the test and incorporates them into an explanatory system.

Several months later (changing Harman's case a bit), Karen learns that the results of the aptitude were not correct; her scores were mixed up with someone else's and they have subsequently been lost. But she still accepts that she has considerable aptitude for science and music and little aptitude for history and philosophy. She forgot that originally her sole reason for accepting this was the original report. Nevertheless, these beliefs are now significantly inferentially integrated in her body of beliefs. She now holds a number of beliefs which support and are supported by her belief about her aptitudes.

The judgment I draw from this case is that Karen's belief after learning about the misleading test is that she remains justified in her belief precisely on account of the overall explanatory virtues of her beliefs. This is not precisely a case for epistemic conservatism since it was never the case that Karen held this belief in empty symmetrical evidence. But it is relevant for the following reason: belief often leads to discovering new explanatory connections. Once those connections are part of a subject's perspective the belief has a new basis and a much better justification. This is how I see epistemic conservatism at work. Some beliefs are held in the state of empty symmetrical evidence, and, given that they have some justification, they can serve as the background for a coherent explanatory story that then further supports the beliefs' justification.

2.5 Conservatism and the perspectival character of justification

I've argued at length that the objections to epistemic conservatism rely on an impoverished conception of the view. Conservatism, properly formulated, is concerned about the special state in which many of our background beliefs are held. In this respect conservatism is a natural view. Yet are there positive arguments for conservatism? One argument appeals to the fact that our epistemic practices are significantly conservative. When we take into account the force of new evidence we follow the maxim of minimal mutilation.[54] This maxim is firmly entrenched in our epistemic practices. While subjects often affirm the consequent, they can learn that this form of reasoning is faulty. Further, they can learn to replace affirming the consequent with explanatory reasoning which explicitly considers relevant alternatives to one's favored conclusion. Yet conservatism differs from natural reasoning errors. Subjects are always and everywhere relying on their antecedent convictions. Even the effort to improve reasoning relies on our trust in unchallenged forms of reasoning.

Another argument for conservatism applies to its necessity for avoiding wholesale skepticism.[55] If I am right that important assumptions are believed in the state of empty symmetrical evidence then many epistemological views requiring positive evidence will land in wholesale skepticism. On those views, we lack justification for thinking that the meanings of our terms are stable and that objects persist through time. If those beliefs are not justified then it is hard to see how any other beliefs can be justified. In Chapter 6 I pick up this argument against a direct acquaintance theory of justification by arguing that an acquaintance theorist cannot provide justification for any belief that lays outside the specious present. The result of avoiding conservatism is a searing skepticism.

2.5.1 The argument from perspective

We have two plausible arguments for conservatism. In the following I pursue a slightly different justification for the doctrine, a justification that comes from the perspectival character of epistemic justification. I argue that if justification is perspectival then conservatism is true. The perspectival character of justification is that the epistemic justification of a subject's beliefs depends on a subject's perspective. Facts that a subject is unaware of do not make a difference to the justificatory status of a subject's beliefs since they are not part of her perspective. The facts relevant for determining justification are facts about a subject's perspective.

The perspectival character of justification is a standard feature of internalist accounts of justification. But even externalists recognize that

---

[54] See Quine (1990); Sklar (1975).
[55] See Sklar (1975, 376). For dissent see Foley (1983).

justification is perspectival. Alvin Goldman, in his famous essay developing a reliabilist theory of justification, recognizes that our judgments of justification depend, not on the actual facts, but our beliefs about the reliability of various ways of forming beliefs. It is so surprising that it deserves to be quoted in full. He writes:

> What we really want is an explanation of why we count, or would count, certain beliefs as justified and others as unjustified. Such an explanation must refer to our beliefs about reliability, not to the actual facts. The reason we count beliefs as justified is that they are formed by what we believe to be reliable belief-forming processes. Our beliefs about which belief-forming processes are reliable may be erroneous, but that does not affect the adequacy of the explanation. Since we believe that wishful thinking is an unreliable belief-forming process, we regard beliefs formed by wishful thinking as unjustified. What matters, then, is what we believe about wishful thinking, not what is true (in the long run) about wishful thinking.[56]

Goldman's claim is reminiscent of Keith Lerher's remark that there is "no exit from the circle of one's beliefs" because justification must always proceed through some belief.[57] Lehrer argues that experience itself cannot provide justification unless experience is underwritten by a belief that the experience is veridical.[58] As Lehrer puts it, "The prick of sense often elicits ready consent, but what we believe in the fact of sensory stimulation depends on our antecedent convictions."[59] The point of both Goldman's and Lehrer's remarks is that justification is perspectival. We rely on our beliefs about what counts as good sources of evidence to determine what beliefs are epistemically good to hold. There is no getting around the fact that judgments of justification and judgments about what we should believe rely on our antecedent convictions.[60] The picture then is that to decide what to believe we must rely on our own beliefs. How could it be otherwise?

The normative backing to the fact that we always must work within our perspective is provided by an internalistic conception of justification. The generic concept of justification is that of satisfying some kind

---

[56] Goldman (1979a, 18).
[57] Lehrer (1974, 187–188).
[58] See also Alston (1993).
[59] Lehrer (1974, 188).
[60] See also Goldman's remarks on Maximalism in Goldman (1979b).

of standard. A subject's belief may be justified on a variety of different standards: pragmatic standards, prudential standards, social standards, and so on. What distinguishes *epistemic* justification is the standard of truth. A belief is epistemically justified if and only if it is likely to be true given what a subject has to go on. But, as I argued in Section 2.1, this notion of 'likely to be true' cannot be entirely unpacked in terms of probability. It needs to rely on some fundamental notion of right reason. BonJour, discussing epistemic justification, writes that its distinguishing feature is "its essential or internal relation to the cognitive goal of truth."[61] The internal relation to the goal of truth is conceptually basic. Our natural judgments about justification provide the basic materials for discovering the nature of this internal relation. Since our natural judgements about justification rely on background beliefs held in empty symmetrical evidence, it is reasonable to hold that conservatism is true. Conservatism is a fundamental epistemic principle; it receives support from our natural judgments about right reason.

I've argued that the claim that a subject in the special evidential situation of empty symmetrical evidence is epistemically justified in maintaining her belief. Because this is a situation of empty evidence there are no specific challenges to her belief. Yet she holds that it is true. This fact about her perspective implies that she has some level of justification for her belief. When challenges arise, though, she loses this justification; but if, by relying on her beliefs, she comes to have a coherent explanatory perspective then her original confidence is vindicated.

2.5.2 Two challenges

In the remaining pages I examine two challenges to this argument.

Externalism

The first challenge to the argument from perspective is that a subject need not rely on her perspective to fulfill the epistemic goal; whether or not a subject fulfills the epistemic goal is a matter of how well the subject's beliefs fare with respect to the truth. If a subject's beliefs are largely true she is doing well and if they are largely false she is not doing well.

This objection assumes an externalist conception of norm satisfaction. It assumes that as long as one's beliefs are mainly true then one is doing well epistemically. But this is false. A subject that gains a true belief

---

[61] BonJour (1985, 5–6).

by sheer luck doesn't thereby improve her epistemic standing. Similarly, a subject that acquires a new reliable belief-forming mechanism by a burst of gamma radiation has not realized a cognitive achievement. She just got lucky. A long-standing tradition in epistemology has been to search for norms to guide our intellectual activity apropos deciding what to believe. The argument for conservatism above is framed within a commitment to internalistic norms for rational beliefs. The proposal is that if one accepts the internalistic project then one must rely on one's perspective to fulfill the main cognitive goal.[62]

Pragmatism

The second challenge is a pragmatist challenge; in the situation of empty symmetrical evidence a subject who believes that p has a pragmatic right to her belief but not an epistemic right. The idea is that given what the subject believes the best prudential strategy is to maintain her belief; after all, if she came to withhold or to disbelieve then she would be acting inconsistent with what she takes to be true. Thus the right to maintain her belief in this special evidential situation comes from purely practical considerations.

In reply, this is a dubious application of the distinction between a prudential and epistemic right. The clearest cases in which these rights come apart are when it is in a subject's practical interest to believe something that is at odds with what her evidence indicates. A subject who learns she has a disease from which recovery is very improbable may still be prudentially justified in believing she will recover. Believing this will increase her odds of survival. But the case of empty symmetrical evidence is not like this. Her belief that p is not *improbable* given her evidence.

What the pragmatist gets right is the availability of a theoretical defense of the subject's belief in empty symmetrical evidence. This defense appeals to the available actions a subject can take to her belief: maintain, suspend, or disbelieve. Given that she takes it that p is true and yet she possesses no legitimate challenges to p, it would be

---

[62] Ernest Sosa's (2009) virtue reliabilism escapes the above argument since on his account the primary item of epistemic value requires apt belief. A significant difference between Sosa's view and mine is the extent of the constraints provided by a subject's perspective. I hold that all the facts that determine justification are facts about a subject's perspective and her explanatory position. As I explain in Chapter 4 this is a kind of mentalist evidentialist view.

inconsistent with her perspective to suspend or disbelieve. But far from a mere prudential concern, this theoretical defense is another way to see that a subject does have epistemic justification to maintain her belief.

Consider, as an example, a subject's belief that memory is reliable. This belief lacks any non-circular defense. Any appeal to evidence to justify that memory is reliable must rely on the assumption that memory is reliable.[63] The belief that memory is reliable is a crucial part of a subject's epistemic perspective. Yet the belief is held in the special situation of empty symmetrical evidence; for any arguments for or against the reliability of memory assume the reliability of memory. Can we even make sense of a subject having a prudential but not epistemic right to believe in the reliability of memory? Even prudence requires justified beliefs about the past. Without epistemic justification that memory is reliable it's hard to see how one could have any prudential rights. So, far from being simply a policy of good prudence, belief in the special state of empty symmetrical evidence makes good epistemic sense.

A related way to resist epistemic conservatism is to adopt a pure coherentist view. Belief in the special state of empty symmetrical evidence is unjustified, but if one's beliefs cohere with everything else one believes then those beliefs are justified. I have some sympathy for this response. But I resist it for two reasons. First, hinge propositions are so fundamental that they lay at the basis for even appealing to the coherentist framework. Consider the assumption that meaning is stable. This assumption is prior to applying any conception of coherence. It would be pointless to argue that one's beliefs were coherent unless one was already convinced that the contents of one's beliefs persisted through the specious present. I do not see any way to provide epistemic justification for this belief apart from conservatism.

Second, I do not see how coherence by itself can provide justification unless the data used for coherence reasoning has some presumption in its favor.[64] Unless the data used for coherence reasoning has some initial plausibility, mere coherence cannot raise the probability of belief.[65]

---

[63] See Alston (1986); Bergmann (2004a) for arguments that we lack non-circular evidence for the reliability of basic sources of belief.

[64] For a good statement of this objection see BonJours, discussion of the input objection in BonJour (1985, 108). BonJour now recognizes that this objection is fatal to pure coherentism. See BonJour (1997) for details.

[65] See Olsson (2005) for a formal proof of this result.

Moreover, it has always seemed to me that the fact that one has a perspective needs to be taken into account. One does not simply reason about propositions one has no commitments on; rather coherentism is an attempt to illustrate the theoretical virtues of the commitments one has. Consequently, in addition to the fact that pure coherence cannot justify belief, a pure coherentist project does not do justice to the subject's perspective.

2.6 Conclusion

Conservatism is an important epistemological doctrine. Anyone attracted to a non-skeptical internalist epistemology must come to grips with the ineliminable role of background beliefs for epistemic justification. Following Neurath's famous metaphor, the entirety of our system of beliefs is like a raft that we rebuild at sea. We seek to continuously improve the raft by adding and subtracting new material but we must always stand on some existing timber. I have articulated a key rationale for thinking that our inability to escape reliance on our own beliefs shouldn't lead to skepticism.

3
Reasons without First Philosophy

We saw in the previous chapter that epistemic conservatism is a viable and important epistemological doctrine. The fact that a subject believes a proposition in the special epistemic state of empty symmetrical evidence confers positive status on that proposition. This conservative view allows for some noninferential justification. In what sense does a view count as 'coherentist' or 'anti-foundationalist'? One of my aims is to answer this question. However, the taxonomic issue of classifying epistemological views is not significant. A more substantive question is whether a view is true and whether it provides a plausible theoretical perspective for addressing perplexing epistemological issues. My primary purpose in this chapter is to argue for a unique coherentist view of reasons which I call 'the framework view of reasons'. This view holds that reasons require an explanatory coherent framework of justified beliefs, where some of those justified beliefs come from noninferentially justified background beliefs. I argue for this view in the context of developing a neglected coherentist argument, the argument against first philosophy. First philosophy is the Cartesian quest for a proper starting point for reason which need not require any additional defense. The argument against first philosophy calls into question the possibility of such a position. On my view we lack a proper starting *point*. Rather we inherit a *map* which we are under the burden to bring into explanatory coherence. I begin with a discussion of the basic reasons dilemma, a problematic dilemma that appears require basic reasons for justification and yet also show that there can be no epistemically justified basic reasons. It is vitally important for a coherentist epistemology to have an adequate theoretical perspective on the nature of reasons. As I will argue, one of the central problems with coherentist views to date has been an ambivalent attitude toward basic reasons and, corresponding to this, an inadequate theoretical perspective on basic reasons. I present and argue for a coherentist account of reasons that is well motivated and distinct from foundationalism. The upshot of this chapter is that the position of Goodman,[1] Quine,[2] Sellars,[3] Harman,[4] Rawls,[5], and Lycan[6] is more plausible than recent history suggests.[7]

3.1 The basic reasons dilemma

A basic reason is a regress stopper. It is a noninferentially justified proposition that supports some other propositions. Basic reasons have two properties: noninferential justification and ability to support another proposition. Coherentists face a dilemma concerning basic reasons: either the view sanctions basic reasons or it does not. If coherentism sanctions basic reasons, then it is just another form of foundationalism and will succumb to arguments designed to undermine foundationalism, specifically the Sellarsian dilemma and the problem of arbitrariness. If, however, coherentism prohibits basic reasons, then it falls prey to circularity objections. On either horn, the prospects of a coherentist epistemology look bleak.

3.1.1 The first horn

The first horn of the dilemma argues for the impossibility of a coherentist view that allows for basic reasons. One reason for this is terminological: no view counts as coherentist if it allows for basic reasons. The other, more important, reason is that the arguments designed to motivate coherentism over its foundationalist rivals demonstrate the impossibility of basic reasons. Let us briefly examine these arguments. I argue later that any form of coherentism should be consistent with the conclusions of the Sellarsian dilemma and the problem of arbitrariness.

---

[1] Goodman (1965, 1979).
[2] Quine (1960); Quine and Ullian (1970).
[3] Sellars (1963).
[4] Harman (1973, 1986).
[5] Rawls (1999, 15–19).
[6] Lycan (1988, 1996, 2002, 2012).
[7] See also Daniels (1996, 2008) for discussion on the method of reflective equilibrium.

The Sellarsian dilemma targets foundationalist attempts to end the regress of reasons in a non-doxastic, experiential state.[8] I discuss and defend the Sellarsian dilemma in Chapter 5. For present purposes I work with a basic form of the dilemma. Either experience has truth-evaluable content or it does not. If experience lacks truth-evaluable content, then it cannot serve as a reason for believing that a claim is true. If, however, experience has truth-evaluable content, then we need an additional reason for thinking that the content of experience is true. On either horn, experience cannot function as a basic reason. If the Sellarsian dilemma is defensible, it constitutes a powerful weapon in the coherentist's arsenal by implying that no truth-evaluable content can support another claim without itself requiring some support.

The second argument against the possibility of basic reasons is the problem of arbitrariness. Peter Klein has rehabilitated this old objection to foundationalism.[9] The arbitrariness problem focuses on allegedly foundational beliefs for which no additional reason need be offered. Such beliefs, it is claimed, need not be supported by additional reasons but yet are justified. Yet, there is a strong natural judgment that a belief's justification requires a reason for its truth. Suppose someone claims to know that the tree in my backyard is a Loblolly Pine. It is natural to ask how they know this. Someone knows that this is a Loblolly Pine only if they possess an adequate reason. Once a reason is offered we can ask about its adequacy. If they claim to have identified it by matching up salient characteristics with a tree identification book then we can ask how reliable or how confident they are that they have correctly identified the tree.[10] It is, of course, natural to end dialogue at some point because no one has time for a persistent Socrates. But, apart from the pragmatic constraints of time and attention, any claim consistent with some skeptical scenarios requires additional reasons. The pragmatic constraints lead us to assume that these skeptical scenarios don't obtain. But epistemological integrity requires additional reasons.[11]

---

[8] See Sellars's essay 'Empiricism and the Philosophy of Mind' in Sellars (1963) and BonJour (1985, Ch. 4).

[9] Klein (1999, 2000, 2004). Klein's discussion has generated a number of responses. See Huemer (2003); Bergmann (2004b); Howard-Snyder (2005); Howard-Snyder and Coffman (2006).

[10] Dendrologists debate the exact number of different species of pine tree.

[11] Many internalist foundationalists claim that experience provides reasons for foundational beliefs. In Chapter 5 I argue against this proposal.

Both the Sellarsian dilemma and the problem of arbitrariness support the claim that basic reasons are impossible. Both arguments focus on the claim that propositions which are capable of support themselves require support. This feature of these arguments lends credibility to the standard coherentist line that there is no noninferential justification. As we will see in the next section I think that this conclusion is not warranted. Before we get to that, let us examine the problems with accepting this claim.

3.1.2 The second horn

The second horn of the basic reasons dilemma states that basic reasons are required to avoid circularity. The problem of circularity has stunted the natural development of coherentism. Circular reasoning conflicts with the aim of demonstration. Consider someone who does not know whether it is a fact that p. Clearly, the aim of demonstrating that p fails if all one does is reason from the disputed proposition. A jury charged with the task of discovering the guilt of a person should not be swayed by the prosecution's argument that he is guilty for the reason that he is guilty. Coherentism has often been maligned as endorsing circular reasoning. Because every proposition requires a reason (anti-foundationalism) and no proposition is justified by an infinite series of reasons (anti-infinitism) then justification requires that one eventually reasons through the disputed proposition. Yet, there is a strong natural judgment that circular reasoning is *never* justified.

This is a problem which plagued Laurence BonJour's coherentism and eventually proved to be the reason for his conversion to foundationalism.[12] BonJour argued that the very feature of a cognitive state that enables it to function as a reason–its assertive propositional content–creates the need for it to be justified.[13] But later on in his book, reflecting on the fact that the data used in coherence reasoning must itself be justified, BonJour recognized that coherence alone cannot justify the data.[14] At the time BonJour reasoned that because any challenge to one's empirical beliefs presupposes that one does have the empirical beliefs thus challenged one may avail oneself of the presumption that one's beliefs about one's beliefs are true. This 'doxastic presumption' provides the crucial unchallenged data for coherentist reasoning.

---

[12] For details, see BonJour (1997).
[13] BonJour (1985, 78).
[14] Ibid., 101–106.

Given that one does have these beliefs, one can then reason about their coherence to come to accept that one's view is mostly true. But BonJour now acknowledges that this move is a desperate attempt to get around the basic problem of justifying the data used in coherence reasoning.[15] Thus, apart from a convincing reply to the circularity objection, coherentism cannot get off the ground.

The basic reasons dilemma illustrates the conflicting forces facing a coherentist philosophy. On the one hand, some positive arguments for coherentism support that there are not basic reasons because any supporter requires support. On the other hand, the problem of circularity supports the conclusion that the data for coherence reasoning requires independent plausibility. My aim in the remainder of this chapter is to offer a view of reasons that relieves these tensions.

3.2 The argument against first philosophy

The basic reasons dilemma shows that coherentism faces powerful forces that threaten its integrity. The dilemma aims to show that coherentism requires basic reasons but cannot have basic reasons. What the coherentists need is a virtuous mean that satisfies the following conditions: first, provides a cogent argument against basic reasons that; second, does not succumb to circularity objections; and, third, avoids the problem of arbitrariness. In the following I advance an argument for a view of reasons satisfying these three requirements.

3.2.1 The nature of basic reasons

A basic reason is an assertive propositional content that need not receive support in order to justify other propositions. A basic reason must be propositional because a reason must represent the world as being one way rather than another, which requires that a reason be consistent with some propositions and inconsistent with others. I understand the notion of 'propositional' here in a weak sense. It picks out a class of things that are representational and have accuracy conditions. To the extent that visual experience provides a reason to believe the world is one way rather than another, it is propositional in this weak sense. The language of 'assertive' contents comes from BonJour's discussion of the doctrine of the given. BonJour claims that the key feature of a cognitive state that enables it to serve as a reason is "its assertive or at

---

[15] BonJour (1997, 14).

least representational content."[16] It is not sufficient for a reason that a content have accuracy conditions; the content must be hosted as true.

Propositions that function as basic reasons for a subject have two properties: (i) a subject has noninferential justification for p, and (ii) the subject can use p in a justifying direct ampliative inference. The dual nature of basic reasons is important. Although not often stressed, foundationalism requires a substantive theory of inference. How do the basic beliefs provide reasons for the non-basic beliefs? I argue in the following that there is a distinctive foundationalist story about inferential support.

According to the foundationalist's story basic reasons provide the foundations for an empirical view. They are the basis upon which one can infer other claims. The kind of inference foundationalism requires is *direct ampliative inference*. Ampliative inference allows one to 'amplify' or expand one's beliefs by going beyond what is given in the premises. The inference from *(a) past As are Bs* to *(b) all As are Bs* expands upon the premise (a) because the conclusion is not a logical implication of the premises. Foundationalism endorses *direct* ampliative inference in virtue of the fact that it denies that every premise in an ampliative argument requires additional support. Some premises in an ampliative argument support the conclusion without themselves requiring additional support.

A direct ampliative inference is a straightforward inductive argument with two properties: the premises of the inductive argument are epistemologically prior to the conclusion, and the premises *exhaust* the evidence for the conclusion. Consider the following inference:

(a) 100 black ravens have been observed.
(b) No non-black ravens have been observed.
Thus,
(c) all ravens are black.

This argument counts as an instance of direct ampliative inference only if the premises are known or justifiedly believed prior to knowledge or justified belief in the conclusion. Suppose that condition is met. Is it a good argument? It is not implausible to think that it is. However, the restriction that (a) and (b) themselves exhaust the evidence for (c) is significant. This restriction prohibits background claims from tacitly serving as additional and unstated evidence for the conclusion. For instance, the claims that 'the color of a raven is a natural kind property'

---

[16] BonJour (1985, 78).

and 'natural kind properties are stable in species' cannot be in the background if the above inference is a direct ampliative inference. One could *add* those background claims to the premises, but then the direct ampliative inference would include law-like claims, and law-like claims are not suitable candidates for basic reasons. As the foundationalist sets up the regress, basic reasons are supposed to be propositions that are directly observable. This illustrates the tension in a foundationalist epistemology between a reasonable reconstruction of ampliative inference and a reasonable account of the nature of basic reasons.

This point about proper restrictions on which premises can be used in direct ampliative inference bears stressing. Direct ampliative inference must not include any premises to the effect that some hypothesis is the best explanation of some other proposition. Direct ampliative inference eschews explanatory premises, lawlike claims, general plausibility considerations, or tacit principles like the principle of induction. The rationale for this is the foundationalist claim that the most fundamental premises to be used in direct ampliative inference must be observational and explanatory and/or lawlike claims are not observational.[17] As I argue in Chapter 6 a principled distinction between observational properties and non-observational properties is vital for foundationalism. If one's empirical view is to be justified by basic reasons the most plausible candidates for basic reasons are observational properties. These properties used in basic enumerative induction is thought to provide the basis for reconstructing empirical knowledge.

A defender of phenomenal conservatism might allow that lawlike claims can provide foundational reasons on the basis of it seeming to one that, for example, the color of a raven is a natural kind property.[18] The phenomenal conservative faces a question about whether there are any restrictions on the content of seemings which provide basic reasons. Suppose it noninferentially seems to one that all non-trivial zeros of the zeta function have as real part $\frac{1}{2}$. It is natural to ask how one has access to such a fact, if it is a fact. Apart from a convincing account it is dubious that any such intuitions provide basic justification. What was plausible about early versions of foundationalism, for example, Russell's acquaintance theory, was that the basic beliefs considered properties

---

[17] One move is to argue that such claims are a priori. Chapter 6 presents an argument that explanatory considerations are required for a priori justification.

[18] For a defense of phenomenal conservatism see Huemer (2001). Also, see Tucker (2013).

which were, arguably, directly present in experience. The more general move to seemings divorces this natural account about why certain basic beliefs are justified.

Direct ampliative inference figures prominently in the regress argument for foundationalism. A foundationalist uses the regress argument to specify the ultimate reasons for one's empirical view, the foundational premises from which one can reconstruct one's view through legitimate inference. The inferential relations between the basic reasons and the next level are construed in a linear manner. The basic reasons constitute premises from which one infers propositions at the next level in the attempted rational reconstruction of one's view. Furthermore, because the regress aims for one's ultimate reasons, these alleged reasons constitute the only evidence for the conclusion in question.

The significance of this conception of basic reasons is that it identifies two distinct elements in a foundationalist theory of reasons: a theory of justification and a theory of inference. The foundationalist theory of justification says that some propositions are noninferentially justified, while the theory of inference specifies that those propositions may be used in direct ampliative inference. The composite nature of this view of reasons opens logical space to consider a view of reasons that denies either of these claims. We've seen in BonJour's work the problem afflicting a view of reasons without noninferential justification. In the following I explore the possibility that some propositions may be noninferentially justified without being able to be used in a justifying direct ampliative inference. On this view there is some noninferential justification, but propositions that possess only noninferential justification cannot support directly ampliative inference, for all ampliative inference involves coherence reasoning. This view makes sense of the conservative element in the previous coherentist epistemologies of Goodman, Quine, Sellars, Rawls, Harman, and Lycan. Moreover, this view fits naturally with the emphasis those philosophers place on the failure of first philosophy.

3.2.2 No first philosophy

A prominent coherentist theme is the revisability of all our beliefs and the fundamental role of the theoretical virtues in revising beliefs. The stress on the theoretical virtues in belief revision conflicts with the possibility of direct ampliative inference. The theoretical virtues of simplicity, conservativeness, and explanatory power do not fit into the simple representation of direct ampliative inference. These virtues are not observational properties and they cannot be inferred by direct ampliative inference from observational properties. They are explanatory properties of sets of information. On my view every good inference assumes a set of background beliefs. These beliefs provide plausibility considerations which govern inference. Conservatism provides the initial justification for these beliefs. In the following I present an argument that all inference involves plausibility considerations. This provides an argument against basic reasons by attacking the claim that some propositions can be used straight off for inference without any background information.

A neglected argument made by the mid-century coherentists supports the claim that all justified ampliative inference is fundamentally explanatory in nature.[19] This argument forms a key contention against foundationalism by arguing against basic reasons. This argument against first philosophy aims to show that "all philosophical arguments are really explicit or implicit comparisons of plausibility."[20] If all arguments are comparisons of plausibility, then any ampliative inference is either explicitly or implicitly a weighing of explanatory virtues. A judgment about the comparative plausibility of various claims relies on judgments (perhaps tacit) about the relative theoretical merits of the respective claims. It is hard to see how one could think that some proposition p is more plausible than another proposition q without having views about the simplicity, conservativeness, or the explanatory power of either p or q. Thus, if there is a good argument that each justifying ampliative inference invokes plausibility considerations, then no noninferentially justified proposition supports direct ampliative inference.

William Lycan presents a version of the argument against first philosophy in his book *Judgement and Justification*.[21] Lycan introduces a position he calls "deductivism," the metaphilosophical view according to which "proper philosophical argumentation consists in the construction of valid arguments with true premises, or more specifically deductively valid arguments whose premises are obvious, self-evident,

---

[19] I will focus on Lycan's development of this argument but comparable arguments can be found in Quine (1960, Ch. 1) and Sellars (1963) (see "Empiricism and the Philosophy of Mind" and "Some Reflections of Language Games"). Similar considerations can be found in Goodman's (1965) discussion of the justification of deductive and inductive rules as well as Rawls's (1999) discussion of the method of reflective equilibrium, which he explicitly grounds in Goodman's discussion. Also see Nozick's remarks on explanation (1981, 13–18). A recent argument for the same conclusion is made by Peter Lipton (2004).

[20] Lycan (1988, 18).

[21] Lycan (1988, 115–122).

indisputably true, or at least uncontroversial."[22] He then argues that on pain of regress deductive inference cannot be the entire story of reasonable belief. The premises themselves must be reasonable. What justifies the premises? In Chapter 5 I consider the traditional appeal to the given and argue that it fails. Assuming the correctness of those arguments, the deductivist is left in one of two uncomfortable positions: either the ultimate premises lack justification or the justification rests on plausibility considerations. Opting for the more feasible latter alternative, the ultimate premises receive justification from plausibility considerations. As Lycan says, "Even if we try to be deductivists ... we seem to be stuck with the conclusion that all philosophical arguments are really explicit or implicit comparisons of plausibility."[23] Any deductive argument can be reformulated as inconsistent set. Consider argument by modus ponens. It shows at best that the following is inconsistent: $\{p, p \to q, \neg q\}$. How should we resolve the inconsistency? Plausibility considerations must guide us; that is, considerations about what is simpler, what explains more, or what fits with accepted belief. Inconsistency alone does not tell us what to believe. We need considerations of plausibility.

Let us examine Hume's criticism of induction given the failure of first philosophy.[24] Hume examines the human tendency to expect more of the same, given the regularities of past experience. But he argues that there is no rational justification of the natural belief that future experience will resemble past experience because any justification for this claim will rely on the disputed claim. One may attempt to argue thus:

1. In the past cases which were then unobserved turned out to resemble observed cases.
So,
2. the presently unobserved cases will resemble the observed cases.

Hume observes that this argument itself depends on the claim the future will resemble the past. The argument projects past successes about the then unobserved cases into the future. This non-deductive argument requires the principle that past successes are reliable guides to the future. But this is the very principle that the inductive vindication of induction seeks to establish.

---

[22] Ibid., 116.

[23] (Lycan 1988 Ibid., 118).

[24] See Hume (2007) 'Of the idea of a Necessary Connection'. Goodman (1965) develops coherentism in response to the Humean skeptic about induction.

On the naturalist reading of Hume,[25] Hume's point is not that inductive beliefs ought not be endorsed, but rather that the Cartesian project of first philosophy is a complete failure. Without a natural belief in the reliability of induction we would be adrift at sea. Hume's point is methodological. Unless we allow room in our epistemologies for natural belief, skepticism reigns.

Opponents of first philosophy see Hume's point as also illustrating the role of plausibility considerations. Our inferential practices resist simple analyses into straight-rule induction or the like. Rather inference rests on plausibility reasoning which is a matter of weighing holistic, explanatory virtues. In the standard inductive cases it is clearly more simple, conservative, and explanatory to suppose that the unobserved cases resemble the observed cases. Any attempt to provide a "more fundamental" justification of these practices is a reversion to first philosophy.[26]

The argument against first philosophy accentuates the ineliminable role of explanatory considerations in belief evaluation. One attempt to escape the role of explanatory considerations is the Keynesian strategy.[27] This strategy claims that the regress of reasons stops with an infallible awareness of probability claims, which are allegedly necessarily true. For instance, one is infallibly aware of the necessary truth that one's experience of seeming to see a red circle *makes it probable* that there is a red circle before one. Awareness of such probability claims would be a significant step towards vindicating first philosophy; for deductivism could be preserved in a probabilistic form.

In the final chapter I consider the plausibility of a general Bayesian epistemology. For present purposes a serious problem for the Keynesian is that it is extremely doubtful that one is actually aware of such probability claims. I am aware of color and shape properties and I am aware of some properties of relations (e.g., *taller than* is transitive and asymmetric), but I am not aware of necessarily true probability claims. Richard Fumerton appears to agree. Writing about the internal relation of making probable posited by the Keynesian, he claims:

> I cannot quite bring myself to believe that I am phenomenologically acquainted with this internal relation of making probable. And in the end, I strongly suspect that the probability relation that philosophers

---

[25] See Garrett (1997); Owen (1999).
[26] For a recent development of this theme, see Maddy (2007).
[27] See Fumerton (1995, 197–203).

do seek in order to avoid skepticism concerning inferentially justified beliefs is an illusion.[28]

In addition to Fumerton's judgment there is a simpler explanation for why persons can be pushed in the direction of thinking such truths exist: these probability claims reflect plausibility judgments. Given the way we think the world works (that is, given our background beliefs), we assign a fairly high probability to the proposition 'I am not in a radical skeptical scenario'. Thus, we assign a fairly high probability to claims that our experiences are truth-indicative. This is far from the Cartesian project of first philosophy.

3.3 Framework reasons

The argument against first philosophy provides a clear line of reasoning against basic reasons by attacking any view of inference that neglects plausibility considerations. In this section I develop a theory of reasons that does not fall back into the problems of arbitrariness and circularity. I begin by explaining how circularity and arbitrariness are avoided and then I formulate the framework theory of reasons.

The circularity problem is that the data used in coherence reasoning requires some presumption in its favor, independent of its use in coherence reasoning. In Chapter 2 I've argued for epistemic conservatism which provides some justification for data that is held in the special state of empty symmetrical evidence. Epistemic conservatism is compatible with the argument against first philosophy. That argument does not challenge the existence of noninferential justification; it challenges the claim that reasons arise independently of any plausibility considerations. A view that combines conservatism with the role of plausibility considerations is not fraught by circularity concerns. This view holds that belief confers some positive epistemic status on its content but that belief alone cannot constitute a reason for another proposition apart from plausibility considerations.

The arbitrariness problem arises in the context of the regress argument in which one aims to specify the basic propositions upon which one can reconstruct by linear inference one's empirical view. We consider some p that supports q that supports r, ..., until one has completed the reconstruction. The arbitrariness objection focuses on the fact that

---

[28] Fumerton (1995, 218).

p is unsupported and yet contingent. One's belief that p is consistent with a class of skeptical possibilities in which p is false and yet one has no additional reason for thinking that p is true. In such a case it is epistemically objectionable to think that p is true.

A conservative view with a more nuanced conception of inference does not succumb to this objection. The argument against first philosophy requires plausibility considerations to support justifying inferences. On this view a reason for another belief requires a framework of justified commitments which together support the inference. The property of being a reason is a property a single proposition has only in relation to a background body of beliefs. Reasons occur only in perspective.

The framework view of reasons can be made more precise by appeal to INUS conditions. J.L. Mackie analyzed the causal relation by way of INUS conditions.[29] On his view x is a cause of y if and only if x is an *I*nsufficient, *N*onredundant condition of a larger *U*nnecessary but *S*ufficient condition for y. The spark is a cause of the fire because the spark, while not sufficient for the fire, is a nonredundant element of a larger set of conditions which are not necessary for fire but collectively are sufficient for the fire. On Mackie's view, causation requires a background set of conditions. Causation is not a two-place relation; rather it is a three-place relation between an event, a background set of conditions, and an effect.

Jonathan Kvanvig appeals to INUS conditions to provide a coherentist account of appearance states.[30] He claims that an appearance state isn't sufficient for a belief's justification because one needs other supporting beliefs. Even so, the appearance state is a nonredundant condition of a larger set of conditions that are not necessary but sufficient for the belief's justification. This provides a clear structural analysis of how an appearance state can play a justifying role within a broader coherentist account.

Kvanvig's idea can be extended to give a structural analysis of a coherentist account of what it is for one proposition to be a reason for another proposition. The similarity between Mackie's account of causation and my account of reasons is straightforward. The relation 'is a reason for' is not a two-place relation; rather it is a three-place relation between a proposition, a background set of beliefs, and a supported proposition.

---

[29] See Mackie (1974).
[30] For details, see Kvanvig and Riggs (1992); Kvanvig (1995b).

We can formulate the account as follows:

Framework Reasons: A proposition p is a reason for a proposition q for a subject S at time t if and only if

1. S is justified in believing p at t,
2. p is an INUS condition for q's justification, that is,
   a. p is insufficient for q's justification,
   b. p is a nonredundant part of a larger set of propositions that are unnecessary but sufficient for q's justification, and
3. S is justified in believing at least one of those larger sets of propositions at t.

In terms of its structural features this view of reasons rules out the circularity objection by conditions 1 and 3. These conditions rule out the possibility that reasons arise from unjustified commitments. The basic materials for reasons are justified commitments. The view addresses the arbitrariness concern by condition 2. Reasons cannot be reduced to justified commitments and simple enumerative inductive. Reasons require a larger framework of coherent commitments. Finally, this theory of reasons fits naturally with the argument against first philosophy.

The framework theory of reasons explains why direct ampliative inference is not a cogent form of inference. Above we observed that in the case of direct ampliative inference to the claim that all ravens are black, the premises of the argument support the conclusion only if one has reason for general principles like 'the color of a raven is a natural kind property' and 'natural kind properties are stable in species.' On a framework theory of reasons (a&b) provides a reason for (c) if and only if (a&b) is an insufficient, nonredundant part of a larger unnecessary but sufficient condition for (c)'s justification. The above argument against first philosophy illustrates why (a&b) are insufficient and also why one needs a larger set of plausibility considerations to underwrite the inference.

Keith Lehrer provides a useful example to illustrate how this view of reasons fits with coherentist themes. Lehrer argues that sense experience does not provide a sufficient condition for justification because to justify sense experience requires that one is justified in believing that the chances of believing in error are small.[31] His general point is that putative sources of reasons require a broader theoretical perspective to justify. He explains, "The complete justification of our perceptual beliefs depends on myriad other beliefs, about ourselves, about others, about

---

[31] Lehrer (1974, 188).

experience, and about the entire universe"[32] Lehrer might be forgiven some embellishment since it is plausible that the complete justification of our beliefs may only extend to our local galaxy cluster. These myriad other beliefs form the supporting perspective which offers a sufficient condition of justification.

How large must the set of information be which provides a sufficient condition for a belief's justification? Is there a least upper bound for the number of elements a set must have to be a sufficient condition on justification? That is, is there some n such that a set must contain at least n beliefs to provide justification? It is dubious to think that this is the kind of thing that can be counted. How many beliefs are required to master a language? The best one can say is that many are required. Moreover, there are ever increasingly large sets of information that are entirely disconnected with no epistemic virtues whatsoever. What matters, as I explain in the following chapter, is the explanatory virtues of the set of information. For reasons I offer in the following chapter I doubt that there is a formal account of explanation and its virtues which would allow us to provide the necessary groundwork to begin to make the question amenable to a formal treatment.

A related question is whether one can get a single proposition to be a reason by conjoining together sufficiently many beliefs? I find this question dubious for similar reasons pertaining to learning a language. It is false that one can conjoin together sufficiently many beliefs into a single proposition such that if one only believed that complex proposition one would master the language. Additionally, for reasons related to the Carroll paradox I doubt that the large conjunction will ever provide enough information to yield a sufficient condition for justification. The framework theory implies that one always needs a background set of information for justifying inference. Even if one conjoins together reasons to form larger and larger propositions, I am inclined to think that there will be some tacit principles that cannot be represented in such a proposition. The fact that modus ponens is primitively compelling is a fact about a subject, but the compellingness of modus ponens cannot be represented in propositional form. In my view this is a feature of many fundamental norms.[33]

---

[32] Ibid., 199.

[33] It is at this point that intellectual skills enter into the picture. Intellectual skills are mental facts about a subject and, arguably, there is something it is like to have a particular intellectual skill. Skillful belief formulation is an achievement by a subject. Thus, intellectual skill is not separable from an agent's perspective.

For the purpose of illustration consider the attempt to fill out the raven argument to get all the crucial premises. Let us add the premises that the color of a raven is a natural kind property and natural kind properties are stable in species.

(a) 100 black ravens have been observed.
(b) No non-black ravens have been observed.
(†) The color of a raven is a natural kind property.
(‡) Natural kind properties are stable in species.
Thus, (c) all ravens are black.

Do these revised premises offer a sufficient condition for the justification of the conclusion? No. The justification of the conclusion requires justification for the claim that no relevant information has not been ignored. This is an assumption in the inference and it is often justified by a host of background information that a subject is right to rely on. But it can't be represented in the argument without turning the argument into a deductive argument.

Selim Berker has objected that this account of reasons implies (‡) is a reason to believe that all ravens are black.[34] Framework reasons implies this because (‡) is a nonredundant part of a larger set of connections which are unnecessary but sufficient for the target belief's justification. While it's true that (‡) is insufficient by itself to justify a subject in believing that all ravens are black, it is nonetheless a crucial part of the overall justification for that belief. Berker's objection highlights the fact that my account of reasons implies that any nonredundant background condition for a belief's justification counts as a reason for it.

Admittedly, this does have unnatural consequences. We can remove some pressure on the account by stressing the difference between *a* reason and *the* reason. Often when there is an assumed background of shared belief, we focus on the contextually salient reasons which our interlocutor might not share. This feature of the Framework Reasons account parallels Mackie's distinction between *a* cause and *the* cause. When our interest is focused on *the* cause of the fire, we are not interested in the presence of oxygen in the room (unless, of course, that is the difference-maker, as may be in a laboratory). We usually identify the

---

Moreover, skill is guided by information. Perhaps, one reason that we cannot entirely offer our reasons for belief is that it involves intellectual skill in so believing. Compare trying to teach someone a new language in one extended dialogue.

[34] Personal conversation.

cause as that which differs from the standard background conditions. The other background conditions are causal factors and in virtue that that they satisfy a weak notion of 'a cause'. On my view, we should understand 'a reason' similarly. A reason is something that has a truth-value, that can be given as a condition on the justification of belief, but by itself does not justify the target belief.

Another point worth stressing is that (‡) does not count as a reason to believe that 'all ravens are black' unless the subject is justified in believing a larger set of conditions that provide a sufficient condition for the belief's justification. Thus, (‡) becomes a reason only once the larger set of conditions are in place. We can thus understand the unnatural consequence that Berker highlights as tracking the correct intuition that (‡) by itself isn't a reason to believe that "all ravens are black."

Berker levels another objection against Framework Reasons worthy of note.[35] (‡) is not *a* reason to believe that "all ravens are black." It's not as if (‡) is one reason and (†) is another. Rather these are all parts of the same reason, viz., the large sufficient condition. One way to develop this objection is that the notion of 'reason' as a count noun is not fundamental. Rather 'reason' is more fundamentally understood as a mass noun. There is more reason to believe this or there is sufficient reason to believe this.[36] So, one way to develop Berker's objection is that my view wrongly takes 'reason' as a count noun, when it'd be better to take it as a mass noun.

I believe my account can accommodate this point. The idea then would be that 'reason' is fundamentally a mass noun, and the sense of 'a reason' is derivative on understanding reason as a mass term. The framework account of reasons, then, is right that any particular proposition is insufficient as a reason because we need first to have the notion of sufficient reason for believing something. Moreover, we have sufficient reason for believing something else in virtue of having a large set of justified propositions which support another proposition and this set is unnecessary for the belief's justification. Yet, when we derivatively use the count noun notion of 'a reason' we specify nonredundant propositions within that larger set. Consequently, we ought not think that reasons are additive when used in the count noun sense. What fundamentally matters is that a reason counts epistemically when it is part of sufficient reason to believe something.

---

[35] Personal communication.

[36] I'm indebted to a conversation with Daniel Fogal for this particular development.

3.4 Weak foundationalism and framework reasons

On the account of reasons I've presented reasons require a framework of justified commitments, where some of this justification comes from epistemic conservatism. This view allows for some noninferential justification but prevents propositions with only such justification for serving as premises for other beliefs. This fits BonJour's characterization of weak foundationalism. He describes the view as follows: "basic beliefs possess only a very low degree of epistemic justification on their own, a degree of justification insufficient by itself either to satisfy the adequate-justification condition for knowledge or to qualify them as acceptable justifying premises for further beliefs."[37] BonJour observes that weak foundationalism has been advocated by no less than Bertrand Russell, Nelson Goodman, Roderick Firth, Israel Scheffler, and Nicholas Rescher.[38] Moreover, he notes the view has promising resources to answer problems such as the alternative systems objection.[39] Nevertheless BonJour resists the view for two reasons: first, a weak foundationalist lacks an adequate account of independent warrant; and second, the idea that weakly justified beliefs can by coherence increase their justification to knowledge-level justification has never been made clear.[40]

Both objections fail. First, Gilbert Harman has distinguished special foundationalism from general foundationalism.[41] Special foundationalism holds that only some special class of beliefs may receive basic justification. Sensory beliefs, for instance, may receive basic justification because of the special relation it bears to sense experience. General foundationalism, in contrast, holds that any belief may have basic justification. Harman observes that epistemic conservatism is a general foundations view. It places no restriction on the type of beliefs that may be justified. I've argued in Chapter 2 that epistemic conservatism is defensible. BonJour's criticisms of weak foundationalism focus on a special foundations view. I agree with BonJour that a special foundations

---

[37] (BonJour, 1985, 28).

[38] BonJour (1985, 232) gives the following references: Russell (1948, Part II, Ch. 11 and Part V Chs 6 and 7), Goodman (1952), Scheffler (1967), and Rescher (1973, 53–71). Interestingly, Goodman and Firth were C.I. Lewis's students. Lewis defended a view similar to weak foundationalism in Lewis (1946).

[39] BonJour (1985, 29).

[40] (BonJour, 1985, 29) Ibid.

[41] Harman (2001).

conception of weak foundationism lacks an adequate defense. However, BonJour's reservations about weak foundationism appear to be unfounded with respect to a general foundations view. In this case the independent warrant comes from the epistemic efficiency of belief in the special evidential state of empty symmetrical evidence.

BonJour's second criticism has been undermined by recent developments. James van Cleve argues that coherence can generate warrant under the conditions imposed by weak foundationalism.[42] Van Cleve frames his discussion in terms of C.I. Lewis's contention that the concurrence of multiple witnesses can raise the probability that their testimony is true. He interprets the weak foundationalist's claim that a witness's individual report provides a small 'bump' in the prior probability of the content of the report, but not enough of an increase to make it more likely to be true than not. He then argues that given constraints on the independence of the witness reports concurrence can significantly raise the claim to which the witnesses report. Van Cleve concludes, "The upshot of our investigation of the witness problem within the framework of the probability calculus, then, is that weak foundationalism is a stable and well-motivated position."[43] I return to the relationship between explanatory coherence and probability in the last chapter but, as far as BonJour's concern goes, van Cleve demonstrates that there is a sound model which vindicates the claim that coherence is epistemically potent given weakly justified beliefs.

Even though an explanationist view allows for some noninferential justification and thus is a kind of weak foundationalism, it is a historically coherentist view. BonJour himself recognizes that weak foundationalism is a hybrid of coherentism and foundationalism. There are two significant reasons for thinking that explanationism can carry the coherentist mantle. First, philosophers who present hybrid epistemological views—for example, foundherentism—stipulate that sense experience can play an epistemic role apart from any other justified beliefs. Earl Conee, for example, argues for a coherentism-cum-foundationalist view according to which "sensory experience does not in turn require substantiation by beliefs in order to act as a constraint on justified belief."[44] This implies that sense experience plays an epistemic role apart from a background perspective which underwrites sense experience. On my

---

[42] See van Cleve (2011).
[43] van Cleve (2011, 372).
[44] Conee and Feldman (2004, 40).

view, experience can play an epistemic role only if it is supported by a broader theoretical framework. Since explanationism captures this dominant coherentist theme it is crucially different from both Conee's and Haack's special foundations version of weak foundationalism.[45]

The second reason that explanationism carries the coherentist mantle is that the virtue that yields noninferential justification–conservatism– is an explanatory virtue. This virtue is a crucial part of the coherentist epistemologies of Goodman, Quine, Sellars, Rawls, Harman, and Lycan. These philosophers saw that justified inquiry is a matter of making adjustments in one's overall view to achieve explanatory coherence. They recognized that this goal is not one achieved from scratch; rather, one begins with a view and works from within that view to bring it into coherence. One's original commitments carry some epistemic presumption themselves. But they only provide reasons for belief when they are members of a larger virtuous system of belief. Admittedly, explanationism is a general foundations version of weak foundationalism, but it has this feature precisely because it stresses that the explanatory virtues of one's informational system determine which attitudes are epistemically appropriate.

3.5 Bergmann on foundationalism and epistemic circularity

I have argued for a framework view of reasons which avoids circularity and arbitrariness. Michael Bergmann has argued that any epistemological view which denies foundationalism must embrace radical skepticism. Moreover, he argues that the cost of avoiding radical skepticism is coming to accept some epistemic circularity.[46] In the following I consider Bergmann's argument in relation to my view. I argue that his crucial argument is unsound.

Bergmann focuses on the core foundationalist thesis

F: There can be noninferentially justified beliefs.[47]

A belief, according to Bergmann, is noninferentially justified just in case "it is justified but not in virtue of being inferred from or based on another belief."[48] His characterization of noninferential justification

---

[45] See Haack 1993.
[46] Bergmann (2006b, Ch 7).
[47] Ibid., 184.
[48] Ibid.

is similar to William Alston's. Alston writes that a subject's belief that p is immediately epistemized if and only if it "epistemized by something other than some relation this belief has to some other epistemized belief(s) by S."[49] The core idea is that immediately justified beliefs receive their justification from some non-doxastic source.[50] Bergmann claims that many epistemologists accept this general thesis F, but accepting F "commits one to approving of (at least some instances of) epistemic circularity."[51]

He begins by arguing that denying F lands in radical skepticism.

1. A belief can be justified only if it is inferentially justified. [i.e. ¬F]
2. A belief can be inferentially justified only if the belief from which it is inferred is a justified belief.
3. Therefore, a belief is justified only if it is justified via logically circular reasoning or it is justified via an infinite chain of reasoning. [from 1 and 2]
4. No beliefs can be justified via logically circular reasoning.
5. None of our beliefs are justified via infinite chains of reasoning.
6. Therefore, none of our beliefs are justified. [from 3, 4, and 5][52]

The argument goes awry at 3. The intermediate conclusion 3 does not follow from 1 and 2. The conclusion follows only if the two relevant options are approving logically circular reasoning or approving of an infinite chain of reasoning. But curiously absent is the holist contention that a belief is justified by the set of other justified beliefs. As Bergmann understands inferential justification for the purposes of denying F, it is the weak claim that a claim is supported by other justified beliefs. Yet, a belief can be justified by its relations to other beliefs without approving either logically circular reasoning or an infinite chain of reasoning. As I explain in the next chapter, if the belief that p is a member of an explanatory coherent set of propositions which beats relevant competitors then a subject has justification for the belief that p. This justification is inferential in Bergmann's weak sense but doesn't require logically circular reasoning or an infinite chain of reasons.

---

[49] Alston (1983).
[50] This is another reason for thinking that epistemic conservatism is not a foundationalist view since the source of justification for a conservatism is doxastic.
[51] Bergmann (2006b, 184).
[52] Bergmann (2006b, 185).

Bergmann does briefly consider coherentism. He argues that the only versions of coherentism worth taking seriously hold premises 2, 4, and 5 and this commits them to approving F.[53] Yet, it is possible for a coherentist to hold that the explanatory relations of a subject's beliefs provide the ultimate justification and yet these *are* relations that hold between other justified beliefs for S. So, it is not clear that any coherentist who accepts 2, 4, and 5 must approve F.

How does a denial of F fit with my defense of epistemic conservatism? As I argued there is some noninferential justification in the special evidential state of belief in empty symmetrical evidence. There is a crucial problem with Bergmann's thesis F in that it is a negative characterization of foundationalism. There are beliefs which are justified but *not* by a relation to other justified beliefs. Later in his chapter, in preparation for showing that F requires approving of some epistemic circularity, Bergmann moves to a different foundationalist thesis:

(a) A subject S has belief sources, X_1-X_n, each of which directly produces noninferentially justified beliefs.[54]

Bergmann doesn't explain the relation between F and (a). He does remark, "Any sensible person who thinks that F is true will, therefore, think that (a) is possible too."[55] Belief sources are sources which causally produce beliefs, sources like perception, introspection, and testimony. His idea is that if you have a basic trust in the deliverances in these sources then, in certain contexts, you can use these sources to come to have justified beliefs about the reliability of the sources. Hence, if one accepts (a) then Bergmann argues one must approve of some epistemic circularity.

(a), however, is a more substantive thesis than F. An epistemic conservative accepts F to the extent that justification of belief in the special state of empty symmetrical evidence does not depend on other justified beliefs. However, as the framework theory of reasons makes clear, these justified beliefs cannot by themselves provide reasons for other beliefs. To get reasons one needs a framework of justified beliefs, a framework, which I explain in the next chapter, has virtuous explanatory properties. Thus, on my view I accept F without accepting (a) and thus I do not

---

[53] Bergmann (2006b, 186).
[54] Ibid., 190.
[55] Ibid.

see that I must endorse the kind of epistemic circularity that Bergmann claims any defenders of F must accept.

It is important to note that accepting epistemic circularity is a significant cost. Bergmann explicitly acknowledges that our natural reaction is to think that epistemically circular beliefs cannot be justified.[56] He thinks, though, that we must abandon this reaction if we are to avoid wholesale skepticism. On his view, we must come to grips with the acceptability of reasoning to the reliability of, for example, memory from a reliance on the deliverances of memory. Yet a general defense of conservatism with framework reasons and explanatory coherence avoids Bergmann's forced choice. We can come to have knowledge-level justification for believing that memory is reliable by our initial belief in the reliability of memory being vindicated by the impressive explanatory coherence of the set of beliefs of which it is a part.

What makes an approval of some epistemic circular arguments seem inevitable is the extremely limited options for understanding what positive reason we could have for the reliability of fundamental belief sources. Unless one is willing to go in for a non-perspectival externalism according to which simple facts about whether or not sources are reliable gives us a right to rely on them, then it looks like an approval of some epistemic circularity is inevitable. A broadly Reidian position on which we have a basic justified trust in some fundamental sources and thus can use their deliverances as reasons appears to be the only game left in town. The view I am encouraging is subtly different. Epistemic conservatism gives us some justification for beliefs about the reliability of fundamental sources but that itself doesn't license us to use that as a reason. Reasons require a framework of justified commitments. The error that lies in approving epistemically circular arguments is that it diminishes the broader framework of justified beliefs a person has. A person has much more to go on in believing that perception is reliable than simply a track record argument; she has an explanatory coherent view that significantly supports that perception is reliable. On my view the idea that we can take parts of a coherent view and use them as isolated premises for reasoning is dubious. All reasoning takes place within a broader framework. Once we add the framework back in, the concern about epistemic circularity lessens.

There is a lingering concern about epistemic circularity. It's epistemically circular to use a broader framework to justify a belief without

---

[56] Bergmann (2006b, 193).

some independent justification for the framework. I grant that this is a lingering worry but it is a concern that is equally expressed in a skeptical worry that all our evidence might be misleading. There is no way to answer that worry without relying on one's own evidence. What evidence does one have for thinking that all one's evidence might be misleading? If the original worry is taken to show that framework considerations cannot be justified without requiring an independent justification then one is left in a radically impoverished skeptical situation. The framework view I've presented shows how one may resist approving of some epistemic circularity.

3.6 Conclusion

I've argued that explanationism has a unique theory of reasons. The framework theory of reasons is supported by the powerful argument against first philosophy. This provides a crucial argument against basic reasons without lapsing into the problems of circularity and arbitrariness. Belief is the starting point in the life of a reason, but it matures to a full reason only once it is part of a framework of justified commitments. This also provides the key materials to avoiding Bergmann's forced choice between either radical skepticism or epistemic circularity. In the next chapter I develop a specific explanationist theory of justification.

4
Explanation and Justification

Explanationism is the view that one's normative standing in the space of reasons is constituted by one's explanatory position. My goal in this chapter is to turn this claim into a clear and feasible theory of epistemic justification. I begin by discussing the nature of explanation and the explanatory virtues. I argue that explanation is a primitive relation between propositions. People offer explanations in an aim to remove a mystery. But what it is to actually remove cognitive dissonance lacks a non-trivial analysis into necessary and sufficient conditions. Next, I present the explanationist theory of justification. I argue that explanationism is a mentalist evidentialist account of epistemic justification. Finally, I examine supporting cases and discuss putative counterexamples with an eye to explaining the plausibility of explanationism.

Explanation is a fecund concept in epistemology. Gilbert Harman has argued that all inference is explanatory inference which helps to explain both why enumerative induction fails in many cases and why false background assumptions can produce Gettier cases.[1] Harman extends his explanationist treatment to handle skepticism.[2] Jonathan Vogel pursues the anti-skeptical power of explanationist reasoning, arguing that the explanatory virtues of the common-sense hypothesis provide good reasons for it over its skeptical competitors.[3] Explanatory inference has been put to other work. Timothy Williamson defends the view that only propositions which one grasps are evidence on the basis of

---

[1] Harman (1965).
[2] Harman (1973).
[3] Vogel (1990).

the fact that only propositions function in one's inferences to the best explanation.[4] Earl Conee and Richard Feldman suggest that "fundamental epistemic principles are principles of best explanation."[5] William Lycan argues that "all justified reasoning is fundamentally explanatory reasoning that aims at maximizing the explanatory coherence of one's total belief system."[6] This chapter continues this theme by arguing that one's explanatory position determines what doxastic attitudes are epistemically appropriate.

4.1 Explanation and its virtues

People offer explanations to remove a mystery. When one grasps an explanation accounting for the occurrence of some phenomenon one understands why it occurred.[7] Why do stars twinkle in the night sky? Because light is refracted by the earth's atmosphere analogously to the way light is distorted as it travels through water. The result is that stars do not actually twinkle; rather light from the star is affected as it travels through our atmosphere. The mystery is removed by tying it to other things we understand.

Is there a successful formal explication of the nature of explanation? Such an explication would provide a substantive, counterexample-free analysis of explanation having this form: a group of statements ϕ explain another statement ψ if and only if X, where X is some set of non-trivial conditions. Six decades of analysis provide strong evidence that such an explication is not to be had. Hempel and Oppenheim provide the first formal explication of explanation.[8] They propose the deductive-nomological model of explanation according to which a group of statements—*the explanans*—constitute an explanation for another statement—*the explanandum*—if and only if the explanans contains a law, has empirical content, and entails the explanandum. An explanation becomes *the* explanation when the explanans are true.

---

[4] Williamson (2000, 195).
[5] Feldman (2008, 97).
[6] Lycan (1988, 128).
[7] How-possible explanations account for the possibility of the phenomenon, not its actual occurrence.
[8] Hempel and Oppenheim (1948).

The D-N model of explanation quickly met a number of devastating problems. First, a valid argument which contains a law in its premises is not sufficient to explain its conclusion. Sylvian Bromberger illustrates this.[9] Suppose a mouse is four feet from the base of a three foot pole. At the top of the pole is an owl. By way of the Pythagorean theorem one can deduce that the mouse is five feet away from the owl. But one has not explained why the mouse is five feet away from the owl. That fact is still very surprising. The deduction does not remove that mystery. The mouse should scurry away because it will be eaten. Hempel and Oppenheim's model does not give a sufficient condition for explanation.

Second, a valid argument is not necessary for explanation. Michael Striven illustrates this via evolutionary theory.[10] Random mutations of DNA together with subsequent fitness properties explains diverse traits of species. The Darwinian explanation works by providing a causal explanation of the diversity of the species. But the explanation is entirely statistical and cannot be used to predict, even with significant probability, that there would be diverse species.

This statistical feature of the Darwinian explanation also undermines Hempel's Inductive-Statistical model of explanation.[11] Hempel proposes this model to handle statistical explanations in science. But his model requires that the explanans make the explanandum more likely than not. Darwin's theory does not meet this criterion. Darwin's theory works by providing a plausible retrospective explanation of the facts as we find them. This retrospective feature of the Darwinian explanation is in sharp conflict with Hempel's argumentative model of explanation according to which an explanation is an argument which leads one to expect the event.

The ensuing debate over the nature of explanation is voluminous.[12] Michael Striven and Wesley Salmon independently purposed a causal theory of explanation. Causality is often central to understanding why something occurred. We can remove a mystery by specifying the cause of the event. But there are many other ways of removing a mystery. Successful explanations may use narrative, analogy, or functional role to provide understanding even though these explanations may not

---

[9] Bromberger (1966). The example I use comes from Keith Lehrer. See Lehrer (2000, 106–107).
[10] Striven (1959).
[11] See Hempel (1965, 381–383, 394–403).
[12] For a good overview see Salmon (1989).

specify causal mechanisms. Moreover, mathematical explanations and explanations of lower-level laws in terms of higher-level laws remove mysteries apart from causal relations. Other approaches to explanation, especially explanation in history, take an entirely different tack. Louis Mink argues that historical explanation significantly differs from scientific explanation.[13] Historical explanation does not aim at the discovery of universal laws, historical events are not repeatable, historical explanations are holistic, and they aim at understanding the events from the perspective of the individual actors. A good historical explanation will remove a mystery but the manner in which the mystery is removed is significantly different from successful explanations in, for example, physics.

It is beyond the scope of this book to rehash the debates over the nature of explanation. The twentieth-century philosophy of science debates over explanation are similar to the epistemological debates over the nature of knowledge. Epistemologists sought the objective relation that turned true belief into knowledge while philosophers of science sought the objective relation that turned some propositions into an explanation for another proposition. In both cases it was widely assumed that since there is an objective relation the relation should be capable of being analyzed into non-trivial necessary and sufficient conditions. In epistemology, the Gettier problem produced a cottage industry which aimed at providing substantive necessary and sufficient conditions for propositional knowledge. Theories were proposed, and quickly met with counterexample. An early solution to the Gettier problem was Michael Clark's "no-false lemmas" approach.[14] In Gettier's original cases the subject reasoned through a justified false belief to a justified true belief. The subject lacked knowledge because he reached the true belief by reasoning from a false belief. Clark proposed that knowledge is justified true belief which is not based on anything false. Yet problematic cases quickly arose to the "no-false lemmas" approach. Other attempts to provide a fourth condition on knowledge met with similar failure.

Timothy Williamson's book *Knowledge and Its Limits*[15] is widely regarded as changing our approach to the Gettier problem. Williamson argues that knowledge lacks an analysis into informative necessary

---

[13] Mink (1966).
[14] Clark (1963).
[15] Williamson (2000).

and sufficient conditions. Knowledge is the most basic factive mental state invoked to explain purposive behavior and to license and criticize assertion and inference. Williamson's argument for the unanalyzability of propositional knowledge proceeds along two lines: first, the failure of the Gettier project to produce an analysis; second, the role knowledge plays in ordinary life.

There is a similar argument for taking explanation to be primitive, that is, to lack an informative metaphysical analysis into non-trivial necessary and sufficient conditions. First, the literature on explanation has failed to produce a metaphysical analysis of explanation. Second, explanation is central to our cognitive lives. We explain purposive behavior. We explain surprising features of the world. Explanation and its virtues are invoked to license and criticize views. We license a view by saying that it can explain a great deal. We criticize a view by claiming that it is too complex, doesn't adequately explain the facts, or doesn't fit with what we already accept. Further, we often ask questions like 'how do you understand this fact in light of that fact'? Preschool children ask many 'why?' questions each day, often leaving their parents exasperated. One hypothesis to account for these data is that *explanation* is a primitive relation between propositions.[16] We can identify criteria for weighing different explanations but explanation lacks an informative analysis in terms of necessary and sufficient conditions. Below I give several further arguments for this primitiveness claim.[17] One of the main advantages of this primitiveness claim insofar as it concerns an epistemological defense of explanationism is that because the nature of explanation is simple it does not require sophisticated intellectual activity to grasp facts of the form 'p explains q'. As I shall argue one need only possess the concept *because* to grasp explanatory facts.

4.1.1 Three arguments for primitiveness

In the following I present three arguments that the nature of explanation is a primitive relation. The primitiveness claim contends that there

---

[16] Keith Lehrer takes this route as well. See Lehrer (1974, 169–170).

[17] Carrie Jenkins (2008) argues for a functionalist account of explanation. Jenkins holds that there are many different realizers of the explanation relation (2008, 71) and that it would be a mistake to identify one of these realizers as the nature of explanation. My primitive account of explanation is one way of making sense of the many different realizers of the explanation relation without adopting a functionalist framework. Jenkins explicitly notes that she is using the term "functionalism" quite loosely (2008, 71).

is no analysis of explanation having this form: a group of statements ϕ explain another statement ψ if and only if X, where X is some set of non-trivial conditions.

The argument from cognition

Metaphysical analysis aims to understand a complex entity, property, or fact in terms of more simple entities, properties, or facts. The Gettier project aimed to understand facts of the form 'S knows that p' in terms of simpler facts: facts about belief, truth, reason, and some extra condition to handle the Gettier problem. One challenge to this is that the use of the word 'know' and its cognates is much more prevalent than any of the terms used in the analysis. We use the word 'know' to evaluate reasoning, assertion, and intentional behavior. This suggests that we grasp facts of the form 'S knows that p' more readily than facts of the form 'S believes that p', 'S has a true belief that p', and so on. Evidence for the centrality of knowledge to cognition comes from the widespread use of 'know' in the English language. According to the Oxford English Dictionary, the word 'know' is the 59th most common word in English (see table below). On the present line of reasoning, metaphysical analysis needs to be sensitive to the ordinary language role of the analysandum.

To the extent that such an argument is successful for the metaphysical primitiveness of facts of the form 'S knows that p', it is successful for an argument that explanation is a primitive relation. The relation between the explanans and the explanandum is the relation picked out by 'because'. The stars twinkle because light from the stars is refracted by the earth's atmosphere. Refraction explains twinkling. There are no even primes greater than 2 because every even number, n, greater than 2 is divisible by itself, 1, 2, and $\frac{1}{2}n$. The latter fact explains the former. The word 'because' is in the 94th most common word in English, having its position on the list between 'want' and 'any'.[18] Preschool children ask over one hundred 'why?' questions each day;[19] parents provide many 'because' answers each day. People's grasp of facts of the form 'p because q' appears to come quite early in the development of cognition.

---

[18] See the *Oxford English Dictionary's* entry 'Facts about the language'.

[19] Reported in *Newsweek* 'The Creativity Crisis', July 10, 2010.

Most common word occurrences in English

1 the	21 this	41 so	61 people	81 back
2 be	22 but	42 up	62 into	82 after
3 to	23 his	43 out	63 year	83 use
4 of	24 by	44 if	64 your	84 two
5 and	25 from	45 about	65 good	85 how
6 a	26 they	46 who	66 some	86 our
7 in	27 we	47 get	67 could	87 work
8 that	28 say	48 which	68 them	88 first
9 have	29 her	49 go	69 see	89 well
10 I	30 she	50 me	70 other	90 way
11 it	31 or	51 when	71 than	91 even
12 for	32 an	52 make	72 then	92 new
13 not	33 will	53 can	73 now	93 want
14 on	34 my	54 like	74 look	**94 because**
15 with	35 one	55 time	75 only	95 any
16 he	36 all	56 no	76 come	96 these
17 as	37 would	57 just	77 its	97 give
18 you	38 there	58 him	78 over	98 day
19 do	39 their	**59 know**	79 think	99 most
20 at	40 what	60 take	80 also	100 us

Answers involving 'because' are often linked to causal explanations. Causation is central to understanding ourselves and our environment. On some accounts of explanation it is the key feature of explanation.[20] Even apart from identifying explanation with a causal account, the aim of removing a mystery is often met by specifying the cause of the mystery. It is not surprising, then, that facts about language reveal the centrality of aiming for 'because' answers.

The prominence of 'know' and 'because' is reflected in other languages as well. In French, 'savoir' *to know* is the 42nd most common word; 'parce que' *because* is the 51st; and 'comprendre' *to understand* is the 98th. In Spanish, 'porque' *because* is 38th, 'saber' *to know* is 46. In German 'da' *since, because (prep); there, here (adv)* is the 75; 'weil' *because* is 84. It is a striking fact that the words corresponding to 'true,' 'truth,' or 'believe' occur less frequently than 'know' and 'because.' This fact seems

---

[20] See Salmon (1998).

to hold across many languages. When it comes to 'because' there is an argument as to why we should expect it to be so prominent.

A crucial step in cognitive development is grasping the distinction between how things appear and how things are. Can we imagine cognitive beings who lack the distinction between how things appear and how things are?[21] Can we imagine beings who can infer, believe, and assert without understanding the difference between *saying that p* or *believing that p* and *the fact that p*, or the distinction between an inference which *seems good* and an inference which *is good*? Any being which lacks an understanding of the distinction between appearance and reality is, at the least, very different from beings like us. But any being that understands this distinction experiences a mystery. Why do things appear different from the way they are? Such a basic question requires explanation, it requires the grasp of at least there being something that would remove the mystery (whether or not there is *actually* something that removes the mystery). The idea that there are facts of the form '*this because that*' appears to be the kind of notion that is not learned by a mastery of more fundamental concepts. It is what explanation seeks. Cognitive beings sophisticated enough to grasp the appearance-reality distinction have this idea. Consequently, they have the idea of what an explanation seeks, a truthful answer of the form 'p because q'.

This argument answers one objection to explanatory coherentism. The objection proceeds as follows: explanation is sophisticated activity that one engages only after one has many justified beliefs. Consequently, it is wrongheaded to think that justification should be understood in terms of explanation. This objection runs together several distinct objections. One, which I address below, is that every justified belief is explanatory. But, for present purposes, this objection begins in error: explanation–the removal of mystery–is fundamental; it is something that preschool children seek and sometimes find. Thus, the cognition argument shows that explanation is not high-brow cognitive art but something that everyone grasps. Explanation is a basic human activity.

---

[21] Perhaps dogs. But in line with the argument in this paragraph, dogs would not be the kind of beings fit for explanations. That seems exactly right. We would then have a firm empirical basis for Sosa's distinction between animal knowledge and human knowledge. Animal knowledge, then, requires just apt belief. But for beings who grasp the distinction between appearance and reality one needs more.

The argument from better explanations in math

Gilbert Harman calls our attention to explanatory differences among mathematical proofs for the same claim.[22] Some proofs in mathematics are more explanatory than others. Consider the rule for summing a series of numbers from 1 to n: $1+2+3+\ldots+n = n(n+1)/2$. One proof proceeds by mathematical induction. Start with the base case $n = 1$. Clearly, $1(1+1)/2 = 1$. Then assume the claim holds up to n. Show that it holds for $n+1$. That is, prove the following: $1+2+3+\ldots+n+(n+1) = (n+1)((n+1)+1)/2$.

This can be proven as follows:

$$1+2+3+\cdots+n+(n+1) = n(n+1)/2 + (n+1).$$

$$n(n+1)/2 + (n+1) = n(n+1)/2 + 2(n+1)/2$$

$$n(n+1)/2 + 2(n+1)/2 = (n+1)(n+2)/2$$

$$(n+1)(n+2)/2 = (n+1)((n+1)+1)/2. \text{ QED.}$$

This proof is adequate but it does not tend to remove the mystery as to why the claim is true.

Now consider a second proof inspired by Gauss.

1 +	2 +	3 +	…+	n
n +	n−1 +	n−2 +	…+	1
n+1 +	n+1 +	n+1 +	n+1 +	n+1

Clearly, this last series is equals $n(n+1)$. Since we added the series twice we need to divide by 2, which gives us $1+2+3+\ldots+n = n(n+1)/2$.

The second proof is more explanatory. The second proof removes the mystery as to *why* the claim is true. The former proof shows us *that* the claim is true but does not reveal *why* it is true. This poses a nice puzzle for a theory of explanation. Why does Gauss's proof remove the mystery but the proof by mathematical induction does not? The Gaussian proof is more visualizable than the mathematical induction; it uses more familiar operations; and it organizes the relevant information in an easily retrievable manner.

---

[22] Harman (1986, 73–74). Harman's case comes from Steiner (1978).

There are similar examples of explanatory differences among mathematical proofs. Consider the following problem. Solve the following equation where each denominator is distinct.

$$\frac{1}{w} + \frac{1}{x} + \frac{1}{y} + \frac{1}{z} = 1$$

One can solve this problem algebraically to determine that $\frac{1}{2} + \frac{1}{3} + \frac{1}{9} + \frac{1}{18}$ is a solution. But the algebraic demonstration may not produce an understanding as to why that solution is correct. One possesses good grounds for believing that it's true but one has not understood the solution. Understanding may be provided by a geometrical demonstration. Take a square and divide it in half. This gives $\frac{1}{2}$. Take the remaining half and divide it into three equal parts. Two of those three parts equal $\frac{2}{3} \times \frac{1}{2} = \frac{1}{3}$. Next take the remaining section—one third of the one half—which is one sixth of the original square. Divide it into three equal areas. Two of those three parts equal $\frac{2}{3} \times \frac{1}{6} = \frac{1}{9}$. The remaining section is $\frac{1}{3} \times \frac{1}{6} = \frac{1}{18}$. One can then see directly that this solution is correct, which shows one why the algebraic solution works.

In both cases of explanatory differences, the more explanatory proof is more readily visualizable, uses more familiar operations, and organizes relevant information in an easily retrievable manner. These properties are features that often accompany good formal explanations but they seem dubious candidates for non-trivial necessary and sufficient conditions in an account of explanation. Capable of being visualized would make the explanatory features of the proofs dependent on good eyesight. Familiarity may be an enabling condition. Organization does seem to be a feature of explanations but the key issue is the kind of organization.

Another datum to account for in a theory of mathematical explanation is the preference for constructive proofs over reductio proofs and brute force proofs.[23] The first proof of the four color theorem—that four colors are sufficient to separate a contiguous plane into different areas such that no adjacent regions have the same color—was by a computer program which showed that for all possible cases there was no counterexample. The brute force proof went through all possible cases. By its nature, brute force proofs lack a kind of generality that would explain why the four-color theorem is true. Similar worries attend reductio

---

[23] Thanks to Jonathan Schaffer for bringing this to my attention.

proofs. Both brute force proofs and reductio proofs provide conclusive grounds *that* a claim is true without removing the mystery as to *why* the claim is true.

Differences in mathematical explanation provide a ripe area for investigation. There are clear explanatory differences among mathematical proofs. One hypothesis is that the explanatory relation is primitive. Another hypothesis is that there is some substantive account of explanation out there such that when such and such conditions obtain we have a mathematical explanation. On my view, the balance of evidence at this point favors the first hypothesis.

The argument from epistemological primitiveness

In the previous chapter I argued that explanatory reasoning cannot be reduced to non-explanatory reasoning. We are always and everywhere in the business of making explanatory judgments. There are no pure deductive or inductive arguments whose justification relies entirely on non-explanatory features. This is to say, explanatory reasoning is epistemically primitive.

How does that bear on the claim that the nature of explanation is metaphysically primitive? The connection lays in the failure to give a counterexample-free, metaphysical analysis of primitive epistemic norms. Consider, for instance, the norm of inferring in accord with *modus ponens*. In many cases, inferring the truth of q from p and $p \to q$ is a good inference. Now, suppose we say that inferring in accord with this norm is epistemically basic. It cannot be reduced to a more fundamental norm. Yet, let us suppose, the norm has a metaphysical analysis. What it is to infer in accord with modus ponens is to follow this rule: Infer q from p and p implies q.

Is this the correct metaphysical analysis of the norm of inferring in accord with modus ponens? No. Many true propositions have implications we are unaware of. In those case, one has no reason to infer q. Suppose we modify the rule to: infer q from a justified belief in p and a justified belief in p implies q. Does that capture the metaphysical analysis of inferring in accord with modus ponens? Arguably, no. Perhaps the act of realizing that p implies q defeats the justification one has for p. The issues here track the issues in the literature on epistemic closure. That literature looks for a counterexample-free analysis of a principle to the effect that knowledge is closed under known entailment. As Harman has stressed, though, there is a significant difference between logic and epistemology and it is a mistake to think that true logical principles are thereby true epistemic principles.[24] What's interesting about Harman's work is that the epistemic primitiveness of certain norms makes those norms resistant to a metaphysical analysis. We can see this at work in the attempt to capture the epistemic norm of inferring in accord with modus ponens. At the level of a theory of content, we can specify a true logical principle; for example, every admissible interpretation that assigns both 'p' and '$p \to q$' true must assign 'q' true. Yet this true principle does not track a metaphysical principle about human inference. Similarly, I contend we see this at work in the literature on the metaphysical analysis of explanation. What makes this relation so difficult to capture is that explanatoriness is epistemically primitive. When we infer in an explanatory manner, we grasp a relation between a set of propositions and another proposition that resists reducibility to other norms. Moreover, this same resistance manifests in an attempt to specify in non-explanatory terms the very nature of explanation.

4.1.2 The virtues of explanation

Explanationism is a general view about epistemic justification. The justificatory status of one's beliefs is determined by the explanatory merits of one's system of beliefs. The justification of a single belief is determined by its role in an explanatory system. Different accounts of explanation and its virtues result in varieties of an explanationist epistemology. In the following I look at one form of explanationism which takes the virtues of explanation to be conservatism, simplicity, and explanatory power. The project of identifying the virtues of explanation I refer to as the *identification problem*. An epistemological defense of explanationism should indicate which virtues are relevant for epistemic justification and address the objection that the virtues are merely pragmatic, that is, non-epistemic goods, which merely reflect human interests. In chapter two I argued that conservatism is an epistemic good. In the following I consider simplicity and power. I indicate how I understand these virtues and then present some arguments that they are epistemic goods. My goal is to argue for a thesis in epistemology: that explanationism is true. I do not, therefore, delve into detail about how these virtues are to be understood. The literature on simplicity is vast and a general epistemological defense of explanationism cannot plumb the depths of this literature.

I acknowledge that some reasons to prefer one explanation over the other merely reflect human interests and are not appropriately

---

[24] Harman (1986).

truth-connected virtues. Consider the virtue of *testability*. One theory is preferred over another because it is more easily tested. Consider this in a specific context. Suppose water does not flow from the faucet. You turn the handle but nothing happens. You consider four explanations. First, the water line into your home is shut off. Second, the water line is not shut off but is damaged. Third, the water line into your sink is blocked. Fourth, the handle is broken. The first two theories imply that water will not run to any other faucet in the house. These theories are more easily tested than the other two. You go to check another faucet. The preference for the first two theories reflects the rational order of testing. Since one can easily go and check whether the water is flowing at other faucets, it makes sense to do that before one begins more laborious investigations. The preference for testability may just come to the preference for easy solutions, so that one can spend one's time doing other things.

Other examples of theory preference on the basis of testability are less straightforward because they tacitly involve other explanatory virtues. To continue with the example, suppose one successfully turns on water to other faucets. Then one has two potential explanations for why water isn't flowing to the sink: a damaged line or a broken handle. The theory that the handle is broken is more easily tested since one can't easily access the water line. One prefers that theory. But this theory is more probable as well since it fits with one's background evidence. The handle often breaks because of a plastic mechanism which opens and closes the water line, and these are known to break periodically. A blockage in the line is rare; it would require an complex series of events. If one believes that the handle is the culprit it may be on account of its epistemic virtues rather than its testability. In some cases the cognitive preference for testability reflects not simply testability but the other epistemic virtues of the theory.

A similar argument holds for the pragmatic virtue of fruitfulness. Fruitfulness is the property of a theory's ability to generate new research programs. A fruitful research project creates excitement because it poses novel questions and leads to promising avenues of unexplored research. Darwin's theory is a fruitful theory because, among other things, it predicted a mechanism which would explain heritable traits. This led to the science of molecular genetics. In simple cases fruitfulness is not a reason to think a theory is true. But in more complex cases the fruitfulness of a theory is tied to its other epistemic virtues. The fruitfulness of Darwin's theory, for instance, might be connected to its broader coherence with reality. Often true theories have unexplored dimensions. A fruitful theory, therefore, may receive some support from the value of diverse evidence or the value of fit with background beliefs.

Explanatory power

The explanatory power of a hypothesis consists in its ability to explain a wide range of phenomena. Hypotheses with greater explanatory power achieve a virtuous unification in overall account. In place of many accounts to explain, a more powerful theory gives us one account. Or, in place of an account and a mystery, a more powerful theory explains and removes previous mysteries. Given the arguments for primitiveness there is not much to say about power. Power is a theory's ability to explain, to remove cognitive dissonance from otherwise puzzling phenomena; the more powerful a theory is, the more it explains.

Why is explanatory power an epistemic good? Relatedly, does the explanatory power of a theory make it more likely to be true? A powerful theory removes many mysteries. As such it unifies an overall set of beliefs by bringing into coherence the various claims we accept. Prior to accepting the account, some statements were accepted but lacked an understanding as to how they fit into an overall account. After accepting the account, those statements are supported by the explanation. Mutual support is a cognitive good.

One challenge to the cognitive goodness of removing a mystery is that explanations are simply rationalizations which make us feel good. Ancient belief in the gods of thunder and lightning may have aimed to remove mysteries, but, surely, so the objection goes, these beliefs were entirely unjustified and the power of such theories to explain simply reflected human desire to have a tidy account of the world that fit their experience. The basic problem with this objection is that it is too strong. Explanation is a cognitive goal in science; arguably, it is the central theoretical goal of science. If this objection succeeded it entirely undermines the goal of science. Of course, it is a legitimate challenge to specific explanatory accounts that it has no power and simply reflects an antecedent desire for a 'nice' account. But such objections must be met in a specific context and answered by the specific information in that context.

Simplicity

We accept simple theories which account for the data and fit with our other beliefs. Simplicity plays a major role in theory choice. Aristotle in the *Posterior Analytics* writes, "We may assume the superiority, ceteris paribus, of the demonstration which derives from fewer postulates or hypotheses." Newton's first rule of reasoning in Book III of *Principia Mathematica* is that "we are to admit no more causes of natural things than such as are both true and sufficient to explain their appearances." Einstein's famously remarks that "Our theories should be as simple as possible, but no simpler." As these remarks indicate simplicity is a virtue, but it is a virtue that must be balanced with explanatory power. Of two theories which both explain the phenomena, the simpler of the two is better.

Discussions of simplicity center on two issues: how should we understand the concept of simplicity, and what is the rational justification for simplicity principles? Discussions on simplicity usually begin by distinguishing between syntactic simplicity (*elegance*) and ontological simplicity (*parsimony*).[25] Syntactic simplicity is intended to measure the number and form of a theory's basic principles. A theory with one basic principle is simpler than a theory with two basic principles. Ontological simplicity is a measure of the quantity of entities postulated by the theory as well as the number of kinds of entities postulated. These two aspects of ontological simplicity are referred to as *quantitative parsimony* and *qualitative parsimony*. I doubt that there is a clear division between elegance and parsimony. Elegance is a feature of the formulations of the theory's principles, but a theory's principles are its laws. The form and number of laws is a matter of qualitative parsimony.

A precise characterization of qualitative parsimony is elusive. Moreover, a comparative measure of two theories qualitative parsimony has also resisted analysis. Is a theory that postulates rabbits and elephants more elegant than a theory that postulates rabbits and rainbows? I will not wade into these turbulent waters. I am doubtful that there is any *a priori* analysis of simplicity which would provide a substantive comparative measure of simplicity. Such an analysis would be desirable, but the lack of an analysis does not imply that we cannot have justified beliefs about the relative simplicity of competing theories. We know that one jar contains more money than another jar without being able determine how much money is in either jar. An explanationist is only committed to the claim that where we can make judgments about the relative simplicity of theories those judgments provide an epistemic reason for believing one theory over another. Given the role simplicity plays in scientific practice, denying its epistemic role amounts to a significant

---

[25] See, for example, Baker (2011).

skepticism. Furthermore, skepticism about science bleeds over to other non-scientific areas.

There is a broader issue here concerning how many fundamental epistemic norms a theory should allow. Many philosophers have aimed to reduce the theoretical virtues to deductive or simple inductive patterns of reasoning. My view is that this project is mistaken and should be turned upside down. As I explain in Chapter 6 one can provide an explanationist justification for simple logical principles. This provides motivation for taking explanation and its virtues as fundamental; other good patterns of reasoning are situated in a broader explanationist context.

Is there a rational justification for thinking that simpler theories are more likely to be true? Advocates of simplicity have offered metaphysical, theological, or naturalistic justifications of simplicity. The metaphysical or theological justifications of simplicity aim to provide a priori arguments that the world is simple and hence that simpler theories are more likely to be true. The argument against first philosophy showed that a priori arguments do not succeed apart from explanationist considerations. An a priori argument for some claim proceeds on the basis of a set of premises from which the desired conclusion is claimed to be entailed. Every argument of this kind can be considered as offering us an inconsistent set of propositions, viz., the premises and the denial of the conclusion. One needs to argue for the premises themselves and these are defended on the basis of explanationist considerations. Thus I see simplicity as playing an ineliminable role in what it is reasonable for us to accept.

I take simplicity to be a fundamental epistemic norm. Alan Baker refers to this justification of simplicity as *the intrinsic value justification*.[26] Evidence for fundamental norms come from reflection on good epistemic practices. Simplicity meets this criterion. Other things being equal, the simplest explanation is the best explanation. Simplicity, conservatism, and power work together as norms to govern belief. I see these norms as flowing out of the fundamental goodness of explanation. Explanations are evaluated by way of simplicity, conservatism, and power. I contend that a subject is epistemically justified in believing a proposition to the extent that that proposition is part of a simple, conservative, and powerful explanation which beats its rivals.

A central challenge to simplicity as an epistemic principle is that it seems to suppose that the world is simple and we have no justification

---

[26] See Baker (2011).

for thinking that the world is simple rather than complex. BonJour rhetorically asks: "why, after all, should it be supposed that reality is more likely to be simple than complex?"[27] The intrinsic value justification is more nuanced than this challenge suggests. The intrinsic value approach claims that when we are faced with two equally conservative and explanatory theories we have *justification* for believing the simpler of the two, if either is worthy of belief. The idea is not that the world is simple and therefore simplicity is an epistemic factor. Rather the claim is that when we are faced with two (or more) competing theories that are otherwise equal, simplicity provides a reason for believing one over the other.

Another challenge to the intrinsic value justification is that some people may prefer the principle of complexity: when two competing theories are otherwise equal, prefer the more complex theory. The principle of complexity may seem to fit actual scientific practice; the more we learn about the world the more nuanced and hence complex our theories become. The primary problem with the principle of complexity is that one can always come up with a more complex theory that is empirically adequate. Take two explanations for a mysterious infectious disease. One theory explains inflection by way of a mutation of a known bacteria. Another theory explains it by way of a double mutation of known bacteria. The principle of complexity implies one ought to believe the real explanation is found in the more complex theory. But then one may devise a competing theory by proposing a threefold mutation. Complexity, as opposed to simplicity, has no limit. There is a crucial difference between a complexity principle and a simplicity principle.

4.2 An explanationist theory of justification

We began with the claim that one's normative standing in the space of reasons is constituted by one's explanatory standing. It is time to turn this claim into a specific account. In this section I argue that explanationism is a type of mentalist evidentialist account of propositional justification. The features which determine the justificatory status of a subject's beliefs are mental facts about that subject. Moreover, the appropriateness of any doxastic attitude of a subject is a function of the evidential situation of the subject. The specific account I propose holds that a subject's evidential situation consists in her explanatory position.

---

[27] BonJour (1985, 181).

The argument is as follows. I begin with a brief discussion of the goal of an account of epistemic justification with an eye towards how a substantive account fits within the Quinean thesis that there is no philosophically interesting distinction between analytic and synthetic truths. Next, I formulate the explanationist theory of justification, Ex-J. Third, I argue that Ex-J is a mentalist account of justification. Fourth, I argue that Ex-J is an evidentialist account. Lastly, I consider the distinction between propositional and doxastic justification from the perspective of Ex-J. The upshot of this section is that Ex-J is a mentalist evidentialist view. Ex-J shares the plausibility of evidentialist accounts of justification. In the final section I argue that EX-J is a plausible account of justification.

4.2.1 The goal

Explanationism attempts to give the conditions under which a subject is propositionally justified in believing that p. This is an internal, structural property of a subject's mental states. Ex-J is intended as a theory about this internal, structural property. A natural evaluation of a subject determines whether a subject has good reason for a specific belief or whether a subject would be rational, given her specific situation, in believing p. This evaluation is one that takes into consideration the mental facts about a subject. Ex-J offers a theory about the nature of this property. In the final section I consider competing accounts of the nature of this property and argue that Ex-J provides the best theory of this internal, structural property.

The project for an explanationist account of justification is thus to understand the conditions under which a subject has justification for believing some proposition. How does this project fit with the explanationist Quinean themes, specifically the failure of a substantive analytic/synthetic distinction? Explanationism is a kind of holism about justification. As I argue in Chapter 6 an explanationist resists the idea that there is a clear separation between the justification of empirical beliefs and the justification of non-empirical beliefs. If one resists this then doesn't that make trouble for the traditional epistemology project of uncovering necessary and sufficient conditions for our key epistemic concepts?

One way of understanding theories of justification is that the ultimate justification for a fundamental epistemic principle is a priori. Once the conceptual terrain is clarified and one understands the arguments for and against the view, one is in a position to grasp with rational insight the correctness of the account of justification. The broadly Quinean view I explore cannot adopt this argumentative strategy. Rather the idea is that an account of justification is itself justified by inference to the best explanation. This is a theoretical evaluation depending on conservativeness, simplicity, and explanatory power. As I argue in the final section, Ex-J fares well by this standard.

4.2.2 The Ex-J account

Explanationism takes explanation and the explanatory virtues to be central to understanding one's normative standing in the space of reasons. One has justification for believing a proposition if and only if that proposition fits within a good explanatory system which beats its competitors. Let us formulate this idea as follows:

> EX-J: S has justification for believing p if and only if p is a member of a sufficiently virtuous explanatory system, E, and E is more virtuous than any competing system E'.[28]

I present a case for Ex-J in the last section. At this point we want to understand Ex-J and how it fits with other theses. Ex-J has three main components. First, there is notion of being a member of an explanatory system. What is it to be a member of an explanatory system? A proposition is a member of an explanatory system by being a part of an *explanans* or part of an *explanandum*. Indispensability arguments in mathematics argue that we have justification for believing certain branches of mathematics because they are an indispensable part of an overall explanation of certain empirical truths. Ex-J holds that if mathematical statements function in this way then we have some justification for believing them.[29]

It is easy to be a member of the explanans or explanandum. Consider *the tacking paradox*. This paradox afflicts the hypothetico-deductive model of confirmation. On this model a law receives confirmation from its consequences. An instance of a black raven confirms the statement that 'all ravens are black'. But if general statements are supported by instances then a black raven would also confirm the statement that 'all ravens are black and there's life on other planets'. Suppose one

---

[28] Strength of justification corresponds to the virtue of the explanatory system and how significantly it beats competitors.

[29] Ex-J is not committed to indispensability arguments being the only way certain branches of math may gain justification. They may be justified on the grounds that they explain or are explained by other mathematical statements.

explains why this specific raven is black by citing the conjunctive statement. Given a bare bones Ex-J account this statement is a member of an explanatory system and *as such* is a candidate for justification. But, even apart from the issue of whether it is a virtuous explanation, there is clearly a better explanatory account, viz., the one that drops 'there is life on other planets'. The lesson is that it's easy to be a member of an explanatory system, but it is more demanding for that system to be virtuous and more demanding still for that system to beat its competitors.

The second component of Ex-J requires that the explanatory system be sufficiently virtuous. It is not enough that a proposition be a member of some account aimed at removing a mystery. The account must be sufficiently conservative, simple, or great in power. As I explained above with simplicity, we do not need an absolute measure of the explanatory merits of each theory to come to be justified in thinking that one theory is a better account than another. In a specific context there is enough shared judgment about how these virtues are to be weighed to make informative decisions.[30] I doubt that when two theories are close explanatory competitors we require some general, a priori metric to resolve the dispute. Disputes between close competitors proceed along the explanatory merits of the cases. Like most substantive theories in epistemology, Ex-J is consistent with there been cases for which it has no helpful advice; it is an epistemological theory, not a decision manual.

The condition that a system be sufficiently virtuous handles the objection that 'the best may not be good'. A common objection to explanatory coherentism is that a specific explanation may be the best among a set of lousy explanations. This is often the case. Some puzzling phenomenon occurs. The explanations we can think of are just not any good. They aren't sufficiently conservative, simple, or explanatory. But there is one that is a bit better than any other. In cases like this Ex-J doesn't imply that one is justified in believing it.

The third component of Ex-J claims that '*E* is more virtuous than any competing system *E*''. In this connection, Ex-J requires for justification that a belief is a member of a system that beats its rivals. If this obtains then the best view a subject has is one in which p is true. Thus, Ex-J secures a natural connection to the truth. It's not enough that p is a part of a good explanatory system; it must be a part of the best.

---

[30] See Laudan (1984).

Explanation and Justification 89

There is a delicate issue over the formulation of the condition about competing systems. An alternative explanationist account holds that

EX-J′: S has justification for believing p if and only if p is a member of a sufficiently virtuous explanatory system, E, and there is no system E' that is more virtuous than E.[31]

The issue between EX-J and EX-J′ concerns the question of ties between explanatory systems. There are two cases: ties between systems which agree on p and ties between systems which disagree on p. Consider the first case. Suppose there are three views E', E'', and E''' all of which agree on p and yet each is equally virtuous. Does one have justification for believing that p is true? One's evidence supports that one of these three views are true and p is a deductive consequence of that. In this case, one has excellent reason to believe that p is true. EX-J′ is intended to handle this case. It implies that p is justified in this case. What about Ex-J? Before we address that question, let us think about the second case.

The second case is one in which a subject has equally virtuous systems which disagree over p: one system includes p, the other does not (by either including ¬p or being silent on p). In this case is the subject justified in believing p? Ex-J′ implies that a subject does have adequate justification in this case. There is no system E' which is more virtuous than E. Yet it is a natural judgment that in this case a subject is not justified in believing p. By her lights there is an equally good explanation that does not require p. Ex-J captures this judgment. It is not enough for a system to be virtuous; it must also beat its relevant competitors. In this connection, Ex-J is more demanding than Ex-J′.

But does Ex-J require abandoning a simple argument that p is true from the three virtuous competing views which all agree on p? It does not. The solution to this puzzle lies in the idea of competing systems. In the case at hand the views do not compete with each other over whether p is true. The competition lies elsewhere. We should understand the idea of a competing system to be focused on a specific proposition or set of propositions. When we consider the justification for some specific proposition p, Ex-J instructs us to consider explanatory systems which compete with respect to p. In the case of ties among systems all agreeing on p, one has justification for believing that p because any system

---

[31] Thanks to Kevin McCain for mentioning this alternative.

not including p is not as virtuous. So Ex-J should be understood as follows:

> EX-J″: S has justification for believing p if and only if p is a member of a sufficiently virtuous explanatory system, E, and E is more virtuous than any p-relevant competing system E'.

The revision to focus competitors on specific propositions or a set of propositions is relevant for understanding Ex-J‴'s holistic implications. It is not a consequence of Ex-J″ that one is justified in believing p only if there is one total explanatory theory which beats out all competitors. A total explanatory theory is informationally complete such that for every proposition (at least, every one of interest to a person) it or its negation is within that system. Complete understanding—the removal of all mystery—aims for a total explanatory theory. But Ex-J″ does not require this. Ex-J″ requires only that the justification for a specific proposition consist in its membership in an explanatory system which beats out relevant competitors. Thus, justification is compatible with several more informationally complete theories each of which are settled on the question of p. For the sake of simplicity, I henceforth refer to Ex-J″ using 'Ex-J'.

What about explanatory systems that a subject does not understand? If a proposition is a member of such a virtuous system but the subject doesn't understand that system does she still have justification for it. On the face of it, Ex-J looks to have this implication. But, on reflection, it does not. The facts about what systems are explanatory for a subject are constrained by the mental facts of a subject. What beliefs a subject has, what propositions she has considered or can consider, and what inferences she can make all constrain the explanatory systems in play. An explanatory system which a subject cannot grasp does not purport to remove any mysteries for that subject. Thus, the explanatory systems in Ex-J are systems that are explanatory for the specific subject.[32]

What about about a case in which a subject has not connected the dots? We are all familiar with that eureka moment when we put the clues together in a crossword to discover the theme and consequently solve a problematic clue. Moments before the subject puts it altogether, did the subject have justification for what is the correct theme? The crossword

---

[32] I argue that this constraint falls out of the nature of explanation in Chapter 6, Section 6.3 "Coherence and Awareness."

answer is a member of a sufficiently virtuous explanatory system and it beats out competitors, although before the realization hits her she doesn't believe it. The justification for the crossword answer arises out of the subject's beliefs about what the clues are, what the other answers are, and what remains to be solved. These are mental facts about the subject. My view is that the realization is a matter of coming to base one's answer on its virtues. I thus hold that the subject in this case does have justification for the crossword answer. Admittedly, though, there are tricky issues with specifying the relevant parts of a subject's mental facts. Do beliefs a subject has that can only be recalled under years of psychological counseling count as relevant for determining justificatory status? Arguably, no. Yet stored beliefs that are easily brought to mind are relevant; even if they are never actually bought to mind. My view, thus, differs from Richard Feldman's view. Feldman holds that only evidence one is currently aware of at a time is relevant for determining justification.[33] A view with greater verisimilitude is that readily retrievable evidence bears on the justificatory status of a subject's beliefs.[34]

4.2.3 Ex-J and mentalism

Ex-J is a mentalist view. Mentalism claims that justification strongly supervenes on the mental facts of a subject. Conee and Feldman state the mentalist supervenience thesis thusly:

> S The justificatory status of a person's doxastic attitudes strongly supervenes on the person's occurrent and dispositional mental states, events, and conditions.[35]

Supervenience is a relation between properties. Properties of one kind, B, supervene on properties of another kind, A, if and only if determining the A-properties determine the B-properties. Supervenience is a kind of dependence relation: the B-properties depend on the A-properties. For example, facts about which team wins depend on facts about the final score. Strong supervenience adds the claim that necessarily there is no change in the B-properties without a change in the A-properties. Facts about which team wins supervene on facts about the final score but do

---

[33] Conee and Feldman (2004, Ch. 9).
[34] See also McCain (2014). McCain argues for a similar view of evidence possession.
[35] Conee and Feldman (2004, 56).

not strongly supervene because there is a world in which winning takes into account not only final score but style of play.

Conee and Feldman hold that facts about justification strongly supervene on mental properties: necessarily, there is no change in the justificatory status of a subject's doxastic attitudes without a change in her mental properties. Ex-J implies this claim on account of the following truth: necessarily, there is no change in the explanatory situation of a subject without a change in her mental properties. The explanatory situation of a subject—what hypotheses are in play, what stands in need of explanation, which sets of beliefs are conservative, simple, and explanatory—strongly supervene on the mental facts of a subject. A crucial argument for this claim comes in Chapter 6 where I argue that the true explanation is not necessarily the best explanation because what is the best explanation is what is best for a specific subject.[36] The true explanation of a subject's perceptual experience can be a fact only an expert could appreciate. In such a case the true explanation is not the best for the novice. The difference between the novice and the expert is a mental difference.

The other argument for the strong supervenience of explanatory position on mental facts is that the other facts about explanatory position—facts about simplicity and power—are necessary facts about a set of beliefs. Because there is no change in necessary truths, they automatically satisfy the strong supervenience thesis. Consequently, once the facts about what beliefs a subject has and what beliefs she can understand are fixed, the facts about simplicity and power are fixed as well. Thus, Ex-J is a mentalist view.

4.2.4 Ex-J and evidentialism

Ex-J is an evidentialist view. Conee and Feldman formulate evidentialism as follows:

> **ES** The epistemic justification of anyone's doxastic attitude toward any proposition at any time strongly supervenes on the evidence that person has at the time.[37]

ES strengthens S by ruling out the possibility that non-evidential mental states partially determine justificatory status. What kinds of mental states are non-evidential? Presumably, these mental states lack assertive

---
[36] See Section 6.3.
[37] Conee and Feldman (2004, 101).

representational content. States like hope and desire have content but the content is not hosted as true. Perceptual states and memorial states, by contrast, represent the content as true. Ex-J entails that contentful states which lack assertive representational content are not relevant for determining the virtues of an explanatory system.

What about mental states pertaining to abilities? The difference between a novice and an expert bird watcher is a difference in their occurrent and dispositional mental states. The expert has an ability that the novice lacks. The expert has more evidence than the novice because she has a specific skill. Similarly, a subject with a good memory has more evidence than a subject with a poor memory even though at any one time they may have the same occurrent mental states. The difference between the two subjects lies in their dispositional mental states. In each case, the expert and the subject with good memory has more available information relevant to the target belief. ES is compatible with the idea that skills make an evidential difference on the assumption that greater skill implies greater evidence.

Some empirical research supports this. Expert chess players recall certain positions in the middle game more readily than novices, and yet this ability does not extend to recalling random chess positions. If the positions are purely random then there is no significant difference in recall ability between experts and novices. A natural explanation of this data is that experts have learned to host certain information in a different way than novices. Thus there is not a pure distinction between evidence and ability to utilize evidence.

There is a crucial divide among evidentialist views over epistemic conservatism and holism. Conee and Feldman's version of evidentialism (CF-evidentialism) appears to be a non-conservative, non-holistic view. They claim that "all ultimate evidence is experiential."[38] They argue, "Believing a proposition, all by itself, is not evidence for its truth. Something at the interface of your mind and the world—your experiences—serves to justify belief in a proposition, if anything does."[39] This argument, though, is consistent with thinking that experience can justify only if one has reason for thinking that experience is reliable. Ex-J implies that ultimate evidence is not experiential. Rather our ultimate evidence for believing anything resides in the virtues of the entirety of a system of beliefs. Experience, as I argue in Chapter 5,

---

[38] Feldman (2008, 88).
[39] Ibid.

provides a reason for belief only if one's perspective supports the claim that experience is reliable. Experience itself is unable to support the reliability of experience; something other than experience—viz., belief—is required.

It's surprising in light of these claims that Conee and Feldman describe their view as "non-standard coherentism" as a kind of "explanatory coherentism."[40] Even so, CF-evidentialism and Ex-J fully subscribe to the claim that "a whole body of evidence entirely settles which doxastic attitudes toward which propositions are epistemically justified in any possible circumstance."[41] The disagreement between CF-evidentialism and Ex-J is over holism and conservatism.

One small issue needs to be addressed. How should we understand the conservative nature of Ex-J in light of Conee and Feldman's thesis E?

> E S is justified in believing p at t if and only if S's evidence at t on balance supports p.[42]

In the special case of conservative justification (see Chapter 2) a subject believes that p even though she has no positive evidence for p and no evidence against p. Her evidence for p is empty; there are no considerations that favor p or not-p. Following the terminology of Chapter 2, this is a case of *empty symmetrical evidence*, which distinguishes it from the standard case of *positive symmetrical evidence*. Epistemic conservatism is a thesis about the epistemic role of belief in the special case of empty symmetrical evidence. Ex-J implies that in the special case of empty symmetrical evidence the system that includes the subject's belief that p is slightly more virtuous than competing systems which do not include p. Therefore, Ex-J implies that belief in this special case yields justification.

Does thesis E imply that epistemic conservatism is false? The simplest response is to grant the objection that Ex-J conflicts with E but then to point out that it doesn't conflict with ES. Thus, ES and E are not equivalent. Indeed, Conee and Feldman in discussing a similar situation—believing or suspending judgment on meager evidence—claim that ES itself does not settle the issue; one needs more specific principles to get substantive commitments in this kind of case.[43] They

---

[40] See Feldman (2008, 98).
[41] Conee and Feldman (2004, 101).
[42] Feldman (2008, 83).
[43] Conee and Feldman (2004, 101–102).

claim that "ES is bedrock evidentialism."[44] Consequently, we should go with ES rather than E. A subject's overall evidential situation apropos p is sensitive to whether or not a subject believes p. In the special case of empty symmetrical evidence E yields the wrong verdict; in all other cases E is a sound principle.

4.2.5 Ex-J and propositional and doxastic justification

Ex-J is a thesis about propositional justification. A subject has justification for believing p just in case p is a member of a sufficiently virtuous explanatory system which beats relevant competing systems. If a subject bases her belief on the virtues of the system then her belief is doxastically justified. Does this require that a subject explicitly believe that her belief is a member of an explanatory system which beats competitors? If so then Ex-J implies that hardly anyone has doxastically justified beliefs.

I do not think this objection succeeds. The basing requirement should not be understood to require that a subject explicitly considers the virtues of her system and its competitors. Jonathan Kvanvig argues that a coherentist account of the basing relation may mirror a foundationalist account of basing in the special case of defeaters.[45] Suppose one believes p on the basis of adequate evidence. The belief is doxastically justified. One then acquires an undermining defeater: the evidence no longer supports the belief. But then one acquires a defeater defeater, a claim which by defeating the underminer reinstates the original evidence. Suppose that defeater defeater is itself defeated and then another claim defeats that. In actual debates this process can be quite complex. If all the defeaters are themselves defeated so that one's original evidence is reinstated many times over, what is one's basis for the belief? It is not the original basis. Rather it is one's total evidence which includes the original evidence and the complex defeater structure. A plausible basing requirement must be consistent with this case; the entire basis is one's total evidence. Whatever problems there may be here for a coherentist carry over to anyone that accepts the total evidence requirement.[46]

---

[44] Ibid.
[45] Kvanvig (1995b).
[46] Ex-J is compatible with either a doxastic or causal account of basing. See McCain (2014, Ch. 5). Ex-J is compatible with McCain's account of the basing relation.

4.3 Supporting cases and putative counterexamples

Ex-J states that a subject has justification for believing a claim if and only if it is part of a sufficiently virtuous explanatory system which beats its rivals. How does Ex-J fare according to this standard? In the following I argue that Ex-J is a virtuous explanatory epistemological view and that it is better than rival accounts about the internal, structural property of a subject relevant to determining whether they are epistemically justified in believing some claim. I begin with a case by case comparison, comparing Ex-J with a standard reliabilist account and CF-evidentialism. The upshot of this section is that Ex-J is a better account than CF-evidentialism and standard reliabilism. In the next subsection I consider counterexamples to Ex-J and argue that Ex-J survives unscathed. The conclusion I draw from this is that Ex-J is plausible and a better account than its rivals.

4.3.1 Case-by-case comparison

Rival views of epistemic justification offer competing accounts of specific cases. In the following I offer a chart of three views and yes/no answers to the question of whether a subject has propositional justification in a particular case. There are eight possible combinations of answers. I focus on cases 3, 4, 5, and 7. The natural judgments about these cases support explanationism over its rivals. The argument can also be understood as a how-possible argument. If one shares these judgments about cases 3, 4, 5, and 7 then Ex-J provides a general theory that captures the correctness of these verdicts. The cases in which all three theories agree or disagree is not interesting for theory choice. Since there is uniform agreement in these cases it does not provide a basis for holding that one theory's account is better than another. Reliabilism, CF-evidentialism, and Ex-J all agree that common sense is justified and, further, that one lacks justification for flights of fancy. The interesting question is where these views disagree and why. The other two cases I ignore are ones in which CF-evidentialism holds that justification is present but Ex-J does not. As I understand Ex-J it is a weaker doctrine than CF-evidentialism, allowing justification where CF-evidentialism does not see any. But in any case in which there is adequate evidence for a claim, Ex-J holds that there is adequate justification of the claim. This follows from the fact that Ex-J is a broader evidentialist view than CF-evidentialism. Consequently cases 2 and 6 are not possible.

Explanation and Justification 97

Logical space of views

Reliabilism	CF-Evidentialism	Ex-J		Cases
Yes	Yes	Yes	1	Common sense
Yes	Yes	No	2	—
Yes	No	Yes	3	Forgotten evidence
Yes	No	No	4	Quiz-show knowledge
No	Yes	Yes	5	New evil demon problem
No	Yes	No	6	—
No	No	Yes	7	Explanatory theories
No	No	No	8	Flights of fancy

Case 3: Forgotten evidence

In case 3 a CF-evidentialist holds that there is no justification while a reliabilist and an explanationist hold that there is justification. The case of forgotten evidence fulfills this role. As the standard account goes, it is a case in which a subject no longer has adequate evidence to support her belief that p but her belief that p was reliably acquired and reliably maintained. Consider Sally who believes that the Battle of Hastings occurred in 1066. She does not recall where she learned this and she cannot bring to mind any specific evidence which supports this specific date. She knows it occurred in the eleventh century but it seems to her that 1086 might be right too. Even so, she's confident it's 1066. Is Sally's belief that the battle occurred in the year 1066 justified? Her belief that it occurred in 1066 is reliable because she did learn it from a good source and has retained it in memory. She has lost a memory of its original acquisition and consequently the date of 1086 has become a competing date for her. But she still holds with conviction that the date is 1066.

A reliabilist maintains that Sally's belief is justified.[47] What does CF-evidentialism and Ex-J say about this case? CF-evidentialism does not countenance as epistemically relevant the fact that Sally believes the date is 1066. CF-evidentialism implies that if there is no positive, non-doxastic evidence that the date is 1066 then her belief is not justified. Conee and Feldman hold that to the extent Sally is justified she has a disposition to bring the belief to mind with the phenomenology of activating memory. To make the contrast between Ex-J and CF-evidentialism sharp, I suppose that Sally now lacks that disposition. Even so, she Sally

---

[47] See, for example, Goldman (2011) on preservative memory.

endorses that the date is 1066.[48] This self-endorsement makes a justificatory difference on my account. Given Sally's beliefs, the system that includes "the Battle of Hastings was 1066" is better than its competitors since the main competing system—which includes that the date was 1086—has one more false belief. Sally's self-endorsement tips the balance in favor of the system with the 1066 date.

The case of forgotten evidence is important. I've argued in Chapter 2 that many crucial beliefs—that memory is reliable, for example—are believed in the state of empty symmetrical evidence. One of the main virtues of externalist accounts of knowledge and justification is that they can provide an answer to radical skepticism. If beliefs of this kind bear the appropriate external relations–track the truth, counterfactual dependence, produced in accord with a design plan aimed at truth, are reliable, and so on—then those beliefs may amount to knowledge and one is justified in believing them. A CF-evidentialist account has a difficult time finding non-questioning begging evidence for fundamental sources of evidence. A common theme in epistemology is that either externalism is true or skepticism reigns. An explanationist account avoids this dilemma. Doxastic facts are relevant for determining justification; it is false that all our evidence is fundamentally experiential.

Case 4: Quiz-show knowledge

In case 4 a reliabilist maintains that there is justification while a CF-evidentialist and an explanationist denies that there is justification. The case of quiz-show knowledge fits this pattern. Suppose Samantha, a contestant on a popular quiz-show, gets all the answers right. When a clue is offered Samantha rings in with the correct answer. She's quite good at this. From a third-person perspective it is natural to think that Samantha knows the answers to the clues; yet from Samantha's perspective the answers just pop into her head. Phenomenology plays little role in this case; it does not *seem* to Samantha that the answers are right and it does not *seem* that they are wrong. What are, in fact, the right answers just occur to her without the phenomenology of activating memory. The "quiz-show knowledge" is for her similar to patients with blindsight.

---

[48] To make this case one of empty symmetrical evidence we need to engage in some fiction. Suppose all historical records relevant to the date of the Battle of Hastings are destroyed and Sally is unable to consult anyone else. In this fictional case, all she has to go on is her conviction that she has it right.

They form beliefs about objects in close proximity but lack any awareness of how this is so. Samantha does not believe that she knows the answer.

This case is designed as an argument against evidentialism. Samantha knows the answers to the questions even though from her perspective she appears to be just guessing. According to reliabilism Samantha has adequate justification for believing her answers.[49] Her 'guesses' are the result of a reliable process even though she thinks she doesn't know the answers. In general, there is nothing about externalist views that requires a particular phenomenology for justification. Justification is a relation between states of the world and belief states. There need not be any specific phenomenological experience in addition to the presence of the right kind of external relation.

CF-evidentialism implies that there is no justification in this case. Samantha's evidence at the time does not support her answers. They appear out of the blue. Ex-J agrees with this judgment. Samantha's perspective does not support the inclusion of this answer over any competing answer. She takes herself just to be guessing. She does not endorse her own answers and is surprised that they are right. Thus, even though these answers are preserved in memory and Samantha can retrieve them, the fact that her perspective doesn't support them implies that she doesn't have adequate justification for her answers.

The case of forgotten evidence and the case of quiz-show knowledge are often presented together as externalist arguments against evidentialism. But Ex-J reveals that these arguments have a crucial difference: the subject's own belief, her self-endorsement. In forgotten evidence Sally endorses the claim that the date is 1066 even though she can't argue on pure evidential grounds that the date 1086 is not right. The fact of her own self-endorsement makes an epistemic difference. In quiz-show Samantha does not endorse the relevant contents. She takes herself to be guessing. This is a crucial epistemic difference.

Case 5: New evil demon

In case 5 a reliabilist holds that there is no justification while a CF-evidentialist and an explanationist maintain that there is. The new evil

---

[49] There is a question about whether or not Samantha actually believes her answers. Whether or not she does, the crucial issue is about propositional justification: is there an adequate basis for belief?

demon problem provides an instance of this pattern.[50] This problem differs from the old Cartesian evil demon problem. Descartes's evil demon problem concerned the question of how we know natural claims like 'I have hands' if it is possible that we are deceived by an evil demon. This problem is fundamentally one of underdetermination: the evidence we possess for many of our beliefs does not entail that our beliefs are correct.

The new evil demon problem addresses a different issue. It concerns the justificatory status of the beliefs of a normal subject and the beliefs of a mental duplicate of that subject in a demon world. The problem is that because both the normal subject and her duplicate have all the same evidence the justificatory status of their beliefs is the same. But this judgment conflicts with standard reliabilism. The subject's beliefs in the demon world are massively unreliable. These beliefs are not formed in a good environment, they do not track the truth, and they are not counterfactually dependent on the truth of her beliefs. Nonetheless, the subject has all the same evidence as we have. Her beliefs form a good explanatory system which beats its competitors. Both Ex-J and CF-evidentialism hold that in this case the mental duplicate in the demon world has justified beliefs.

Case 7: Explanatory theories

Is one ever justified in believing an explanatory theory on the basis of its explanatory merits? Many of the views we accept purport to be justified in this way. Scientific theories are advocated on the basis of their explanatory merits. Historical and philosophical views are defended by their ability to account for a wide range of phenomena in a simple and conservative manner. Even the view bequeathed to us by our ancestors—common sense—is an explanatory theory. If it turns out that no one is justified in believing a theory on the basis of its explanatory merits then the reach of skepticism is vast.

Yet there is a simple argument to the effect that we are never justified in believing any explanatory theory. Theories requires a large number of commitments, each of which is less than certain. In Lakatos's terms, a theory has its core commitments but also requires a large surrounding protective belt and a positive heuristic. The protective belt fills out the theory so that it gains empirical traction and the positive heuristic provides a defensive strategy for addressing challenges. An explanatory

---

[50] See Cohen (1984).

theory is best thought as the combination of the hardcore, the protective belt, and the positive heuristic. Yet, the conditional probability of any explanatory theory is low. Given the conjunctive rule of probability, summing the probabilities of numerous uncertain propositions quickly leads to the total probability of a theory being considerably low. Unless one is justified in accepting a view whose probability is low, no one is justified in believing any explanatory theory.

Reliabilism implies that no one is justified in believing an explanatory theory. Reliabilism may secure justification for some components of an explanatory theory but the process of believing a theory on the basis of uncertain propositions is massively unreliable. Reliablism looks to be a good indicator of the commitments of other externalist theories in this respect. Externalism accounts for knowledge and justification by way of external relations one tracks to one's environment. But explanatory theories attempt to explain features of one's environment, features that are not readily detectable by the senses. Explanatory theories require the use of reason by formulating hypothesis, generating implications, testing those implications, and comparing them with the results of other views. Externalists views are poorly positioned to make sense of the way explanation and its virtues work to justify our views. The relevant facts that explanation adopts to grasp are too subtle for the senses.

The commitments of CF-evidentialism are not clear because it is a non-holistic, non-conservative interpretation of ES, the thesis of epistemic supervenience. A plausible way of filling out CF-evidentialism implies that no one is justified in believing an explanatory theory. This specific view adopts thesis E which requires that one's beliefs be positively supported by the evidence and interprets positive support as requiring a probability greater than .5. The simple argument from the conjunctive rule of probability implies that explanatory theories have a probability less than .5. This version of CF-evidentialism implies that no explanatory theory is justified.

It is overwhelmingly plausible that *some* explanatory theories are justified on the basis of their explanatory merits. I've argued that Ex-J can make sense of this. Given Ex-J the final conjunctive probability of a theory is not relevant for determining justification. Rather what is relevant is the explanatory merit of the theory in comparison with its competitors. If the theory itself is simple, fits with background evidence, explains, and beats its competitors then one has justification for that theory. The fact that the final conjunctive probability of a grand theory is low does not itself provide any specific challenge to one's view. The cost of an explanatory theory is available at no lower cost.[51]

Conclusion from the cases

The best explanation of the following verdicts is that Ex-J is true. It provides an account of justification in these cases and beats competing accounts. Philosophers disagree. They propose alternative accounts which they claim better explain the cases, and thus should be accepted rather than Ex-J. My challenge to such philosophers is to specify the epistemic role of such explanatory arguments. If they claim that their preferred account is the best explanation of the relevant data then why should this fact give us justification for believing that the account is right? Is it because their account is simpler, more conservative, or more explanatory? If so then how does this judgment fit with a general denial of Ex-J? Consider, for example, Chisholm's theory of justification. Chisholm has a number of fundamental epistemic principles. Why should we accept those epistemic principles? The principles do not support themselves. Rather the argument seems to be that the best explanation of our diverse judgments about justification are that these principles are true. But then the ultimate justification for Chisholm's principles relies on inference to the best explanation. Why then ought we take Chisholm's principles as fundamental rather than taking inference to the best explanation as fundamental? Reflection on questions like this support the fundamental role of explanatory judgments for justification. An explanationist account makes sense of this; alternative epistemological accounts must take seriously the role of explanatory arguments. This is a significant reason Conee and Feldman think that "fundamental epistemic principles are principles of best explanation."[52] I go one step further: the fundamental epistemic principle is inference to the best explanation.

4.3.2 Putative counterexamples

Ex-J implies that a belief is justified only if it is part of a virtuous explanatory system which beats its competitors. A belief can be a part of such a system by either explaining, being explained, or being a part of an explainer or explainee. In this section I examine several putative counterexamples to this claim. These alleged counterexamples help clarify Ex-J. The purported counterexamples arise from a mistaken

---

[51] To echo a remark made by Mark Kaplan. See Kaplan (1996, 119).
[52] Feldman (2008, 97).

application of the difference between propositional knowledge (knowledge that) and explanatory knowledge (knowledge why). The mistake is to assume that since propositional knowledge is prior to *specific* explanatory knowledge, propositional knowledge can be had without any explanatory knowledge. The following cases concern a subject who knows that a proposition is true without knowing why it is true.

The prediction–explanation asymmetry and Lehrer's counterexamples

The first putative counterexample involves a case in which a subject comes to know *that* a proposition is true without knowing *why* it is true. The distinction between propositional knowledge and explanatory knowledge goes back to Aristotle's *Posterior Analytics*. It is a platitude that one may know that a proposition is true without knowing why it is true. If Ex-J implies that propositional knowledge entails explanatory knowledge then the view is false. Mysteries arise because we have knowledge we cannot adequately explain.

I address this issue by considering the asymmetry between prediction and explanation. On Hempel's deductive-nomological account of explanation any deduction of an event by way of boundary conditions and a law constitutes an explanation of the event. As we saw in Section 1 this view wrongly implies that deducing that a mouse is five feet away from a owl via boundary conditions and the Pythagorean theorem implies that we know why the mouse is so close to the owl.

Keith Lehrer claims this as a counterexample to explanatory coherentism.[53] One has adequate justification for believing the mouse is five feet from the owl but one lacks an explanation for why the mouse is so close. However, to provide a counterexample to Ex-J it must be false that one's justification consists in the fact that the proposition that 'the mouse is five feet from the owl' is part of a virtuous explanatory system which beats its competitors. Yet this claim is dubious. One's belief follows from the boundary conditions and the Pythagorean theorem which are parts of a virtuous explanatory system which beats competitors. One's justification for accepting the claim about the mouse depends on one's justification for accepting the theorem and the boundary conditions, and the justification for those claims consists in being a part of a virtuous explanatory system.

---

[53] Lehrer (2000, 114).

Even though Lehrer's case isn't a counterexample to Ex-J, it is useful to illustrate the difference between *propositional knowledge* and *explanatory knowledge*. Explanatory knowledge is a specific kind of propositional knowledge; it is propositional knowledge which removes a mystery. Explanatory coherentism is not committed to the claim that everything a person is justified in accepting comes with an explanation. Rather, Ex-J implies that justification is a holistic matter determined by the explanatory virtues of a set of information. It is not committed to the claim that there are no mysteries within that set. It is just committed to the idea that the mysteries that arise do not favor abandoning those beliefs for another more explanatory system.

Lehrer's second putative counterexample illustrates this.[54] He considers a case involving David Hume who, in the eighteenth century, sees a dead man. Hume believes that this man was sexually conceived and he is fully justified in this belief. But conception does not explain death. Consequently, Lehrer maintains, one has full justification without any explanatory considerations.

In reply, Hume's belief that "this man was conceived" is part of a virtuous explanatory system which beats its competitors. Conception explains this man's life and the facts about human mortality explain death. Hume accepts all this. This set of beliefs beats any competitors that the man was not conceived. Again, knowledge and justification do not always come with a specific explanation. In this case, Hume possesses no explanation for why this man died yesterday rather than a week, a month, or a year from now. But his justification consists in the explanatory merits of his system of beliefs.

Lehrer explicitly considers this kind of reply, viz., the explanationist reply that one's justification in these cases consist in the way the conclusions and premises function in an overall explanatory system. Lehrer rejects this for the following reason. He considers a group of *anti-explanationists*,[55] individuals who avoid asking any why-questions, and satisfy themselves with accepting observations and using deduction and enumerative induction to extend belief. Lehrer alleges that anti-explanationists are justified in believing that "the mouse is five feet from the owl" and "this man was conceived" on the basis of purely deductive and non-explanatory inductive considerations. He concludes that explanatory considerations are not necessary for justification.

---

[54] Ibid., (114–115).
[55] Lehrer (2000, 115).

On the face of it this case is simply a rejection of Ex-J. Suppose Lehrer had designed the case in the following way: imagine a group of people who use just deduction and enumerative induction. They have justified beliefs but it's false that their beliefs is part of a virtuous explanatory system. This isn't an argument against Ex-J; rather it is a statement that the view is false.

Is there an argument here against Ex-J? It's not clear that there is. Ex-J holds that a necessary condition for justification is that a subject's belief is part of a virtuous explanatory system which beats competing system. Is this condition false in Lehrer's case? Given the objectivity of explanatory relations, it is either a fact or not about whether a subject's system of beliefs is a virtuous system. If it's not then the subject lacks adequate justification and if it is then the subject has adequate justification.

The most charitable way to understand Lehrer's case is that it focuses on the role of higher-order beliefs. Suppose the anti-explanationists beliefs are part of a virtuous explanatory system. Yet they eschew any notion of explanation. They take themselves to accept that, for example, 'the flag pole is three feet' on the basis of simple induction. It's been measured and all the times in the past measurements are accurate, so the pole is three feet. They claim that is the only basis for their belief. One question is whether these anti-explanationist subjects have any justification of thinking that the ruler is a standard ruler, that the measurements are taken in normal conditions, and so on.[56] This is clearly relevant to whether the argument is good because if they lack any justification for thinking that the rule is a standard ruler then they lack justification for thinking the pole is three feet. Suppose the ruler was purchased at a hardware store from a bin of other rulers marked with the sign 'Rulers'. This is evidence which supports the belief. It's relevant and, protestations to the contrary, it needs to be represented in the overall argument. As I argued in the previous chapter, direct ampliative inference is not a sound form of inference; explanatory considerations are required. Consequently, Lehrer's argument faces a dilemma that either the subjects lack explanatory considerations to support their belief or not. If they lack explanatory considerations then, given my earlier argument, they are not justified. But if they do have such considerations then they are justified.

---

[56] For example, whether the store is a standard hardware store, not some gag store which sells misleading rulers.

What about their own reflective stance on their beliefs, specifically the anti-explanationist stance that they eschew any explanatory considerations? Given the centrality of why-questions to adult cognition and our desire to remove mystery, it's difficult to conceive of such people. Can we imagine people that accept appearances without any explanatory considerations? Appearances conflict. A square tower looks round from a distance. Some explanation is called for. Do anti-explanationists accept that the tower is square close up and round from a distance? Do they accept that geometrical shapes shift from one's perspective, so that a tower can be both round and square? An anti-explanationist is stuck with conflicting appearances. One needs to explain why some appearances are not veridical. The role of explanatory considerations is tied to the appearance–reality distinction. If there were no appearance reality distinction then, perhaps, anti-explanationists would be possible. But given the distinction and its central role in the development of cognition, it's hard to make sense of the thought that anti-explanationists have justified beliefs. In the final analysis, then, to the extent that Lehrer stresses that the anti-explanationists eschew any explanatory considerations and accept all appearances then this group of people have little justified beliefs. They have conflicting appearances which stand in need of resolution.

Goldman's counterexamples

Alvin Goldman reject's Conee and Feldman's suggestion that epistemic principles are principles of best explanation on the grounds that justification does not require explanatory considerations.[57] Goldman considers three cases: introspective beliefs, preservative memory, and arithmetical inference. I consider introspective beliefs in the next chapter on the justification of phenomenal beliefs. Let us address these last two cases.

Goldman argues that *preservative memory* is a case of justification without explanatory considerations. He gives the following case:

> Years ago Ichabod formed a belief in proposition q by acquiring it in an entirely justified fashion. He had excellent evidence for believing it at that time (whether it was inferential or non-inferential evidence). After ten years pass, however, Ichabod has forgotten all of this evidence and not acquired any new evidence, either favorable or unfavorable. However, he continues to believe q strongly. Whenever

---

[57] Goldman (2011, 276).

he thinks about q, he (mentally) affirms its truth without hesitation. At noon today Ichabod's belief in q is still present, stored in his mind, although he is not actively thinking about it. I stipulate that none of his other beliefs confers adequate evidence either for believing q or for disbelieving it. Since Ichabod remembers q's being the case, and since he originally had excellent evidence for q, which was never subsequently undermined, Ichabod's belief in q at noon today is justified.[58]

Goldman declares that this is a counterexample to explanationism as well as to mentalist evidentialism. The core problem, he explains, lies in the evidentialist requirement that "justifying evidence must be possessed at the same time as the belief."[59] Is this a consequence of mentalism? It is not. Mentalism counts as relevant dispositional mental states of a subject. An expert bird watcher may be unjustified in her belief that the bird before her is a Wilson's Plover even though she is in the same occurrent state as a novice who believes the same thing. The difference is that an expert has the disposition to recall defeating information which the novice does not.

Even so, CF-evidentialism may have a problem with this case for the reasons we discussed in the case of forgotten evidence. But this is not a problem for Ex-J. The conservative nature of Ex-J counts belief as epistemically relevant. There remains, though, a substantive disagreement between my Ex-J account and Goldman's view over the issue of knowledge-level justification. Justification adequate for knowledge requires more than mere belief. It requires a supporting virtuous explanatory system. In the case of Ichabod he lacks this supporting perspective. Thus, I take it that Ichabod does not know.

Goldman's second case against explanationism concerns *arithmetic inference*. He considers the inference from (1) *there are two squirrels on the patio* and (2) *there are two birds on the patio* to the conclusion that (3) *there are four animals on the patio*. The belief that (3) is epistemically justified on the basis of this inference but Goldman asks:

> Is it a case of explanatory inference? Surely not. How does there being four animals explain there being two squirrels and two birds? It doesn't. Still, here is a justified belief that some epistemic principle

---
[58] Goldman (2011, 260).
[59] (Goldman 2011 Ibid., 261).

must cover. But that principle, in turn, cannot be grounded in terms of best explanation.[60]

In reply, this case does not conflict with Ex-J. One's belief that there are four animals is part of a virtuous explanatory system which beats competitors. Each of the premise beliefs are justified on grounds of inference to the best explanation. Squirrels have thus and so characteristics and the animal before one best fits those characteristics. One's belief that there are four animals does not do any specific explanatory work but Ex-J isn't committed to this idea. Justification is holistic, having to do with the virtues of one's system of beliefs.

Statistical syllogism and Ex-J

The final case I consider is one that other explanationists—Harman and Lycan—have found troubling. The problem is that some inductive inferences are not explanatory. Some inferences simply provide grounds for belief. This poses a problem for a rabid explanationist claim that all justifying inference is explanatory inference. William Lycan appears committed to this claim, writing that "all justified reasoning is fundamentally explanatory reasoning that aims at maximizing the explanatory coherence of one's total belief system."[61] But Ex-J is not committed to the claim that all reasoning is explanatory reasoning. Ex-J entails that one's justification for a belief consists in the overall explanatory virtues of one's system of belief. There may be particular inferences which are not explanatory. But the justification for the conclusion of the inference consists in its being a part of an overall virtuous explanatory system.

Let us consider this in context. The specific problem that concerns Harman and Lycan is statistical syllogism.[62]

N% of Fs are Gs (where N > 50, by a good margin).
So, The next F will be a G.[63]

Lycan remarks that it is difficult to reconstruct this inference in explanatory terms. The conclusion that *the next F will be G* does not explain the premise that *N% of Fs are Gs* and the premise does not

---

[60] Goldman (2011, 277–278).
[61] (Lycan, 1988, 128)
[62] (Lycan 1988 Ibid., 183–188).
[63] (Lycan 1988 Ibid., 184).

explain the conclusion. But explanatory considerations are not far from hand. This argument generates the rational expectation that the next F is G because we have grounds for believing that the statistical premise is not accidentally true and that the next F is not atypical. These background, explanatory beliefs must be operative in a justifying use of statistical inference. Consider the following inference:

> 99% of students at Ronald Reagan College are men.
> So, Cynthia, a student at Ronald Reagan College, is a man.[64]

This argument is an instance of statistical syllogism but the conclusion is not justified. The reason is that we have grounds for thinking that Cynthia is not a typical student at Ronald Reagan College.

The lesson I draw is that even though Ex-J isn't committed to the thesis that all inferences are explanatory inferences, explanatory considerations are never far from hand. Justifying inferences require plausibility considerations and require normality conditions. These are straightforwardly conditions that are justified on the basis of simplicity, conservativeness, and power. Consequently, even though some inferences in particular contexts are not explanatory, the ultimate justification for those inferences rests upon explanatory considerations.

4.4 Conclusion

I've argued that Ex-J is a plausible account of justification. Ex-J relies on a primitive concept of explanation. On the specific Ex-J account the virtues of better explanation are simplicity, conservativeness, and explanatory power. Ex-J is a mentalist evidentialist view which differs from Conee and Feldman's evidentialism over holism and the explanatory virtues. I've examined supporting cases in the context of rival views and have argued that Ex-J beats its rivals. The counterexamples to accounts like Ex-J do not succeed. Ex-J doesn't require that every belief and every inference is explanatory. Rather Ex-J holds that justification is a holistic matter of the virtues of one's explanatory system.

---

[64] Lycan (1988, 186).

5
BonJour and the Myth of the Given

Laurence BonJour's epistemology is marked by careful reflection on the consequences of epistemic internalism for an overall theory of epistemic justification. Epistemic internalism requires that the facts which determine whether a subject's belief is justified are internal or mental facts, facts that, in some sense, a subject is aware of. BonJour formerly argued that epistemic internalism implied epistemic coherentism. A crucial part of this overall argument was a defense of the Sellarsian dilemma. This dilemma attacks foundationalist internalist views that attempt to ground basic beliefs in experiential states such as appearances, seemings, immediate apprehensions, direct awarenesses, or intuitions. BonJour argued that the requirement that these states do not require further reasons conflicts with the internalist requirement that these states provide reasons for a subject to believe that some proposition is true.[1]

BonJour has renounced this argument and has defended a form of internalistic foundationalism.[2] My goal in this chapter is to defend BonJour's earlier coherentist view about the Sellarsian dilemma from his later foundationalist epistemology. I seek to accomplish this by arguing that his latest attempt to solve the Sellarsian dilemma does not succeed. I begin with an overview of BonJour's anti-foundationalist argument and his defense of the Sellarsian dilemma contained in his book *The Structure of Empirical Knowledge*. This will set the stage for evaluating his latest position, which comes in the second section. In the final section, I consider David Chalmers's recent attempt to defend a position closely similar to BonJour's by appeal to phenomenal concepts. I argue that

---
[1] BonJour (1978, 1985, Ch. 4).
[2] BonJour (1999, 2000, 2001c, 2001d, 2004); BonJour and Sosa (2003).

Chalmers's view faces similar problems to BonJour's. It is not possible to consider every attempt to defend the doctrine of the given, but, as the last section aims to show, there is a common core to many attempts to defend that doctrine. I argue that the common core conflicts with the requirements of epistemic internalism. Thus, I take this argument to have shifted the burden of argument back to epistemic internalists who aim to defend a foundationalist view.

5.1 BonJour's anti-foundationalist argument and the Sellarsian dilemma

BonJour formulates a basic argument against foundationalism in chapter 2 of his book *The Structure of Empirical Knowledge*. The argument aims to show that epistemic internalism implies that foundationalism is false. BonJour's argument is heavily influenced by Wilfrid Sellars's essay 'Empiricism and the Philosophy of Mind.'[3] In section VIII 'Does empirical knowledge have a foundation?' Sellars argues that knowledge requires justification that in some sense must be recognized by the knower. Sellars writes, "We have seen that to be the expression of knowledge, a report must not only *have* authority, this authority must *in some sense* be recognized by the person whose report it is."[4] This conflicts, Sellars claims, with the requirement that there can be basic knowledge. William Alston accuses Sellars's argument of a levels confusion.[5] Sellars's argument is defensible against Alston's charge but that is a story for another occasion. In the following I examine BonJour's formulation of the argument.

BonJour's anti-foundationalist argument:[6]

1. Suppose that there are basic empirical beliefs, that is, empirical beliefs (a) which are epistemically justified, and (b) whose justification does not depend on that of any further empirical beliefs.
2. For a belief to be epistemically justified requires that there be a reason why it is likely to be true.
3. For a belief to be epistemically justified for a particular person requires that this person be himself in cognitive possession of such a reason.

---

[3] Sellars (1963).
[4] Ibid., 168.
[5] Alston (1980).
[6] BonJour (1985, 32).

4. The only way to be in cognitive possession of such a reason is to believe with justification the premises from which it follows that the belief is likely to be true.
5. The premises of such a justifying argument for an empirical belief cannot be entirely a priori; at least one such premise must be empirical.

Therefore,

6. The justification of a supposed basic empirical belief must depend on the justification of at least one other empirical belief, contradicting (1); it follows that there can be no basic empirical beliefs.

Premise (1) of this argument is a stipulation. Premises (2) and (3) function to specify epistemic internalism. Premise (5) indicates that the justification of any empirical belief cannot be entirely a priori. The key premise is (4). BonJour supports this premise by the Sellarsian dilemma. The conclusion of the dilemma states that experience can provide a subject with a reason for a belief only if it is the kind of thing that itself requires justification. The core dilemma can be formulated as follows:[7]

The Sellarsian dilemma

7. Either a potentially justifying state has assertive, propositional content or it does not have assertive, propositional content.
8. If a state has assertive, propositional content then, while it can provide justification, it also requires justification.
9. If a state does not have assertive, propositional content then it cannot provide justification.

Consequently,

10. Only states with assertive, propositional content can provide justification and these states also require justification.

For our purposes of evaluating BonJour's later attempt to refute the dilemma, it will be helpful to consider how BonJour formerly defended this argument. I focus on BonJour's argument against C.I. Lewis's doctrine of the given.[8] Lewis defends a sophisticated foundationalist account of empirical knowledge which rests upon statements whose truth is determined only by experience.[9] BonJour argues that Lewis's

---

[7] See BonJour's summary of the basic problem with givenness (1985, 78).
[8] What follows is based on BonJour (1985, 72–79).
[9] See Lewis (1946, 172).

view fails because the apprehension of the given can provide epistemic support only if it is construed in a way that it thereby requires support.[10]

How does C.I. Lewis understand "the given"? In *An Analysis of Knowledge & Valuation* Lewis characterizes the given by that which is picked out by the use of expressive language which includes constructions like "it appears as though," "it seems to be that," and "it looks as if." Expressive language signifies *appearances*, which is "confined to the description of the content of presentation itself."[11]

Appearances, according to Lewis, are the subject matter of foundational empirical beliefs. The belief *it appears that there is a red item before me* may be justified by the appeal to the given. For this belief to be justified, however, it's not sufficient that a subject believe it or even that the subject be in the particular appearance state. Rather a subject must *grasp* or *apprehend* that the content is present. As BonJour observes it is this *grasp* or *apprehension* of the given that does the justificatory work.[12] C.I. Lewis himself finds it necessary to talk of the "apprehension of the given," though he is not explicit about the relation between the given and the apprehension of the given.[13]

BonJour then presses the Sellarsian dilemma against the claim that *the apprehension of the given* provides basic justification. Is this a propositional, conceptual state or is it a non-propositional, nonconceptual state? If the former then the apprehension *that* there is something red before one can provide justification but it is the kind of thing that one requires justification. If, however, the apprehension of the given is construed as a non-propositional, nonconceptual state then it does not give the subject a truth-evaluable reason to believe that some proposition is true. Thus, it's difficult to see how the apprehension of the given can provide basic justification.

BonJour profitably discusses two potential replies a defender of Lewis may offer.[14] The first reply denies that there is a substantive distinction between "the given" and "the apprehension of the given." One may hold that the given is by its nature *self-apprehending*. The given thus doesn't require a separate act of apprehension.

---

[10] BonJour (1985, 72).
[11] Lewis (1946, 179).
[12] BonJour (1985, 74–5).
[13] BonJour observes this too (1985, 75).
[14] (BonJour, 1985, 75–78). The following discussion relies heavily on BonJour at this point. I explicitly indicate where my discussion diverges from BonJour's discussion.

BonJour acknowledges that this reply has "a certain intuitive plausibility" but, he argues, it ultimately fails.[15] He contends that the same dilemma can be offered to this response. BonJour asks, "Is the apprehension which is allegedly built into the given experience cognitive or noncognitive, judgmental or nonjudgmental?"[16] If the apprehension is cognitive or judgmental then there is a logical distinction between a red experiential content and the apprehension of it. On this option the apprehension of the given is "propositionally formed, capable of being true or false, and capable of serving as the premise of an inference," whereas the given is "literally red."[17] Against the noncognitive, nonjudgmental option, BonJour contends that there seems to be no clear reason for distinguishing between the given and its apprehension. The motivation for moving to the requirement that the given be apprehended is that the noncognitive state of givenness was insufficient for the justification. Because we lack a clear conception of noncognitive apprehension, this move inherits the original problems with the given itself.[18]

The second potential reply available to a defender of Lewis is to attack the distinction between cognitive states and noncogntive states. Perhaps, the apprehension of the given is a special kind of state that is not strictly cognitive nor strictly noncognitive.[19] This would be a kind of state a subject can be in prior to language use, and, yet, also a state that involves a representation that some specific state of affairs is true. But, BonJour argues, if a state involves the representation that something is the case then there is logical space to distinguish between correct and incorrect representation. Given this space, one needs justification for thinking that the representation is correct.[20]

The logical space between the given and its apprehension is significant. One way to press this further (in a way BonJour doesn't) is to consider the given in connection with the specious present. The specious present is the duration one is immediately aware of, a temporal length in which (presumably) memory plays no role. Acts of apprehending the given occur within the specious present. Given the distinction between the given and its apprehension, one can legitimately seek out

---

[15] BonJour (1985, 76).
[16] Ibid.
[17] Ibid.
[18] Ibid.
[19] Ibid.
[20] Ibid.

the nature of one's justification for thinking that when one putatively apprehends that *there is a red appearance* the appearance is the same as the way red things have appeared in the past? The defender of the given can answer this question only by appealing to items within the specious present. But within the confines of the present *now* there is little to support the thought that my belief that this appearance is red tracks my former belief that red things appear this way. Thus, the defender of a view like Lewis's is caught between reducing the content of the apprehension of the given to only that which can be defended within the specious present or allowing one to rely on beliefs that cannot be justified within the specious present.[21]

In summary the Sellarsian dilemma is a powerful argument against foundationalism. Given a commitment to epistemic internalism, the view that epistemic reasons arise only from within a subject's perspective, the dilemma attacks foundationalism. As we've seen from discussing BonJour's defense of the dilemma, it is a compelling case against internalistic foundationalism views that aim to end the regress of reasons in experiential states. In the next section I turn to BonJour's new foundationalist view, which, he claims, solves the Sellarsian dilemma.

5.2 BonJour's new foundationalism

Given BonJour's former defense of the Sellarsian dilemma, it is surprising that he has now adopted a form of C.I. Lewis's view.[22] BonJour's change in view is akin to a Gestalt switch; what he formerly saw as an inherent difficulty with an internalist foundationalist views, he now sees as no longer problematic. My goal in this section is to layout BonJour's considered response to the dilemma and then to argue that his new response fails. I will focus on his claim that a non-propositional, nonconceptual awareness of sensory content can provide a subject with a basic reason for belief. I argue that experience can provide justification only if a subject can recognize the fit between the character of her experience and a conceptual description of it. This recognition requirement conflicts with BonJour's nonconceptualist solution to the dilemma, and it introduces adequacy conditions for experiential justification that cannot be justified within the specious present.

---

[21] As we will see below, Chalmers's account of direct phenomenal beliefs has this consequence.

[22] BonJour (1999, 2000, 2001c, 2001d, 2004); BonJour and Sosa (2003).

5.2.1 BonJour's nonconceptualism

BonJour's new nonconceptualist response to the Sellarsian dilemma aims to show that a nonconceptual experience can provide a subject with a reason to believe that some specific proposition is true. At the outset we should set aside a trivial objection. There is a banal sense in which a nonconceptual experience provides a subject with a reason to believe some proposition. For any experience, a subject has a reason to believe the proposition 'I am experiencing.' This is not relevant to the debate because the main issue is whether a nonconceptual experience can provide a subject with a reason to believe some specific proposition concerning the character of one's experience. The main issue is whether a nonconceptual experience can provide a subject with a reason to believe that, for example, one is experiencing a red, round object. BonJour's task is to formulate a view that yields a positive answer to this question.

BonJour formulates this view in his book with Ernest Sosa.[23] He presents a view of justification with three components, which together form an argument against the nonconceptualist horn of the Sellarsian dilemma. The following is my formulation of BonJour's argument.

BonJour's nonconceptualist argument

11. One has a constitutive or built-in awareness of nonconceptual sensory content.
12. A relation of description exists between a nonconceptual object—an experience that has a nonconceptual character—and a conceptual description.
13. If this relation holds and one is aware of the nonconceptual character of the sensory experience then one has a reason for thinking that the relevant proposition—the proposition that is the conceptual description of the nonconceptual character of one's sensory experience—is true.

These three claims imply,

14. If one has an experience with such and such nonconceptual character then one has a reason for thinking that the relevant proposition—the proposition that is the conceptual description of the nonconceptual character of one's sensory experience—is true.

---

[23] BonJour and Sosa (2003).

What justification does BonJour offer for the premises? He argues for (11) by an analogy between the awareness of belief content and the awareness of sensory content. He begins by suggesting that "an essential and intrinsic aspect of having any occurrent belief just *is* being consciously aware of ... two correlative aspects of its content: first, its propositional content ... and, second, the assertory rather than, for example, questioning or doubting character of one's entertaining the content."[24] These two aspects of occurrent belief can be referred to as the *constitutive awareness of the assertive character of one's occurrent beliefs*.[25] When one occurrently believes that *it is raining* one is thereby aware of the thought that *it is raining*. To be consciously aware of that thought it is sufficient that one occurrently hosts the thought; one need not have a second-order thought the content of which is *one believes that it is raining*. Belief, according to BonJour, is itself a form of conscious awareness of content.[26]

Next, BonJour suggests that we have a similar built-in constitutive awareness of the content of one's own experiences.[27] When one has an experience, that experience has a certain character. Because experience is a form of awareness, it follows that one has an awareness of the character of one's experience in virtue of having that experience. BonJour observes that this kind of built-in awareness is infallible because there is no logical room for one to experience something with a specific character and *not* experience something with a specific character.[28] As BonJour understands it (11) should be understood as the statement that when one undergoes a specific experience, one has an experiential awareness of the specific content of the experience.

Understood in this way (11) is the triviality that *experience makes one experientially aware of the character of one's experience*. Regardless of the complexity of the character of one's experience, one is always experientially aware of its complexity. No one, however, is moved to think that a normal subject has basic justification for thinking that, for example, a hen has 39 speckles when one is in the relevant experiential state. As we will see in a moment BonJour modifies (11) to avoid this objection.

Premise (12) states that a relation of description exists between a nonconceptual object and a conceptual description. This relation is a

---

[24] Ibid., 62.
[25] Ibid., 63.
[26] BonJour and Sosa (2003, 62–63).
[27] Ibid., 70.
[28] Ibid.

descriptive relation "having to do with the accuracy or inaccuracy of fit between a conceptual description and a non-conceptual object that the description purports to describe."[29] If, for example, one perceptually experiences a red square then one is in a state whose nonconceptual object fits the description a red square. His aim in specifying this descriptive relation is to argue that in virtue of having a constitutive awareness of the nonconceptual character of one's experience one has a reason to believe that this description is true. This is precisely what premise (13) does; it connects the descriptive relation and constitutive awareness of the nonconceptual character of one's experience with having a reason to believe that a conceptual description is true.

5.2.2 Nonconceptualism and justification

The core problem with (13) is that constitutive awareness of nonconceptual sensory content does not have the right kind of cognitive significance for justification. As we just saw, BonJour understands this built-in constitutive awareness to be infallible. It is the kind of awareness one has of experiential content simply in virtue of experiencing. This suggestion runs up against the problem of the speckled hen.[30] When one perceptually experiences a 39 speckled hen one is in a visual state that registers information that the hen has 39 speckles. But that perceptual information is too detailed and specific to provide normal subjects like us a basic reason for believing that the hen has 39 speckles. BonJour recognizes the force of this problem and significantly modifies his view to handle it, but the changes he makes ends up abandoning nonconceptualism.[31]

BonJour acknowledges that in speckled-hen type cases the constitutive awareness of the nonconceptual character of experience does not provide one with a reason to believe the associated speckled hen type description.[32] To have justification one must *attend to* the relevant feature of one's experience. BonJour considers, as an example, a large painting containing various colored shapes.[33] You look at the painting at close range and in good light. Someone suggests to you that there is a

---

[29] (BonJour and Sosa 2003 Ibid., 72.)

[30] See Chisholm (1942) for the original discussion of the speckled hen problem and see Fumerton (2005) for a more recent discussion of the problem.

[31] See section 10.3 BonJour and Sosa (2003, 190–197) entitled 'Sosa's Critique of the Appeal to the Given'.

[32] BonJour and Sosa (2003, 191–192).

[33] Ibid., 191.

dark green equilateral triangle in the painting. Initially you do not spot the triangle, but after looking around you see it. BonJour suggests that the change in your experience is that you went from having an experiential awareness of the feature to *recognizing* the agreement between this aspect of your experience and a conceptual description. To have basic justification via experiential awareness BonJour claims one must "apprehend or recognize the agreement ... between the aspect of experience being attended to and the conceptual description given by the belief."[34]

This apprehension requirement is similar to Lewis's move from the given to the apprehension of the given. How does BonJour's later view escape the argument that Lewis's appeal to the apprehension of the given is unsuccessful? The objection to Lewis's view was that any representation capable of providing justification must involve propositional representation, a representation *that* something is the case. But propositional representations have accuracy conditions and one needs justification for thinking that those accuracy conditions are satisfied. BonJour's new position holds that experiential awareness is infallible; one cannot have an experience with a specific character and fail to be experientially aware of that character. BonJour now adds to this requirement that one focus on the specific feature and come to see that that feature fits a particular description. He claims, though, that one does not need a separate cognitive act to realize this. Rather, he thinks that the experiential awareness *itself* allows one to come to see that a feature of one's experience satisfies a particular conceptual description.[35]

BonJour's suggestion that no independent cognitive act is required to satisfy the recognition requirement is not plausible. BonJour's own case of the painting with various colored shapes shows that at one time a subject is in a specific experiential state which includes the presence of a green equilateral triangle and the subject *does not* realize it is there. At another time the subject is in the same experiential state and the subject *does* realize it is there. This is excellent evidence that the subject's *realization* that there's a triangle is a separate state from the original experiential awareness. When a subject comes to see *that* a particular description fits the character of her experience this is a distinct propositional state from an infallible experiential awareness.[36]

---

[34] BonJour and Sosa (2003, 193).
[35] BonJour and Sosa (2003, 193).
[36] See Bergmann (2006a, 686–7) for a similar argument against BonJour's position

BonJour now concedes that the act of "seeing the fit" is a distinct cognitive act.[37] But he resists the idea that this impugns foundationalism. He argues that this additional cognitive act does not require any additional justification because the original infallible experiential awareness is sufficient to provide all the justification necessary. He claims that the cognitive act of "seeing the fit" enables one "to grasp both the content of the proposition and the non-propositional situation that make it true, and see directly and immediately that the truth conditions for the proposition are satisfied."[38] The result is that a propositional judgement is justified entirely by a cognitive act that takes into account the feature of one's experience.

I find BonJour's reasoning at this point difficult to follow. The claim that the original experiential awareness is sufficient to provide justification is wrong. BonJour admits as much. How then does the original experiential awareness provide justification for the more complex cognitive act of "seeing the fit"? Perhaps, the most charitable understanding of BonJour's remark is that the cognitive act of "seeing the fit" is an infallible propositional awareness. The infallibility is guaranteed by the factive nature of "seeing the fit" rather than the kind of assurance such a kind of awareness offers. One cannot 'see the fit' between a conceptual description and a nonconceptual feature of one's experience unless one's experience has that feature and the relation between that feature and the conceptual description holds. But, as reflection on the specious present shows, one can have an awareness that is phenomenologically indistinguishable from seeing the fit without actually seeing the fit.

To illustrate this possibility, suppose one's phenomenal concepts are switched so that what you formerly conceived of as a green appearance you now think of as a red appearance (and vice versa). When presented by a paradigm red object, you think that you are undergoing a green appearance. There is nothing within the specious present to correct for this error. In a normal case one's justification for thinking that you are undergoing a red appearance depends on one's justification for thinking that one is undergoing an appearance whose character is similar to the way red things have appeared in the past. But in this case appearances are deceptive. Your standing phenomenal concepts have been switched so that what you formerly conceived of as a red appearance, you now conceive of as a green appearance. To be sure, the character

---

[37] BonJour (2006, 746).
[38] Ibid., 747.

of your experience is the same as before but it's uptake in cognition has switched. We will see below in Chalmers's framework a vindication of this argument.

There is a fundamental tension in BonJour's new foundationalist epistemology between internalism and foundationalism. Internalism claims that every justified belief has a reason that is possessed by a subject. Foundationalism claims that the justification of some beliefs need not depend on the justification of any other belief. BonJour attempts to bring these views together by an infallible propositional awareness of the nonconceptual character of sensory experience. If there were such an awareness then this would provide a basis for internalism and foundationalism. But the problem is that any propositional awareness has adequacy conditions which cannot be adequately justified within the confines of the specious present. If, however, BonJour dropped the infallibility requirement then he would run up against my argument in Chapter 3 that inductive inferences always depend on plausibility considerations.

5.3 The phenomenal concept strategy

David Chalmers has recently taken up the defense of an acquaintance theory of the justification of phenomenal states.[39] Chalmers lays out a detailed theory of phenomenal concepts and argues that direct phenomenal beliefs are foundationally justified. His account of phenomenal concepts clarifies some of the difficult issues in this debate as well as helps to identify a crucial problem with the justification of phenomenal beliefs. The upshot of the argument in this section is that the difficulty we found in BonJour's view is not idiosyncratic; it lies at the center of foundationalist attempts to justify phenomenal beliefs by direct awareness or direct acquaintance with phenomenal states.

Let us begin with the notion of a *phenomenal concept*. A phenomenal concept is a concept of the phenomenal character of an experience. When one has an experience of a characteristic red object in normal conditions, one's experience has a certain character; there is something-it-is-like to undergo that experience. The phenomenal character of experience is what it's like to undergo the experience.

---

[39] See Chalmers (2010, Chs 8 and 9). See also Gertler (2001, 2011) for a similar defense of an acquaintance theory.

In what follows it will be helpful to be familiar with Frank Jackson's famous thought experiment about Mary.[40] Mary is a neuroscientist specializing in color vision who knows every physical fact about color vision. Mary has been raised in a black and white room and has never seen a red tomato in normal conditions. One day, Mary leaves the black and white room and sees for the first time a ripe tomato. Upon having this experience, Mary learns something new; she learns what it is like to see to see a red object. That is, she learns about the phenomenal character of typical red experiences.

Chalmers helpfully distinguishes between several types of phenomenal concepts.[41] When Mary steps outside the monochromatic room and attends to her new experience, her experience instantiates the property of phenomenal red, R. Chalmers distinguishes two relational phenomenal concepts about R. First, there is the *community relational concept, red$_C$*. This concept indicates "the phenomenal quality typically caused in normal subjects within my community by paradigmatic red things."[42] The second type of phenomenal concept is the *individual relational concept, red$_I$*. This concept indicates "the phenomenal quality typically caused in me by paradigmatic red things."[43] Red$_C$ and red$_I$ are distinct concepts. An abnormal subject may have red–green color inversion in which case her concept red$_I$ picks out a different phenomenal quality than red$_C$ denotes.

Chalmers observes that R can also be picked out by using a demonstrative concept. One may refer to the phenomenal quality of one's experience by using the phrase 'this quality' or 'this sort of experience.' Let us refer to this demonstrative concept as *this$_E$*. This demonstrative concept picks out whatever quality is present on the specific occasion. It functions in the same way one may pick out one's location by 'I am here'. The function of that expression picks out one's location, wherever one happens to be.

Chalmers claims that each of these concepts fixes the reference to phenomenal redness relationally, either through external objects or acts of ostension. He then argues that there is a fourth phenomenal concept that picks out phenomenal redness "directly in terms of its intrinsic phenomenal nature."[44] He terms this a "pure phenomenal concept."

---

[40] Jackson (1982).
[41] Chalmers (2010, 254–260).
[42] Ibid., 255.
[43] Ibid.
[44] Chalmers (2010, 256).

Chalmers argues that there are pure phenomenal concepts by reflection on the case of Mary. When Mary steps outside the black and white room she learns that red experiences have "such and such a quality." She learns that red experiences cause experiences of such and such quality and she learns that the quality is now extending is such and such. Chalmers refers to this as "Mary's 'such-and-such' concept."[45] This is Mary's pure phenomenal concept R. This concept R picks out the phenomenal quality R.

Chalmers then argues that the concept R is distinct from the concepts red_C, red_I, and $this_E$. His argument relies on using cognitive significance tests for difference between concepts. When Mary steps outside the monochromatic room and sees a red object in normal conditions she gains the following beliefs:

$red_C = R$,
$red_I = R$, and
$this_E = R$.

The first two beliefs are cognitively significant. She learns that the quality typically caused in normal subjects in her community by paradigmatic red things is R. Similarly, for the second identity, Mary learns that the quality caused in her by paradigmatic red things is R.

A crucial question is whether $this_E = R$ is cognitively significant. The belief expressed by this identity is the claim that "the quality she is now ostending is such-and-such."[46] Chalmers needs to successfully argue that this thought differs in content from the trivial thought that *this quality is whatever it happens to be*.

Two lines of argument support the cognitive significance of $this_E = R$. First, no a priori reasoning supports $this_E = R$ because a priori reasoning cannot rule out the possibility that the quality being ostended is different than it is. Compare the situation with the thought expressed by 'My location is here'. This thought has a character that implies one can know a priori that any occasion of use will pick out a true sentence.[47]

---

[45] Ibid.

[46] Ibid., 257.

[47] Arguably, the situation is more complicated. Imagine a person whose location changes every second but whose experience stays the same. It's not pellucid that the thought expressed by 'My location is here' is knowable a priori because the person's location changes so quickly. This suggests that some indexical expresses require a certain amount of stability. 'I' functions to pick out the subject of thought, but, arguably, it succeeds only if the subject of thought is constant.

However, Mary's thought that $this_E = R$ picks out the phenomenal quality, R, which is not guaranteed by any a priori feature of the linguistic situation.

The second line of argument that $this_E = R$ is cognitively significant proceeds on analogy with other kinds of demonstrative knowledge.[48] Consider a demonstrative concept of a shape $this_S$, which intuitively picks out 'this shape, whatever it happens to be'. Jill tells Jack she is about to show him her favorite shape. She shows him a circle and Jack forms the thought that *Jill's favorite shape is $this_S$*. '$This_S$' picks out the shape of a circle. Jack can form the non-demonstrative thought that *Jill's favorite shape is a circle*. This thought uses a qualitative concept of a circle. Jack might also form the thought that *$This_S$ is circle*. This thought takes the object of demonstration and attributes to it a substantive qualitative property. Chalmers claims that it's inessential to this example that the concept *circle* is a public language concept. He claims that Jack might acquire the qualitative concept of circularity for the first time and thereby be able to think the substantive thought that *$This_S$ is circle*.

Chalmers asserts that Jack's thought that $this_S$ is circle is analogous to Mary's thought that $this_E = R$. He explains "Like Jack's thought, Mary's thought involves attributing a certain substantive, qualitative nature to a type that is identified demonstratively. This qualitative nature is attributed using a qualitative concept of phenomenal redness, acquired upon having a red experience for the first time."[49] The qualitative nature of Mary's thought, though, is difficult to express in a language. The term 'phenomenal redness' express the concepts of either red_C or red_I. The concept R, by contrast, is a non-relational concept which directly picks out the phenomenal quality currently instantiated in Mary's experience. The non-relational character of concept R makes it difficult to see how the thought that $this_E = R$ can have much cognitive significance. I turn to argue for this now.

Chalmers explicitly states that the lifetime of a direct phenomenal concept like R is "limited to the lifetime of the experience (or the instantiated quality) that constitutes it."[50] This implies that a direct phenomenal belief—a belief of the form $this_E = R$—exists only within the lifetime of the experience. Direct phenomenal beliefs exist only within the specious present. Furthermore, as Chalmers acknowledges,

---

[48] Chalmers (2010, 257–258). The following paragraph summarizes Chalmers's discussion.
[49] Chalmers (2010, 258).
[50] Chalmers (2010, 272).

beliefs of the form "R is phenomenal red" are not direct phenomenal beliefs. This kind of belief involves the pre-existing phenomenal concept expressed by 'phenomenal red' which is a relational phenomenal concept, red_C or red_I.[51] Similarly, a belief like 'I am in pain' involves a relational concept of pain, either the community relation concept of pain ($pain_C$) or the individual relational concept of pain ($pain_I$). This kind of belief is not a direct phenomenal belief.

The consequence that direct phenomenal beliefs exist only within the lifetime of the relevant experience puts significant pressure on Chalmers's insistence that direct phenomenal beliefs are cognitively significant.[52] Chalmers argues for the significance of these beliefs by claiming that a direct phenomenal belief constrains the class of a priori epistemic possibilities.[53] His thought is that when Mary forms the belief that '$this_E = R$' her belief is false at all worlds (considered as actual) in which Mary is not experiencing phenomenal redness. Mary's belief is cognitively significant because her new experience significantly constrains the possible worlds prior to having that experience. For instance, prior to leaving the black and white room it was epistemically possible that Mary form the belief that '$this_E = G$', but now, having had the relevant experience, that thought is no longer epistemically possible.

This sounds as if direct phenomenal beliefs are cognitively significant, but appearances are deceptive. The direct phenomenal beliefs exist only within the specious present, and so they only constrain epistemic possibilities within the present 'now'. Mary's thought that '$this_E = R$' constrains epistemic possibilities only for a fleeting moment; let it pass and it is an epistemic possibility that a similar thought '$this_E = G$' is true. What makes this an epistemic possibility is that judgments of identity, similarity, and difference are not direct phenomenal beliefs. When one thinks that 'R is phenomenal red' one identifies a present quality with a relational quality. One's evidence that this identity is true relies on a host of background information that is not contained within the specious present. If the relational quality is red_C then one needs evidence both that this quality exists (i.e., that the members of your community do not experience different properties when faced with red things) and that the majority of other people experience the same quality as you do.

---

[51] Ibid., 278.
[52] Ibid., 282.
[53] Ibid.

There is a real puzzle here about how to understand the significance of Mary's knowledge when she leaves the black and white room. She gains a new belief '$this_E = R$' which exists for the present 'now' of her experience. Suppose Mary stares at the ripe tomato thinking 'wow, this is what it's like'. On Chalmers's account, this is a direct phenomenal belief only within the fleeting present. If Mary were to look away and attend to another red object, her belief that '$this_E = R1$' would be a different direct phenomenal belief. But her belief that '$R = R1$' is not a direct phenomenal belief. If Mary's knowledge is restricted to direct phenomenal beliefs then she has no way to knowingly identify or compare any pure phenomenal qualities. To the extent that Mary can knowingly identify and compare phenomenal qualities she must rely on a wealth of information that is not contained within the specious present. She relies on her beliefs that memory is reliable, that sensations do not change faster than she realizes, and that other people experience the same sensations. None of these beliefs are given in the specious moment. But to the extent Mary gains new knowledge, she relies on these beliefs.

If you take these beliefs away and consider only what Mary knows in the specious present via direct acquaintance with a phenomenal quality, the best one can do is get a belief like '$this_E = R$'. But this belief has little cognitive significance. To the extent it constrains epistemic possibilities it constrains them momentarily. The space of epistemic possibilities contracts and expands with every passing moment. Mary cannot hook up this new belief with any other beliefs, at least apart from coherence considerations. She cannot, for instance, reason that 'phenomenal redness is R' because 'phenomenal redness' is a public language term.

The problem here is similar to Descartes's problem in reaching a substantial ego via the indubitability of the cogito. Descartes could not doubt that on any occasion of use "I think" picked out a true sentence, but he wondered "what is this 'I' that thinks"? As many commentators have pointed out it's consistent with the indubitability of the cogito that the subject of thought changes with each token thought. Descartes cannot rule this possibility out by the method of doubt. If we think of the epistemic possibilities that are ruled out by the cogito we may think that they are significant. On the one hand, on each occasion of thought the epistemic possibilities are significantly constrained. Every possibility in which someone or something other than the actual thinker thinks that token thought are thereby eliminated. The function of 'I' picks out a single thinker and on each occasion of use the actual thinker is different from the many merely possible thinkers. But, on the other hand, this elimination of possibilities does nothing to identify or discriminate between possible thinkers. It does not pick out an actual thinker as René Descartes or David Hume. For René Descartes is a person with a particular history who endures over time. Nothing about that history is contained within the passing moment of thinking. Moreover, once the fleeting moment of the cogito passes, the epistemic possibilities expand again.

Part of the problem Descartes faces is supporting the inference from "I think" to "I was thinking."[54] This inference requires that the second use of 'I' has the same content as the former use. If there is an enduring self that is picked out by the two occasions of use of 'I' then the beliefs have the same content. But more than sameness of content is required for justification. One needs a reason for thinking that there is an enduring self. It's not sufficient that, in fact, there is an enduring self.

Similarly, direct phenomenal beliefs should support the inference from '$this_E$ is R' to '*that was R.*' But, this requires that the second use of the concept R has the same content as the first use. This is not revealed within the specious present. And the fact that the first thought constrains epistemic possibilities does nothing to constrain the relevant epistemic possibilities for the second thought. Chalmers acknowledges that this is a problem for his account, but he claims that no one has "a good account of what is it is for one token of a concept to be a 'descendant' of another in a manner that allows it to inherit justification."[55] As he observes more than sameness of content is required for justification because a new concept with the same content could be formed 'de novo.'[56] One needs a natural persistence relation between concepts. Furthermore, one needs some justification that such a persistence relation obtains. And yet the options for providing justification are quite limited. My view is that the best option for this kind of justification is a conservative coherentist account. These kind of fundamental background beliefs are held in the special state of empty symmetrical evidence. Conservatism is well suited for providing justification for these crucial, background beliefs. The explanatory coherence of an entire system of beliefs which includes these vindicates the initial conservative justification.

---

[54] The other part is to knowingly identify and discriminate the subject of thought from other possible thinkers.

[55] Chalmers (2010, 298).

[56] Ibid.

5.4 Conclusion

We have seen that BonJour's new solution of the Sellarsian dilemma does not adequately address the nonconceptualist horn. Furthermore, I have argued that reflection of Chalmers's detailed defense of an acquaintance theory of phenomenal concept vindicates this judgment. I've argued that reflection on the specious present undermines this account of justification. To the extent one can have a direct phenomenal belief it has little cognitive significance. The upshot of my argument is that cognitive significance requires a wealth of background information that is not contained within the present 'now.'

6
Is Foundational A Priori Justification Indispensable?

Laurence BonJour argues for a rationalist position according to which pure reason can discover substantive truths about the world.[1] Rationalism has been dominant throughout the history of philosophy, but in recent years the development of philosophical naturalism has diminished its prestige. Naturalism holds that reason's putative grasp of these truths can either be explained away in terms of convention or dismissed entirely. The first move explains reason's putative grasp of these claims in terms of definitions and trivial implications between synonyms. This view is associated with *moderate empiricism*. The other naturalist move takes aim against the distinctions and concepts upon which the traditional debate over the a priori relies. BonJour focuses on Quine's *radical empiricism* in this connection. One of the themes I return to is that BonJour doesn't appreciate the depth of Quine's criticism of the traditional rationalist-empiricist debate. I restrict my attention to BonJour's indispensability arguments. He argues that unless one is a radical skeptic about justification, there must be some substantive a priori justification.[2] BonJour refers to this argument as "the master argument" of his book.[3] He argues that unless there is some substantive a priori justification then no reasoning is ever justified and no one is ever justified in believing any claim that transcends experience. My primary aim is to rebut these arguments. There is a gap in BonJour's indispensability arguments that undermines their force. This lacuna corresponds to BonJour's failure to mine the depths of explanatory coherentism. I aim, therefore,

---

[1] BonJour (1998).
[2] Ibid., 3.
[3] BonJour (2001b, 626).

to explain this explanationist alternative in the context of responding to BonJour's indispensability arguments. In contrast to BonJour's avowals, explanatory coherentism is a coherent and plausible account of the a priori.

At the outset I want to make it clear that I will not be arguing for the connection between naturalism and explanatory coherentism. These positions develop within Quine's philosophy, and Quine's naturalism can be seen as developing out of explanatory coherentism. In my estimation, much contemporary work on philosophical naturalism can be interpreted as extending explanatory coherentism.[4] My primary purpose is to defend the coherence of an explanationist account of the a priori from BonJour's criticisms. I also want to distinguish my argument from a Quinean indispensability argument for the a priori. A Quinean indispensability argument aims to show that apparent a priori truths are justified by being embedded in a broader theory that has significant empirical confirmation. This kind of argument has come under significant fire.[5] I do not intend to enter the fray over the merits of this Quinean argument. Rather, I argue for a position much closer to Goodman's justification of inductive and deductive rules.[6] We start with various beliefs about the necessity of certain claims and by reasoning in a coherentist fashion come to have justification for believing that these claims are true. The argument I develop is compatible with our being justified in believing various branches of higher mathematics that are not embedded in any successful empirical theory. Our justification for these branches of mathematics consists in their overall coherence with the rest of our beliefs.

6.1 BonJour's indispensability arguments

BonJour argues that substantive a priori justification is indispensable for three reasons. First, there are putative a priori truths like $2 + 2 = 4$ and *nothing can be both entirely green and red at the same time*. BonJour argues that only a rationalist view of the a priori can account for their justification. Second, there are claims which transcend immediate experience. Nothing in my current experience indicates that *I was asleep last night*, but I am currently justified in believing this. BonJour contends that only a rationalist conception of the a priori can account for the justification

---

[4] See Quine and Ullian (1970); Lycan (1988); Hylton (2007).
[5] See, for example, Jeffrey Roland's recent article (2009).
[6] See Goodman (1965).

of these claims. Third, BonJour claims, reasoning itself requires robust a priori justification. Even a simple application of modus ponens requires a grasp of its goodness, and only a rationalist view can provide suitable justification for it.

Each indispensability argument raises significant challenges for an explanationist who claims that the justification of any claim is a function of how well the belief fares with respect to the explanatory virtues—simplicity, conservativeness, and explanatory power. In the following I tackle BonJour's indispensability arguments. I begin with his argument concerning observation-transcendent claims because our discussion of these issues will carry over to the other indispensability arguments.

6.1.1 Observation-transcendent inference

Many beliefs concern matters removed from present experience. I believe that *the Battle of Hastings occurred in 1066*, that *it will rain somewhere in England over the next week*, and that *many people are presently asleep*. These beliefs are not based on current observation, but concern matters in the distant past, in the future, and about presently unobserved events. Call beliefs like these 'observation-transcendent beliefs' or simply 'transcendent beliefs.' How are transcendent beliefs justified? BonJour claims that these beliefs are justified only if some substantive a priori beliefs are justified. What is his argument for this claim?

BonJour begins with the supposition that some beliefs are justified entirely on the basis of present experience. Call beliefs of this kind 'immanent beliefs'. According to this assumption, one's belief that there is a red, circular disk directly ahead is justified entirely on the basis of one's current visual experience; one need not have justification for any transcendent beliefs to be justified in this belief. BonJour assumes that immanent beliefs provide the starting points for the justification of transcendent beliefs. He then assumes that the inferences from immanent beliefs to transcendent beliefs must be based on principles that are justified a priori.[7] According to him the only way to resist this conclusion is that experience provides the links between immanent beliefs and transcendent beliefs. But transcendent claims require something besides experience to have justification, which BonJour concludes must be supplied by the a priori.[8]

---

[7] BonJour (1998, 4).

[8] See BonJour (2001a, 625–626) for a concise statement of this argument.

BonJour's argument assumes a traditional foundationalist view according to which some beliefs are properly basic, and the remaining, non-basic, beliefs are justified only if they are properly related to the basic beliefs. In the previous chapter I argued that no empirical belief is properly basic. Even beliefs about the given rely on a host of background assumptions. But within this foundationalist conception of justification, it is difficult to see how the transitions or inferences involved in observation-transcendent inference could come from experience. However natural BonJour's line of reasoning appears, his conclusion depends crucially on the assumptions that (1) there is a clear distinction between observational and non-observational beliefs and (2) non-observational beliefs are justified by being inferred from observational beliefs. These assumptions lend more credibility to BonJour's argument than it actually has.

Consider the distinction between observational and non-observational beliefs. BonJour glosses over this distinction by way of a rough characterization of beliefs based on direct experience. These beliefs are "particular rather than general in their content and are confined to situations observable at specific and fairly narrowly delineated places and times."[9] BonJour's characterization is vague, but on a plausible way of understanding his remark it implies that when one observes a piece of litmus paper turning red and believes that *this liquid is acidic* then that belief is a direct observational belief. But, plainly, this is not a direct observational belief.

What, then, is a direct observational belief? This is a difficult question, and BonJour cannot simply assume there is a principled distinction between observation and inference in an argument for traditional rationalism. Given the argument of Chapter 5, a direct observational belief would be one in which the justification for the belief relies wholly on what is given in the specious present. But I've argued that no such justification exists. Even beliefs about the given rely on a host of background beliefs for their justification.

This theme resonates with Wilfrid Sellars who argued that a subject must have theoretical beliefs in order to entertain observational beliefs.[10] Evidence from cognitive psychology and the history of science strongly suggests that higher-level cognition significantly influences

---

[9] BonJour (1998, 3–4).
[10] Sellars (1963, "Empiricism and the Philosophy of Mind" sections III 'The Logic of Looks', VIII 'Does Empirical Knowledge have a Foundation', and XII 'Our Rylean Ancestors')

lower-level information processing.[11] BonJour's indispensability argument gains considerably more plausibility than it has by ignoring this crucial issue. If transcendent beliefs are necessary conditions for immanent beliefs, then the justification of immanent beliefs is not simple and straightforward. Moreover, if it is true that the content of every belief is influenced by theory, then there is no basis for identifying a subset of our beliefs as the epistemically privileged ones by which all other beliefs must be justified. In place of this, one may adopt Neurath's claim: each belief has some presumption in its favor and should be abandoned only to improve one's overall doxastic position.[12] It is therefore no surprise, in this connection, that epistemic conservatism arose alongside the realization that theory was always involved in any attempt to determine what one should believe.

6.1.2 Putative a priori truths and the parade argument

The strongest case for a substantive doctrine of the a priori appeals to apparently self-evident a priori claims. Consider the following list of putative a priori claims:[13]

1. No surface can be uniformly red and uniformly blue at the same time.
2. No statement can be both true and false at the same time and in the same respect.
3. Everything is identical to itself.
4. If the conclusion of an inductive argument is contingent, it is possible for the premises of that argument to be true and its conclusion to be false.
5. $2 + 3 = 5$ is necessarily true.

This is an impressive parade of seemingly obvious a priori truths. Indeed, BonJour remarks, "it is no accident that the vast majority of historical philosophers, from Plato on down to Leibniz and Locke, would have regarded this general line of argument as both obvious and conclusive, so much so that the issue of whether there is a priori justification scarcely arises for them at all."[14] Yet, what is this "line of argument"? BonJour intends to elicit the response that there is substantive a priori justification by parading before one's view standard cases of

---

[11] Brewer and Lambert (2001).
[12] See Harman (2001, 657–658) for a similar point.
[13] See Beebe (2011, 583) for a longer list.
[14] BonJour (1998, 2).

a priori truths. Let us call this 'the parade argument.' BonJour recognizes that this argument is not entirely convincing given the formulation of non-Euclidean geometries and the rise of moderate and radical empiricist accounts of the a priori. To properly appreciate the force of the parade argument one must clear away confusions that encumber the argument. BonJour seeks to accomplish this task by arguing against moderate and radical empiricism.[15] After having removed obstacles to the parade, BonJour holds that one can grasp, directly and immediately, that these claims are true in such a way that requires substantive a priori justification.

What should the explanationist say about the parade argument? The explanationist prefaces an answer with two general remarks. First, because the parade argument is intended to support rationalism it is not sufficient that the examples illustrate the necessity of non-experiential justification. As we saw above the distinction between observational truths and transcendent truths is philosophically dubious. Each claim is justified only if some non-experiential claims are justified. It comes as no surprise to the coherentist that there must be non-experiential justification. This is a central coherentist theme: every belief, insofar as it is justified, requires non-experiential justification. But the justification comes not from some mysterious faculty that supposedly directly grasps necessary features of reality, but rather from explanatory considerations. Thus, BonJour needs to argue that once the conceptual terrain is clarified, we clearly grasp these truths with direct immediate insight.

Second, discussions over the status of putative a priori truths are often confused with whether putative a priori claims are possibly false. Of course, to show that a putative a priori claim is possibly false is to thereby show that one did not grasp the necessity of the claim. Gilbert Harman, for instance, raises possibilities that threaten the necessity of various examples of the putative a priori.[16] BonJour replies that Harman is not making any sense or is changing the subject. This quick descent to brute intuition about whether a statement is genuinely necessary should be avoided if possible. My strategy is to grant to the rationalist that many putative a priori claims are necessary truths (or, at least that the balance of evidence indicates so). I then inquire about the epistemology of putative necessary claims. I argue, however, that the parade argument does not support a foundationalist epistemology.

---

[15] This is BonJour's task in chapters 2 and 3 of BonJour (1998).
[16] Harman (2001).

The pivotal issue is over the autonomy, or singularity, of rational insight. BonJour claims that the rationalist is committed to the autonomy of rational insight. He writes, "According to the moderate rationalist position, each instance of apparent rational insight or apparent self evidence, each alleged case of a priori justification, should be construed as *epistemically autonomous, as dependent on nothing beyond itself for its justification.*"[17] The autonomy of apparent rational insight does not imply that apparent rational insight is indefeasible. Rather, as BonJour acknowledges, apparent rational insight can be undermined "by further a priori reflection, by considerations of coherence, or by (partly) empirical considerations."[18] Even so, an initial, apparent grasp of the necessity of a claim is sufficient, all by itself, to justify one in believing the claim.

What exactly is an autonomous rational insight? Is it a matter of thinking that a claim *must* be true without having any idea *why* it's true? Is it as if one has the thought that, for example, "nothing can be both entirely red and green at the same time" along with an indescribable conviction that this must be so? This is Alvin Plantinga's conception of basic a priori beliefs. Plantinga holds that basic a priori beliefs are ones in which you are utterly convinced that they are true and could not be false.[19] Furthermore, these convictions are accompanied by an indescribable feeling often indicated by saying one "sees" it.[20] BonJour resists Plantinga's characterization of basic rational insights, writing that the conviction based on rational insight is not "as Plantinga seems to suggest, a matter of a conviction of necessity accompanied by some peculiar, indescribable phenomenology."[21] Rather BonJour explains that "I at least seem to myself to see with perfect clarity just why this proposition holds and even to be able to articulate this insight to some extent."[22] BonJour expands, writing about the proposition that *nothing can be both entirely red and green at the same time*:

> it is in the nature of both redness and greenness to exclusively occupy the surface or area that instantiates them, so that once one of these qualities is in place, there is no room for the other; since there is

---

[17] BonJour (1998, 146, emphasis added).
[18] Ibid.
[19] Plantinga (1993a, 105).
[20] Ibid.
[21] BonJour (1998, 108, fn12).
[22] Ibid., 108.

no way for the two qualities to co-exist in the same part of a surface or area, a red item can become green only if the green replaces the red.[23]

This ability to articulate the content of a rational intuition is not peculiar to the red–green case; for BonJour remarks that one can give similar accounts of other rational insights.[24]

To what extent is rational insight autonomous or singular, capable of justifying a claim "all by itself"? Plantinga's characterization has the virtue of rendering the autonomy of rational insights intelligible; one has a thought accompanied by an indescribable feel that things have to be this way and couldn't have been otherwise. This bare conviction need not be articulated to any extent at all to justify belief. Yet BonJour resists this line because it makes it difficult to understand how one could be justified in believing on the basis of indescribable feelings. However, BonJour distinguishes his view only at the cost of significantly muddying the waters. Given what he says about how it is possible to articulate the content of the intuition, it's hard to recover the thought that a rational insight can stand alone and still justify. What's more, one natural paraphrase of BonJour's remark that he is "able to articulate this insight" is that he can explain the insight. An explanationist may be forgiven for understanding BonJour's remarks as contradicting his avowal that rational insights are autonomous. The explanationist sees matters thus: BonJour has a strong belief that *nothing can be entirely red and green all over at the same time* and this belief fits with his other beliefs. He can explain this belief by embedding it in an explanatory coherent story about the nature of redness and greenness, the nature of space, what it is for a space to instantiate a quality, the nature of qualities, co-existence, and so on. As the explanationist sees things all these features of BonJour's story support to an impressive degree that BonJour's intuition is true. The intuition does not stand alone and does not justify apart from its impressive coherence with other elements of the story. In short, BonJour's position seems to support coherentism rather than annihilate it.

6.1.3 Reasoning

BonJour's third indispensability argument focuses on principles of reasoning and the process of reasoning. He argues that a substantive

---

[23] Ibid.
[24] Ibid.

rationalist position is indispensable for a justification of both the principles and process of reasoning. BonJour's most sustained remarks on this occur in a later section responding to the mysteriousness objection that unarticulated rational insights cannot provide justification. As we just saw, BonJour's response was to stress the context in which these insights can be filled out and articulated. In this passage BonJour backtracks and defends a view much closer to Plantinga's. BonJour focuses on the objection that singular rational insights cannot provide justification by themselves "precisely because of their unarticulated character, there can be . . . no genuine basis for ascribing rational cogency to them – and in particular no reason to think that beliefs adopted in accordance with them are likely to be true."[25] BonJour replies that this objection overlooks the necessity of immediate, rational insights involved in the process of reasoning.[26] Any operation of reasoning "must ultimately rely on immediate insights of the very same kind that the objection is designed to impugn."[27] BonJour provides two reasons for this judgment.[28] First, any criterion or rule that legitimizes reasoning must itself be justified, and, apart from immediate rational insights, there would be a vicious regress. Second, one needs discernment to see that a rule is applicable to a situation. But this discernment requires "the very same sort of rational insight or intuition that the rationalist is advocating."[29]

BonJour's first reason that simple rational insights are inescapable raises the specter of the regress of reasoning. Any attempt to justify a rule will have to provide reasons and then those reasons can come under scrutiny. The examination of those reasons requires further reasons, which themselves need additional reasons, and so on. To escape this vicious regress, one must stop with an immediate insight. But the coherentist objects that a linear regress of reasons is not the only option for justifying the rules or criteria. The coherentist holds up the coherence of her rules and criteria with her other judgments and claims that the overall coherence of these rules and judgments provides her with an excellent reason to believe them.

BonJour's second reason that simple rational insights are required for the process of reasoning does not conflict with coherentism. BonJour

---

[25] BonJour (1998, 131).
[26] Ibid.
[27] Ibid.
[28] Ibid.
[29] BonJour (1998, 131).

writes, "There is no apparent alternative to the reliance on immediate, non-discursive insights of some sort as long as any sort of reasoning or thinking that goes beyond the bounds of direct observation is to be countenanced."[30] The alternative to this is "a mode of intellectual process that is entirely a function of criteria, rules, or steps, that is somehow purely discursive in character, requiring no immediate insight or judgment of any kind."[31] The explanatory coherentist can accept that 'the reliance on immediate, non-discursive insights' is about the psychological process of reasoning. Some reasoning is explicitly discursive in character, but even that sort of reasoning relies on immediate judgments. Those immediate judgments, though, are justified along coherentist lines. Reasoning cannot continue forever. As the coherentist understands this situation, we all start with beliefs and dispositions. Reasoning is a combination of what you believe and what you are disposed to do. One can justify the rules of reasoning by their coherence, and this justification may attempt to justify certain dispositions we have to reason in certain ways. But none of this requires a substantial rationalist view of the a priori.[32] After all, as BonJour recognizes, if psychologically immediate judgments simply amount to a contextless thought accompanied by an indescribable feeling then it is difficult to understand how that could justify one in believing that the thought is correct.[33]

6.1.4 Taking stock

BonJour's indispensability arguments do not support rationalism over coherentism. His observation-transcendent argument assumes a principled distinction between observational and theoretical beliefs which lends undue credence to BonJour's strict foundationalist view of how transcendent beliefs are to be justified. BonJour's parade argument does not require rationalism because the putative examples of simple a priori beliefs turn out, on BonJour's preferred analysis, to be embedded in a coherent story. His final argument about reasoning fails to address a coherentist justification of the rules of reasoning

---

[30] Ibid., 133.

[31] Ibid., 132.

[32] See Nelson Goodman (1965) on a coherentist justification of the rules of deductive and induction.

[33] See Boghossian (2001, 639) for similar remarks and BonJour (2001b) for a rejoinder. BonJour's reply either lapses back into the errors of Plantinga's view or reiterates the point that reasoning requires psychologically immediate judgments.

and runs together the issue of the justification of reasoning with the psychological process of reasoning. At one point BonJour recognizes that a coherentist justification of the a priori may succeed in very many cases, but replies that a complete coherentist theory of the a priori is impossible.[34] In the next section I consider this argument.

6.2 BonJour's anti-coherence objection

BonJour has consistently held that a coherence theory of the *a priori* is inadequate. In the appendix to *The Structure of Empirical Knowledge* entitled 'A Priori Justification', BonJour argues that a thoroughgoing coherentist view is impossible because "*a priori* knowledge is essential to provide the very ingredients of the concept of coherence (one of which is logical consistency) and thus could not without vicious circularity be itself based on coherence."[35] In his recent book *In Defense of Pure Reason*, BonJour repeats this charge:

> Any conception of coherence, however restricted, will presuppose certain fundamental premises or principles that define the conception in question and thus cannot be assessed by appeal to it.[36]

BonJour recognizes that some might be tempted to offer a coherentist justification of the *a priori* but replies that "this overlooks the fact that coherence depends essentially on principles, such as the principle of non-contradiction and others, that must be justified in some other way."[37] My aim in this section is to answer these charges. Coherentism, specifically explanatory coherentism, escapes BonJour's criticisms. In the first subsection, I explain how an explanationalist may view the justification of the law of noncontradiction. The second subsection addresses BonJour's charge that coherentism cannot offer a non-circular justification of logical principles. The third subsection addresses BonJour's charge that any conception of coherence presupposes the law of noncontradiction. The result of the arguments in this section is that logical principles do not pose any special problem for explanatory coherentists.

---

[34] BonJour (1998, 118).
[35] BonJour (1985, 193).
[36] BonJour (1998, 118).
[37] Ibid., 148, fn 12.

6.2.1 Explanationism and noncontradiction

Explanationism is the view that a subject has propositional justification for a claim if and only if that claim is a member of a virtuous explanatory system which beats relevant competitors. As I explained in Chapter 4, the virtues are simplicity, conservativeness, and explanatory power. It is not enough that a claim is a member of a system that beats competitors, the system itself must be sufficiently virtuous. On the face of it, an explanationist has an elegant justification for the law of noncontradiction. The law is simple, conservative, and has great explanatory power. It beats every rival; in fact, dominates rivals. The explanationist may continue to laud the principle as one of the guiding axioms of first-order logic, a logic whose virtues lie in its accessibility and simplicity. The principle is confirmed over and over again in experience; to this date no one has managed to both order an espresso and not order an espresso. A denial of the principle would lead to a radical revision of our understanding of logic, inference, and evidence. In short, on purely explanationist grounds, the principle of noncontradiction has the highest level of justification.

I take this to be a significant reason that BonJour's charge against explanatory coherentism lacks a proper foothold. I now turn to two specific objections. First, any coherentist justification of the law of noncontradiction is circular. Second, any conception of coherence requires the law of noncontradiction.

6.2.2 Coherence and circularity

BonJour charges that any coherentist justification of the law of noncontradiction is circular. His charge is not that the coherentist is guilty of *premise circularity*, of arguing for the law of noncontradiction by taking the law of noncontradiction as a premise. Rather his charge is that the coherentist is guilty of *epistemic circularity*, of assuming that the law of noncontradiction is true in order to get justification that contradictions cannot be true. BonJour reasons that any conception of coherence must presuppose that contradictions cannot be true, and therefore it is circular to justify the principle by its coherence. Is this charge well-placed? I think not. As we saw at the end of Chapter 3, Michael Bergmann argues that any non-skeptical epistemology must own up to some epistemic circularity.[38] Bergmann argues that in at least some cases epistemic circularity does not undermine one's justification

---

[38] Bergmann (2004a, 2006b).

or knowledge.[39] Bergmann observes that it's overwhelmingly plausible that subjects can acquire justified beliefs from perception and memory. Yet given those justified beliefs, one can use simple deductive and inductive reasoning to come to justifiably believe that perception and memory are reliable. Yet this argument depends on the reliability of perception and memory in order to justify that perception and memory are reliable.

In Chapter 3 I argued that the framework theory of reasons escapes Bergmann's attempt to foist epistemic circularity on all non-skeptical epistemologies. In this present case, Bergmann's argument can be wielded against BonJour's rationalism. BonJour argues that the justification for any belief that extends beyond the directly observable requires *a priori* justification. Yet, unless BonJour denies that one can ever have any justification for thinking that rational insight is reliable, he must approve of an epistemically circular argument for the reliability of rational insight. This argument is exactly parallel to the argument Bergmann offers to show that any non-skeptical epistemology must come to grips with some epistemically circular arguments. Hence, BonJour's charge that any coherentist justification of the principle of noncontradiction is circular must appeal to specific considerations pertaining to coherentism that show the ensuing circularity is both importantly different from the kind Bergmann discusses and epistemically vicious.

There is not any special problem for coherentism here. First, as I argued in Chapter 3, a framework theory of reasons escapes Bergmann's argument that every epistemological view must accept some epistemic circularity. A framework theory of reasons draws a distinction between noninferential justification and reasons, and allows that one may have noninferential justification for some claim but that that claim functions as a reason only if it is part of a larger explanatory coherent view. The explanationist can maintain that the principle of noncontradiction can function as a reason in this way.

Second, even if the framework theory of reasons does not completely escape epistemic circularity, the kind of circularity that afflicts the coherentist is no different in kind from that which afflicts BonJour's rationalist view. Consider a simple version of coherentism, according to which a belief is justified if and only if it is logically consistent with a subject's other beliefs. According to this simple view logical consistency is *the* source of justification. Perceptual beliefs are justified if consistent.

---

[39] Bergmann (2004a, 711).

The justification of these beliefs does not depend on any theoretical beliefs nor does it depend on any beliefs about the source of perception. Furthermore, beliefs about logical consistency are themselves justified if consistent. Like other non-skeptical epistemologies, the simple view must come to grips with some epistemic circularity; one may rely on the fact that logical consistency is a source of justification to come to believe that logical consistency is a source of justification. But this circularity is similar to the circularity of relying on the reliability of perception to come to believe that perception is reliable.[40]

What goes for the simple view goes for explanationism as well. Explanatory coherentism upholds the explanatory virtues as the materials for a belief's justification. Just as BonJour's rationalist view and the simple view approve of some epistemic circularity, explanationism will also approve of some circularity. One can come to be justified in believing that the explanatory virtues are a source of justification by relying on the virtues themselves. Epistemic circularity poses no special problem for coherentism. Explanatory coherentism eschews premise circularity, but, like other non-skeptical epistemologies, must come to grips with some rule circularity.

6.2.3 Coherence and presupposition

Let us turn to BonJour's claim that any conception of coherence presupposes the principle of noncontradiction.[41] As BonJour conceives of the situation, *before* a coherence view of justification can get up and running one must first specify the nature of coherence. This specification will involve certain principles which themselves cannot be abandoned without giving up the coherence view of justification. Furthermore, while some principles may be more peripheral to the notion of coherence, the law of noncontradiction is at the core. Thus, BonJour concludes, a coherence theory of justification requires some unrevisable logical principles. This criticism feeds into BonJour's general criticism that coherentist views neglect the importance of the a priori. In the following I tackle this charge: the notion of coherence needn't presuppose the principle of noncontradiction. Our conception of coherence is itself driven by our desire for adequate explanation, which can put pressure on the principles we use to specify our conception of coherence. I follow BonJour by focusing on the principle of noncontradiction. I assume that

---

[40] However, one important difference is that perception is a causal process that produces beliefs, whereas consistency is an internal relations between beliefs.

[41] BonJour (1998, 118).

our conclusions regarding the role of this principle also hold for other principles involved in specifying the nature of coherence.

Let us approach this issue by considering Graham Priest's dialetheist view that some contradictions are true. Priest argues that it is rationally acceptable to believe some contradictions.[42] He writes, "I believe, for example, that it is rational (rationally possible—indeed, rationally obligatory) to believe that the liar sentence is both true and false."[43] In addition to the liar sentence, Priest considers other logical paradoxes such as the Russell set, truths of our own making, and contradictions arising in physics, and then argues that the best explanation of the enduring difficulties with alternative accounts aimed at avoiding contradictions is that the theories are true and consequently we have a good argument for some contradictions.

Priest's methodological strategy in arguing for dialetheism is admirable. Consider our very best theory of some set of phenomena. If it is well-confirmed and its explanatory merits far outstrip any alternative theory then we have a good reason to accept that the theory is true. If the theory implies that some proposition is true then we have a reason to accept that proposition; by our present lights, we have a good argument for some claim. Priest applies this explanatory strategy to contradictions; if a good argument implies that a contradiction is true then we should accept that some contradictions are true. Why should we resist this argument? Priest considers several arguments that there cannot be true contradictions and argues that they are unpersuasive.[44] We do not have space to repeat these arguments other than to say that he defends the overall coherence of a position that maintains true contradictions by developing and defending a paraconsistent logic that prevents contradictions from entailing everything.[45]

Even so, dialetheism seems incoherent. Priest explicitly acknowledges that dialetheism is extremely odd. He writes:

> I ... believe that the Russell set is both a member of itself and not a member of itself. I do not deny that it was difficult to convince myself of this, that is, to get myself to believe it. It seemed, after all, so unlikely. But many arguments convinced me of it.[46]

---

[42] Priest (1985–1986, 1998).
[43] Priest (1998, 410).
[44] Priest (1985–1986, 1998).
[45] For details see Priest (1998).
[46] Priest (1985–1986, 103).

Are we to dismiss dialetheism as incoherent, as a position that no one could ever rationally hold? David Lewis appears to think so. He replies to Priest: "No truth does have, and no truth could have, a true negation. Nothing is, and nothing could be, literally both true and false. This we know for certain, and *a priori*, and without any exception for especially perplexing subject matters."[47] Lewis acknowledges that his response is dogmatic, and, further, that the principle of noncontradiction is indefensible against Priest's challenge because it calls so much into question that there are no grounds to argue against it.[48] But, Lewis holds that the principle of noncontradiction is not only *a priori* but certain.

Is Lewis right that the principle is apodictic? Explanationists hold that the principle has the highest level of justification. Arguably, the law of noncontradiction is so central to the very nature of reasoning, thought, and representation that its denial amounts to a position that is barely intelligible. Given the centrality of noncontradiction, our current view dominates any rivals that deny the principle. This justification of the law ties its justification to its role in human cognition. Given our understanding of evidence we can acquire evidence against a proposition by acquiring evidence for its negation. When a subject asserts a proposition we understand the subject as implying that its negation is false. Furthermore, the nature of representation confirms the law of noncontradiction. One cannot represent, at least by way of a picture, a truth and its true negation. This is all so close to our common cognitive practice that it is hard to take seriously the thought that some truths may also have true negations. But the nature of the justification proceeds along explanationist grounds. Views that include the law of noncontradiction have much greater explanatory virtues than views that deny it.[49]

A defender of a Lewisian position that the principle of noncontradiction may dig in one's heels; the signs the explanationist point to are signs of apodicity. Why not hold the principle is apodictic instead of just having the highest level of justification? The answer is that, in

---

[47] Lewis (1982, 434).

[48] Lewis (1982, 434).

[49] See Field (1996) for a similar proposal. Field defends an even stronger proposal according to which empirical evidence is irrelevant to the epistemic status of classical logic. Field argues for the empirical indefeasibility of classical logic along, by my lights, explanationist grounds. Field argues that there are no clear alternatives to classical logic for use in reasoning and furthermore that classical logic has significant confirmation by use in empirically successful theories.

short, one is not forced to. Taking the law to have the highest level of justification can do all the epistemic work that it needs to do. There is no principle for which we have a better justification; so positions that imply a contradiction give us strong reason for rejection. This explanationist justification avoids the problematic notion of purely autonomous rational insight. Autonomous rational insight can be puzzling; how are human creatures about to latch onto modal space with a singular act of rational insight. A better view is that creatures like us are about to latch onto modal space by triangulating their position by other claims they have some justification for believing. In this respect the explanationist has a simpler view than the rationalist. It gets the same judgments about the functional profile of putative a priori principles but without the metaphysical story rationalist append to an account of the a priori.[50]

6.3 Coherence and awareness

To this point I have argued that an explanatory coherentist alternative undermines BonJour's arguments that a priori justification is indispensable and that this explanationist alternative is plausible. There is one final consideration to address. Is it enough that one's belief *be* coherent, or must one be *aware* of the coherence of one's beliefs? BonJour held that coherence alone was not sufficient for justification; one had to be aware that one's beliefs were coherent. But then it was implausible to think that a person was aware of the entirety of her body of beliefs, let alone the coherence of her beliefs. This problem led BonJour to formulate the *Doxastic Presumption*: the presumption that one does have the system of beliefs one believes oneself to have.[51] BonJour later realized, though, that this presumption was ad hoc, and that the epistemological issues arising from an awareness requirement could not be addressed within the confines of a coherentist epistemology.[52]

One solution to this problem is to adopt an externalist form of coherentism. If a subject's belief are coherent then, regardless of whether a subject is aware of this, her beliefs are propositionally justified. This solution must address the challenging problem of distant, unknown

---

[50] Field's Field (1996) justification of the empirical indefeasibility of classical logic also avoids appeal to the autonomy of rational insight.
[51] See BonJour (1985, 104).
[52] See BonJour (1997) for details.

coherences. Richard Fumerton forcefully presses this worry:

> Suppose I believe twenty-eight very complex propositions. Suppose further that I reached those conclusions in an extraordinarily silly way. I was reading a book far too difficult for me and to amuse myself I decided to believe every fifth proposition I encountered. As it turns out, by a remarkable coincidence there is an extremely sophisticated proof that interrelates all these different propositions, a proof that only a handful of logicians in the world would be able to grasp. Is there any plausibility at all in holding that my beliefs are rational?[53]

Fumerton's objection works only against a simple externalist version of coherentism. A better version of coherentism is explanatory coherentism which holds that propositional justification is determined by the explanatory virtues of a subject's beliefs. In Fumerton's case the subject's new beliefs have little, if any, explanatory value. These new beliefs do not fit with the rest of what the subject believes and do not perform any explanatory work (by either explaining or being explained). The subject's explanatory position is worsened by gaining these new beliefs.

An adequate explanation is constrained by facts about a subject. A good explanation for a brilliant logician differs from a good explanation for an undergraduate. The facts that constrain adequate explanations are the mental facts of the subjects. A subject's beliefs and abilities affect the form and content of a good explanation. Thus, on an explanationist account, explanatory virtue does not float free from the mental facts of a subject. In this connection an explanationist is well positioned to offer a better account of an awareness requirement for justification. Given that goodness in explanation is constrained by the mental facts of a subject, there is no relevant distinction between a subject's beliefs merely having the explanatory virtues and a subject being aware of her beliefs having those virtues. To be sure, one can distinguish between a subject's beliefs having the virtues and a subject having an explicit belief about her belief's having the virtues. But explanationism does not require an explicit meta-belief about the virtuousness of one's beliefs. Rather, it must be a fact about a subject's belief that they are explanatory coherent. This fact itself reflects facts about a subject's mental abilities—what hypothesis she can entertain, what kind of evidential relationships she can appreciate, and so on.

---

[53] Fumerton (1995, 155). William Lycan addresses this objection in Lycan (2012, 16). My response is similar to Lycan's.

This feature of explanationism answers a worry that Richard Feldman presses. Feldman considers the following case:

> Three people, Expert, Novice, and Ignorant, are standing in a garden looking at a hornbeam tree. They have a clear and unobstructed view of the tree. The visual appearance present to each of the tree people in the garden is exactly the same. Expert knows a lot about trees and can easily identify most trees, including this one, immediately. Novice knows a little about trees but is unfamiliar with hornbeams. Ignorant does not know anything about trees. He does not know which of the things in the garden is a tree and which is a flower.[54]

Feldman then argues:

> In one use of the phrase "best explanation," it seems to be true that the best explanation of Novice's experience was that there was a hornbeam tree in front of him. After all, nothing else would look just like that. But then [given that one is justified in believing the best explanation] Novice is justified in believing that he sees a hornbeam. But this is the wrong result.[55]

I agree with Feldman that Novice is not justified in believing that there is a hornbeam tree before him. But explanationism does not imply that Novice is justified. Feldman's argument relies on the dubious claim that what counts as the best explanation is not sensitive to facts about the subject. The mental facts of Expert are different from the mental facts of Novice, a difference which lies in their occurrent and dispositional mental states. Expert has more relevant beliefs about trees than Novice. Thus what counts as the best explanation of Expert's visual experience differs from what counts as the best explanation of Novice's experience. There is a temptation to think that the true explanation is the best explanation regardless of the mental facts of a subject. But the history of science is replete with examples of people who are justified in believing a theory on explanatory grounds even though it is not true. To take one example, until people rejected an Aristotelian theory of motion and accepted the Galilean view, the best explanation of the astronomical data was not that the earth was hurtling through space in orbit around the sun. Given their beliefs and experiences, that view was massively disconfirmed by

---

[54] ?, 147.
[55] ?, 150.

common experience of a stable earth together with the background Aristotelian theory. The lesson is that the best explanation is best relative to some set of information. In the case of Novice, the true explanation is not conservative. It doesn't fit with what Novice believes. He knows that he can't identify hornbeam trees, and thus the true explanation in this case isn't the best. Crucially, inference to the best explanation is constrained by mental facts about an agent. An agent's beliefs and dispositions fix what is, for her, the best explanation.

6.4 Conclusion

I have argued that BonJour's indispensability arguments for foundationalism about the a priori fail. Explanationism offers a coherent and plausible view about the justification for apparently necessary truths. Furthermore, I have argued that there is no fundamental incoherence with a complete coherentist justification of the a priori. Even if our reasoning rests on principles such as the principle of noncontradiction, it is possible to give a coherentist justification of this principle. Finally, I've argued that the fact that goodness of explanation is relative to a subject's beliefs and abilities avoids the problems with BonJour's access requirement and his resulting doxastic presumption. The upshot is a coherent and plausible explanationist account of the a priori.

7
Bayesian Explanationism

The explanationist view I have defended maintains that propositional justification consists in a subject's overall explanatory position. There is no purely autonomous justification that provides a subject with autonomous reasons, whether from experience or intuition. Rather a subject has justification for a claim only if that claim is part of a virtuous explanatory view which beats relevant competitors. One final challenge to this view comes from Bayesianism.

The ascendency of Bayesian views of scientific methodology is one of the success stories of twentieth-century philosophy. Bayesians take an elegant mathematical theory of probability and apply it to modeling inductive confirmation. As I explain in the first section Bayesianism has many virtues. It provides a tractable theory that can account good methodological rules and make good sense of how a person's degrees of belief should develop in response to new evidence. Yet the Bayesian structure is silent about explanation and its virtues. How do the explanatory virtues fit into a Bayesian story? An old methodological rule is to seek the most simple, powerful, and conservative explanation (i.e., the 'best' explanation) of some phenomena and to believe the best explanation when it is good enough.[1] It is not apparent from the Bayesian apparatus why the norm to seek good explanations should be reflected in a Bayesian view of inference.

My goal in this chapter is to argue for a new compatibilist position regarding the relationship between Bayesianism and explanationism. I argue that explanationism is consistent with Bayesian requirements of coherence and conditionalization. Furthermore, I argue that inductive

[1] See Harman (1965).

confirmation requires explanatory information. Adding in explanatory considerations to undergird the Bayesian framework makes for a more powerful theory. The view I stump for may be described as *explanatory Bayesianism*. It requires that a subject's prior probability distribution reflect explanatory virtues. A Pr-function ought not have priors that give simple theories lower priors than complex theories. A Pr-function should reflect the power of an explanatory hypothesis in the relevant likelihoods. A Pr-function should distribute probability over the most fundamental explanatory parameters instead of the Platonic heaven of all possible explanatory parameters. In light of new mysteries, one should seek a new prior distribution that departs least from one's previous prior distributions while maximizing simplicity and explanatory power. This explanationist Bayesian view then offers a tractable theory that builds upon the merits of the formal Bayesian machinery.[2]

7.1 Bayesianism

Bayesian treatments of induction provide a relatively new way of thinking about inductive inference. Even though Bayes's theorem was formulated in the eighteenth century by the Reverend Thomas Bayes, Bayesian approaches to confirmation did not begin in earnest until after the reprinting of Bayes's essay in 1940 and then in 1958.[3] Since the 1960s there has been an explosion of interest in Bayesianism, leading to the new and fruitful field of Bayesian statistics. My aim in this section is to explain the nature and appeal of Bayesianism with an eye to its relationship with explanationism.

There are natural commonalities between a Bayesian theory of inference and an explanationist theory. Bayesianism provides a formal theory that makes sense of holism in that the confirmation of a theory by some evidence is dependent on a host of other background assumptions. Alan Chalmers writes, "An important aspect of the Bayesian theory of science is that the calculations of prior and posterior probabilities always take place against a background of assumptions that are taken for granted, that is, assuming what Popper called background knowledge."[4] One of the important lessons of a Bayesian analysis of Hempel's discussion on confirmation is that, *pace* Hempel, the confirmation relation

---

[2] This general position has been anticipated by Huemer (2009) and Weisberg (2009).

[3] Earman (1992, 1).

[4] Chalmers (2013, 162).

is a three-place relation between two statements and a background body of information. This Bayesian analysis of confirmation fits strongly with the explanationist's contention that justified belief requires a background theory. Moreover, many of these background assumptions come from belief, or more generally, informational states of a subject. Subjective Bayesians hold that a subject's initial probability function is a reflection of their personal informational states. This captures a crucial part of the dimension of justification that depends on personal background theory. Furthermore, both Bayesians and explanationist stress the importance of coherence and that coherence is a holistic property of a belief system.

7.1.1 An introduction to Bayesianism

The starting point of Bayesianism is an elegant theorem of the probability calculus that relates the probability of a hypothesis on a piece of evidence to other values. Let 'h' represent a hypothesis and 'e' a piece of evidence then the simplest version of Bayes's theorem is

$$Pr(h \mid e) = \frac{Pr(e \mid h)Pr(h)}{Pr(e)}$$

Bayes's theorem relates the probability of a hypothesis on a piece of evidence—known as the *posterior probability of the hypothesis*—with three terms. First, there is the *prior probability* of the hypothesis, Pr(h). By Bayes's theorem the posterior of the hypothesis is directly proportional to its prior. Second, there is Pr(e|h), referred to as the *likelihood* of the hypothesis. This probability reflects the degree to which a piece of evidence is expected if the theory is true. If some evidence is strongly predicted by a theory but not so by its rival, then the theory gets more confirmation from it than its rival. The third value on the right-hand side of Bayes's theorem is in the denominator, Pr(e), known as the *prior probability of the evidence*. This value is naturally conceived of as the degree to which the evidence itself is to be expected. The posterior probability of the hypothesis is inversely proportional to the value of Pr(e). By the rule of total probability, Pr(e) = Pr(e | h)Pr(h) + Pr(e | ¬h)Pr(¬h). This reflects an explanationist insight that the degree to which a piece of evidence is expected is dependent on theoretical judgments about how likely it is on various hypotheses and how likely are those theories.

One of the main appeals to Bayes's theorem is that it naturally equates the probability of a hypothesis with cognitive values. A hypothesis is confirmed by a piece of evidence to the extent the hypothesis is plausible, it predicts the evidence, and also to the extent the evidence was surprising. These three values—*plausibility*, *prediction*, and *surprise*, all explanatory aspects—are located in Bayes's theorem by the prior, the likelihood, and the prior of the evidence. One of the main arguments for Bayesianism, the unification argument, appeals to these cognitive virtues.

To use Bayes's theorem to evaluate the relevance of evidence one must have probabilities for the terms on the right-hand side of Bayes's theorem. Bayesians appeal to the mathematical theory of probability and instruct agents to have degrees of belief that satisfy the probability calculus. The standard axioms for the probability calculus are the Kolmogorov axioms.

> Axiom 1: The probability of any proposition is a positive real number inclusively between 0 and 1.
> Axiom 2: The probability of a tautology is 1.
> Axiom 3: The probability of any countable sequence of mutually exclusive propositions is given by the sum of their probabilities.

In addition to these axioms, the conditional probability of a proposition, A, given another, B, is defined as the ratio of A&B cases to all B cases. That is,

$$Pr(A|B) = \frac{Pr(A\&B)}{Pr(B)}.$$

Once probabilities are in place, Bayes's theorem determines the posterior probability of a hypothesis. Bayesian approaches to confirmation assume that a piece of information is evidentially relevant to a hypothesis if and only if it is probabilistically relevant to the hypothesis. That is,

> e is evidentially relevant to h if and only if $Pr(h|e) \neq Pr(h)$.

Bayesians then propose various relevance measures of confirmation aimed to measure the magnitude of evidential relevance e has to h. The simplest of these measures is *the difference measure*. The degree of confirmation e offers for h—$c(h,e)$—is

$c(h, e) = Pr(h|e) - Pr(h).$

Where e is positively relevant to h, $c(h,e)$ is positive; where e is neutral, $c(h,e) = 0$, and where e disconfirms h, $c(h,e)$ is negative. It is not hard to see the general appeal of Bayesianism. The mathematical structure is clear. Bayes's theorem precisely relates the evidential support of a hypothesis to other cognitive values. And there is a clear way of measuring evidential relevance.

One central question for Bayesianism is how we should interpret the mathematical theory of probability? That is, how should we understand the notion of 'probability' the Kolmogorov axioms formalize? In simple cases such as selecting a ball from an urn it is natural to think that the probability that a particular ball is selected is the ratio of favorable cases to total number of cases. This ratio can be given by the frequency of those events to occur given the composition of the urn and the mechanism used for selection. But other propositions are not amenable to this treatment. What is the probability that general relativity is true? The urn-model is not helpful in this case. How should we understand the total number of cases, or even the favorable cases? What counts as a 'favorable' case for general relativity? Is it a favorable case for Einstein's theory if one of the parameters of general relativity is off by a slight degree? These are unanswered questions.

There are three broad approaches to understanding probability. One approach is the logical approach. A *logical* interpretation of probability aims to assign probabilities to propositions by an a priori examination of the space of possibilities.[5] A second *objective* approach identifies the probability of a proposition with the frequency of the corresponding event happening.[6] The probability that this coin will land heads is identified with the chance of the event-type of this coin landing heads over all possibilities. Finally, a *personalist* approach identifies the probability of a proposition with the degree of confidence a person has in that proposition.[7] If Jones has complete confidence in the event of rain or shine and his confidence in both is the same then his probability for sun today is $\frac{1}{2}$.

Bayesians typically identify probabilities with a person's degree of beliefs. Bayesians then put forward two characteristic claims: *probabilism* and *conditionalization*. The thesis of probabilism maintains that a rational subject has degrees of belief that satisfy the axioms of the probability calculus. Conditionalization is the thesis that a subject who acquires new evidence should update her degrees of belief in accord in Bayes's theorem. I examine Bayesian arguments for these claims below.

---

[5] See Carnap (1950).
[6] See von Mises (1957); Popper (1959).
[7] See Howson and Urbach (1993).

7.1.2 Arguments for Bayesianism

To model inductive inference via the mathematical theory of probability Bayesians require that propositions have probabilities and that these probabilities be coherent, that is, satisfy the Kolmogorov axioms. Since Bayesians are typically personalists about the interpretation of probability, this amounts to the claim that humans have degrees of belief for propositions and that these degrees of beliefs should be coherent. To this end Bayesians offer Dutch Book arguments, representation theorem arguments, and scoring rule arguments for these conclusions.[8] A final argument for Bayesianism is what I will call 'the unification argument.' This argument takes a different route by arguing for a Bayesian view of induction on the grounds that it unifies many natural methodological principles via the mathematical theory of probability.

Dutch Book arguments

The most prominent argument for probabilism is the Dutch Book argument. A Dutch Book is a series of bets that is guaranteed to lose money. The Dutch Book argument for probabilism shows that any subject whose degrees of belief violate the probability calculus should accept as fair a series of bets that is guaranteed to lose money. Consider Mike who is placing bets on which team will win the SuperBowl. Mike is fully confident that one of five teams will win. He has the following degrees of belief about the chances of each of those five teams. He believes that the Packers, Bears, and Niners each have a 25% to win the SuperBowl. He also thinks that the Patriots have a 20% chance of winning and the Steelers have an outside shot at 10%. Given those beliefs Mike should find fair the following odds: 1:3 for the Packers, Bears, and Niners; 1:4 on the Patriots; and 1:9 on the Steelers. Mike places bets of $50 on each team with 1:3 odds, $40 on the Patriots, and $20 on the Steelers. Mike's series of bets is guaranteed to lose $10. This series of bets costs him $210 but he is guaranteed only to make $200 regardless of whichever team wins.

The core intuition about the Dutch Book argument is that Mike's probability assignments are irrational because they can be criticized on a priori grounds that it guarantees a monetary loss. David Christensen takes this core intuition to argue for a depragmatized Dutch

---

[8] I will not discuss the new scoring rule arguments. This argument is a non-pragmatic argument for probabilism which aims to show that given certain goals which beliefs aim to realize one is subject to Bayesian coherence requirements. See Joyce (1998, 2009).

Book argument for probabilism.[9] Early Dutch Book arguments aimed both to identify degrees of belief with betting preferences and to argue for probabilism. Christensen argues this involves dubious metaphysical assumptions about the nature of degrees of belief. Furthermore, the criticism that certain degrees of belief lead to a guaranteed monetary loss is pragmatic rather than an epistemic criticism of those degrees of belief. One way to avoid a Dutch Book argument is to adopt the policy of never placing any bets. If probabilism is to offer a normative epistemic constraint on degrees of belief, a Dutch Book argument should be freed as much as possible from these pragmatic assumptions.

Christensen attempts to do this. He begins with the judgment that if a subject has a degree of belief in p of $\frac{2}{3}$ then, from the subject's perspective, this sanctions as fair the odds of 2:1 on a bet on p.[10] Next, Christensen introduces the idea of a simple agent who values only money and values it in a linear manner (that is, an increase of $1 is worth the same for a simple agent regardless of the agent's current wealth).[11] This assumption fixes the preference of a simple agent as well as the structure of the agent's preference. Christensen then proposes the following principle:

Sanctioning. A simple agent's degrees of belief sanction as fair monetary bets at odds matching his degrees of belief.[12]

Sanctioning establishes a normative connection between degrees of belief and fair betting odds. Given this normative connection, Christensen's depragmatized dutch book argument follows the normal pattern of other Dutch Book arguments. He proposes a plausible principle about when bets are defective:

Bet Defectiveness. For a simple agent, a set of bets that is logically guaranteed to leave him monetarily worse off is rationally defective.[13]

A simple agent who cares only about money in a linear manner will not satisfy his preferences by playing a series of bets guaranteed to

---
[9] Christensen (2004).
[10] Ibid., 116.
[11] Christensen (2004, 117).
[12] Ibid.
[13] Ibid., 118.

lose money. The last principle Christensen proposes connects rational defectiveness in a set of bets to a rational defect in the degrees of belief that sanction those bets. That is,

> *Belief Defectiveness.* If a simple agent's beliefs sanction as fair each of a set of bets, and that set of bets is rationally defective, then the agent's belief are rationally defective.[14]

With these three principles in place the Dutch Book theorem[15] implies,

> *Simple agent probabilism.* If a simple agent's degrees of belief violate the probability axioms, they are rationally defective.[16]

The key principle in Christensen's Dutch Book argument is *Sanctioning*. This principle gains considerable plausibility from the characterization of a simple agent. Such an agent values only money and values it in a linear manner. Given these assumptions, the claim that a simple agent's degrees of belief provide the basis for sanctioning a series of monetary bets is plausible. If an agent countenances as fair a series of bets then, by that agent's lights, those bets should leave him with at least an equal chance of success as not. When one shows that bets fail to satisfy those conditions then one infers that something is amiss with the agent sanctioning those bets as fair.

Christensen's depragmatized Dutch Book argument for probabilism is compelling for simple agents. Yet it does not threaten an explanationist epistemology. The explanationist may wonder about the adequacy of the simple agent model to real world subjects with an interest in understanding the nature of the world. Scientific and philosophical inquiry is far removed from Christensen's simple agent model. Igor Douven shows that a subject who is interested in being in a position to assert the truth reaches this goal more quickly and safely by violating Bayesian diachronic constraints.[17] Agents who are interested in understanding the nature of the world are not simple agents. They value gaining wisdom and, occasionally, value it more than money. Yet, it's still true

---

[14] Ibid., 119.

[15] That is, if an agent's degrees of belief violate the probability axioms, then there is a set of monetary bets, at odds matching those degrees of belief, that will logically guarantee the agent's monetary loss. Christensen (2004, 121).

[16] Ibid.

[17] Douven (2013).

that for simple agents wisdom lies in probabilism. Certainly, any agent who failed to be coherent is under a more general obligation to explain himself. Probabilism and conditionalization, then, do not float free of broader explanatory considerations.

Representation theorem arguments

While Dutch Book arguments are the best-known arguments, representation theorem arguments are taken more seriously by probabilists.[18] Representation theorem arguments aim to support probabilism by examining a set of natural principles that constrain the structure of an agent's preferences. One such principle is the transitivity of preference: if a subject prefers *a* to *b* and *b* to *c* then a subject prefers *a* to *c*.[19] What the representation theorem argument shows is that if a subject's preferences satisfy these constraints then a subject can be represented as an expected utility maximizer with a coherent set of degrees of beliefs. Usually, a representation theorem argument assumes that if a subject can be represented by a set of utilities and degrees of belief then the subject has that set of utilities and degrees of belief. Consequently, such arguments show that if a subject's preferences satisfy those constraints then the subject has a coherent set of degrees of belief. To the extent subject's preferences ought to satisfy those constraints a subject should have a coherent set of degrees of belief.[20]

Christensen provides an overview of a representation theorem argument.[21] He offers three principles which jointly imply probabilism. The first principle states the naturalness of the constraints:

Preference Consistency. Ideally rational agents' preferences obey constraints C.[22]

The next principle is the representation theorem:

Representation Theorem. If an agent's preferences obey constraints C, then they can be represented as resulting from some unique set of

---

[18] Christensen (2004, 124).
[19] See Kaplan (1996, Ch. 1) for a list of these principles.
[20] See Meacham and Weisberg (2011) for a recent discussion and criticism of representation theorem arguments.
[21] Christensen (2004).
[22] Ibid., 125.

utilities U and probabilistically coherent degrees of belief B relative to which they maximize expected utility.[23]

These two principles are not sufficient to establish that a subject who satisfies those constraints in fact has that set of utilities and degrees of beliefs. The next principle closes that gap by taking the availability of such a representation to imply that the subject has those utilities and degrees of belief. That is, a normal representation theorem argument assumes:

Representation Accuracy. If an agent's preferences can be represented as resulting from unique utilities U and probabilistically coherent degrees of belief B relative to which they satisfy expected utility, then the agent's actual utilities are U and her actual degrees of belief are B.[24]

Probabilism, the thesis that ideally rational agents should have probabilistically coherent degrees of beliefs, follows from these three principles. By *Preference Consistency* the preferences of an ideally rational agent will obey constraints C. The *Representation Theorem* guarantees that an ideally rational agent's preferences can be represented as resulting from a combination of coherent degrees of beliefs and values such that they maximize expected utility. *Representation Accuracy* secures that an ideally rational agent in fact has those coherent degrees of beliefs and values. Thus, an ideally rational agent has a coherent set of degrees of beliefs.

One might worry about *Representation Accuracy*.[25] In place of this principle, Christensen thinks that the constraints are normative rather than metaphysical. Christensen recognizes the possibility that an ideally rational agent might not have the unique set of credences and utilities she can be represented as having, even though he thinks an ideally rational agent should have those degrees of beliefs. Christensen's argument is similar to Mark Kaplan's.[26] Both Christensen and Kaplan hold that the constraints are normative ideals, that departures of the constraints are failures of complete rationality. In response to these concerns Christensen imposes a normative requirement connecting preferences with degrees of belief:

---

[23] Ibid.
[24] Ibid.
[25] See Christensen (2004, 126–135) for Christensen's concerns.
[26] Kaplan (1996).

Informed Preference. An ideally rational agent prefers the option of getting a desirable prize if B obtains to the option of getting the same prize if A obtains, just in case B is more probable for that agent than A.[27]

Informed Preference is appealing. Suppose we hold fixed everything an agent values and she has a choice between two ways of winning a desirable prize. She can bet on either A being true or B being true. A rational agent should prefer the first bet over the second if and only if she takes A to be more probable than B. Even if we recognize the possibility that preferences and degrees of belief can come apart *Informed Preference* is plausible. Suppose an agent violates *Informed Preference*. She believes there's a better chance that A is true than B, but she is indifferent between the two bets. While this is metaphysically possible, it's difficult to understand as rational indifference. By her own lights, she'd do better by taking taking the first bet. If she persisted in being indifferent, her rationality is undermined apart from an adequate explanation of her indifference.

The representation theorem argument for probabilism is consistent with explanationism. Nothing about *Informed Preference* requires violating explanatory constraints and the constraints arising from the explanatory virtues do not conflict with it. The constraints in *Preference Consistency* are themselves supported by explanatory considerations. There are arguments for the constraints and replies to challenges to the constraints. The constraints are justified on overall explanatory grounds in line with the argument in the previous chapter for an explanationist justification of the principle of noncontradiction. An agent who violates the constraints or *Informed Prefence* is under a more general obligation to explain herself.

The unification argument

The Dutch Book and representation theorem arguments provide support for probabilism and conditionalization. An entirely different argument defends a Bayesian approach to explaining inductive confirmation. The conclusion of this argument is that Bayesianism provides an accurate account of what it is for some evidence to confirm or disconfirm some hypotheses. When this is applied to human epistemic agents the claim

---

[27] Christensen (2004, 137).

is that probabilism and conditionalization offer the correct materials for inductive inference.

This unification argument appeals to the theoretical virtues of Bayesianism by arguing that it provides the correct account of inductive confirmation on the basis of its elegant, unified treatment of natural methodological principles. Whereas the Dutch Book argument and representation theorem argument focus on the structure of an individual's degrees of belief, the unification argument focuses directly on methodological principles that undergird our judgments about inductive confirmation. Kevin Kelly and Clark Glymour observe that the unification argument is what truly motivates Bayesian confirmation theory. They write:

> Bayesian confirmation theorists have some foundational arguments for their methods (e.g., derivation from axioms of "rational" preference, Dutch book theorems) but one gets the impression that these are not taken too seriously, even by the faithful. What really impresses confirmation theorists is that Bayesian updating provides a unified, if highly idealized, explanation of a wide range of short-run judgments of evidential relevance.[28]

Martin Curd, J.A. Cover, and Christopher Pincock express a similar sentiment. They write:

> A considerable part of the attraction of the Bayesian approach is that, on the basis of a simple theorem of probability—Bayes's theorem–and a few assumptions about rationality and degrees of belief, Bayesianism promises a unified explanation of a wide range of accepted principles and truisms of scientific methodology.[29]

Curd et al. offer a summary of natural methodological principles and other judgments that figure in this argument.[30] These principles and judgments include:

1. Surprising predictions have special evidential value.
2. Simple theories are more likely to be true.
3. Ad hoc additions to theories to address problematic evidence reduce the plausibility of those theories.

---

[28] Kelly and Glymour (2004, 100–101).
[29] Cover Curd and Pincock (2013, 515).
[30] Ibid., 515–516.

4. Diverse sets of evidence lend stronger support to theories than narrow sets of evidence.
5. Not every theory is equally well confirmed by the evidence it entails.
6. There is an elegant Bayesian solution to paradoxes of confirmation such as the raven paradox and Goodman's riddle.

In the next section I examine several examples of Bayesian unification to illustrate the depth and power of the Bayesian explanation of these virtues. But at this point let us pause and consider the overall unification argument. Does this argument show that explanationism is false or that explanationism is inconsistent with Bayesianism? No. The argument requires that the methodological principles are true in order to get a compelling argument for Bayesianism. The argument does succeed in showing that there is a general, unified, and tractable theory that captures these correct judgments. But that itself is a reason to believe that Bayesianism is right only if a theory's ability to unify accepted judgments is itself a good making feature of a theory. Drawing the conclusion that explanationism is wrong from the unification argument would be like concluding that paper and pencil arithmetic is mistaken because there are calculators. The unification argument isn't a reason to reject the old explanationist methodology; rather it's a vindication of it.

7.1.3 Examples of Bayesian unification

Let us consider three examples of Bayesian unification and consider how this fits with general explanationist themes: the ability to explain the evidential value of surprising predictions, the value of diverse evidence, and finally a theoretically elegant response to the ravens paradox.

Surprising predictions

In 1919 Arthur Eddington and his colleagues observed that light from a distant star shifted in the presence of a strong gravitational field. This discovery threw significant empirical weight behind Einstein's theory of general relativity, which was previously accepted on elegance considerations and its ability to explain the precession of the perihelion of Mercury. The data in this case is that light bends in a strong gravitational field. According to Newton's theory, light travels in a straight line. Thus, Eddington's observation significantly disconfirmed Newton's theory while confirming Einstein's theory.

Why did Eddington's observation provide so much empirical support for Einstein's theory? One reason was that the data was completely unexpected. Bayesians explain this via the extremely low value of the evidence, Pr(e). By Bayes's theorem if the evidence has an extremely low probability then it has the power to significantly confirm a theory. The evidential value of surprising evidence is a simple and straightforward consequence of Bayes's theorem. The explanationist agrees with all this but has a more illuminating explanation of why a probability function with this shape has the properties it does. First, people did not believe that light could bend; rather, according to accepted theory at that time, it was assumed that light traveled in straight lines. Second, Einstein's theory, if true, explained how light would bend in a strong gravitational field. Thus, when people came to accept the results they had significant explanatory reasons to accept Einstein's view. General relativity removed the mystery of Eddington's experimental result; Newton's theory left the mystery unaccounted for.

Let us engage in some fiction. Suppose prior to Einstein's prediction that light bends in strong gravitational fields, a contemporary of Newton observed this to be so. Does this observation falsify Newton's theory? Does it make it irrational to believe Newton's theory? Our judgment on these questions is highly sensitive to specific contexts. It is not unreasonable to suppose that given the impressive explanatory achievements of Newton's theory and the lack of viable alternatives, one would still be rational in believing Newton's theory. For Quine–Duhem reasons, one may make other adjustments. One could introduce an experiential error factor that would account for the apparent observation of the bending of light. One could introduce some extra factor in Newton's theory to account the observation. This fictional scenario is parallel to the postulation of Neptune's position and mass to account for irregularities in Uranus's orbit, movements that, apart from Neptune's position and mass, are unaccounted for on Newton's theory. As I've argued in Chapter 4, rational belief is sensitive to one's overall explanatory position. Unless one has a devastating objection to one's view, the explanatory merits of a view can make it rational to maintain belief in it until a better explanatory view comes along. Extremely improbable data can be dismissed as an anomaly until some explanation comes along to the effect that given some other conditions and laws it was not completely unexpected after all. The evidential value of the surprise factor is not independent from overall explanatory considerations.

The value of diverse evidence

As we saw above, a natural methodological principle is that diverse evidence confirms more strongly a theory than narrow evidence. Carl Hempel writes, "The confirmation of a hypothesis depends not only on the quantity of the favorable evidence available, but also on its variety: the greater the variety, the stronger the resulting support."[31] Newton's theory received more support from both terrestrial and celestial observations than just terrestrial observations. Howson and Urbach compare the support in these two cases. Case 1: we observe on a Tuesday and then on a Thursday that the rate of fall of a given terrestrial object is r, as Newton theory predicts. Case 2: we observe that the rate of fall of a given terrestrial object is r and that the position of a heavenly body on a specific date is p, both as predicted by Newton's theory. Case 2 confirms Newton's theory more strongly than case 1.[32]

Bayesians provide a clear, simple account of the evidential value of diverse evidence. To explain this I follow Branden Fitelson's account of the confirmational significance of evidential diversity.[33] Fitelson explicates evidential diversity in terms of independent evidence. Two items of evidence are confirmationally independent regarding H if and only if the support each provides for H is independent of whether the other piece of evidence is already known. That is,

Definition of confirmational independence: E_1 and E_2 are (mutually) confirmationally independent regarding H according to c if and only if both $c(H, E_1 \mid E_2) = c(H, E_1)$ and $c(H, E_2 \mid E_1) = c(H, E_2)$.[34]

The notation '$c(H, E_1)$' is the degree of confirmation that E_1 provides for H and '$c(H, E_1 \mid E_2)$' is the degree of confirmation that E_1 provides for H given that E_2 is known. Bayesians have proposed several relevance measures of confirmation, measures that satisfies Bayesian accounts of evidential relevance. A Bayesian account of evidential relevance states that e is evidence for h if and only if $\Pr(h \mid e) > \Pr(h)$. Accordingly, a relevance measure of confirmation satisfies the conditions that it is positive when e raises the probability of H, negative when e is reduces the probability of H, and 0 when e doesn't change the probability of H. For our purposes, we can work with the simple difference measure of confirmation according to which $c(h, e) = \Pr(h \mid e) - \Pr(h)$. Intuitively, the difference measure is one way of measuring the magnitude of change that e makes to h's probability.

---

[31] Hempel (1966, 34).

[32] Howson and Urbach offer this case as an example of evidential diversity (Howson and Urbach, 1993, 169).

[33] Fitelson (2001).

[34] Ibid., 125.

Fitelson shows that the difference measure (among others) satisfies natural principles about evidential independence. One such principle is what Fitelson calls the "fundamental Peircean desiderata." C.S. Peirce claims that when two arguments are entirely independent then when they both occur they should produce an level of confidence equal to the sum of the levels of confidence each would produce separately.[35] Fitelson interprets this Peircean claim as the following:

($\mathcal{A}$) If E_1 and E_2 are confirmationally independent regarding H according to c, then $c(H, E_1 \& E_2) = c(H, E_1) + c(H, E_2)$.

Fitelson proves that the difference measure (among others) satisfies ($\mathcal{A}$).[36] Applied to case 2 above with Newton's theory, this amounts to the claim that the degree of confirmation by both pieces of evidence should be additive.

The other natural methodological principle is the value of diverse evidence. Fitelson interprets this principle in Bayesian terms as follows:

($\mathcal{D}$) If each of E_1 and E_2 individually confirms H, and if E_1 and E_2 are confirmationally independent regarding H according to c, then $c(H \mid E_1 \& E_2) > c(H \mid E_1)$ and $c(H \mid E_1 \& E_2) > c(H \mid E_2)$.

The proof that the difference measure satisfies ($\mathcal{D}$) is a simple corollary of the proof that it satisfies ($\mathcal{A}$). What both ($\mathcal{A}$) and ($\mathcal{D}$) give us is clear statements of the evidential significance of independent and diverse evidence. Bayesians take this as a good example of how Bayesianism yields more clarity to methodological rules than other accounts of induction. The explanationist can accept this as a precisification of deeper methodological norms. Again, this isn't an argument against Hempel's broader explanationist principle that diverse evidence is confirmationally more significant than narrow evidence, but rather a vindication of it.

Bayesian treatment of raven paradox

The ravens paradox is a classic paradox of confirmation, first formulated by Hempel.[37] The paradox is centered on the judgment that observing a white shoe does not confirm that all ravens are black. Yet this judgment

---

[35] See Fitelson (2001, 125).
[36] See the proof for theorem 1 regarding measure *d* on (Fitelson, 2001, 135).
[37] Hempel (1945).

conflicts with two very plausible principles about confirmation.[38] The first principle, known as Nicod's condition, states that instances provide confirmation for universal claims. Formally,

(NC): For any object a and any predicate 'F' and 'G', the proposition that 'Fa & Ga' confirms the proposition that every F is G.

The other principle is that confirmation transfers over logical equivalence, that is

(EC) for any propositions H1, H2, and E, if E confirms H1 and H1 is equivalent to H2 then E confirms H2.

Given NC, a non-black, non-raven—for example, a white shoe—confirms that all non-black things are not ravens. And, given, NC this confirms that all ravens are black. Accepting (NC) and (EC) lead to the paradoxical result that observing any non-black, non-raven confirms that all ravens are black.

The classic Bayesian treatment of the ravens paradox dates back to I.J. Good's paper.[39] My discussion of this treatment follows Fitelson and Hawthorne's explanation.[40] Bayesians respond to the ravens paradox by first observing that (NC) is ambiguous. (NC) fails to specify the nature of one's background evidence. Bayesians, as well as the framework theory of reasons, understand confirmation as a three-place relation between a hypothesis, a body of evidence, and background knowledge. e confirms h relative to k just in case $Pr(h \mid e\&k) > Pr(h \mid k)$. (NC) should be reformulated to include specific reference to one's background evidence. Once this is done there are different choices for what to include in k. We might restrict k to our actual background information or take k to include only tautological or a priori information. Bayesians then prove that relative to our actual background information the observation of a black raven offers more significant confirmation for the hypothesis that all ravens are black than does the observation of a white shoe.

The key to this Bayesian solution is that our background evidence includes the proposition that there are many more non-black things

---

[38] The following is a summary of Fitelson's and Hawthorne's explanation of the paradox. See Fitelson and Hawthorne (2010).

[39] Good (1960).

[40] See Fitelson and Hawthorne (2010). Fitelson and Hawthorne prove that a Bayesian solution to the ravens paradox need not require the substantial assumptions made by the classic treatment.

than ravens, that is, $Pr(\neg Ba \mid K) > Pr(Ra \mid K)$. Bayesians typically show that if the background evidence includes two independence claims then the observation of a black raven provides greater confirmation than the observation of a non-black, non-raven. These two independence assumptions are: (a) the probability that something is a raven is independent of whether all ravens are black and (b) the probability that something is non-black is independent of whether all ravens are black. These three claims imply the desired conclusion.

Fitelson and Hawthorne prove, however, that the independence claims have undesirable consequences.[41] For instance, the independence assumptions together with the claim that there are many more non-black things than ravens implies that the observation of a black, non-raven disconfirms that all ravens are black. Fitelson and Hawthorne take this unnatural consequence to motivate the search for a weaker condition to get the relevant confirmational asymmetry. They find this in a condition which says that "learning H does not dramatically increase one's estimate of the ratio of non-black objects to ravens."[42]

Fitelson and Hawthorne's treatment identifies a condition on one's background evidence that accords with natural judgments about evidential sampling strategies. Sampling ravens to see whether they are black has greater confirmational power than sampling the non-black things to see if they are non-ravens. This Bayesian treatment of the ravens paradox has significant affinities to my explanationist view. The confirmatory power of a piece of evidence or sampling strategy depends on one's background knowledge. In the ravens paradox, one's background evidence must include the (natural) assumption that there are many more non-black things than ravens and that the hypothesis that all ravens are black doesn't significantly change the proportion of non-black objects to ravens.

7.1.4 Summary

Bayesianism develops out of the ashes of deductivism. Both deductivists and Bayesianism aim to provide formal accounts of inductive confirmation and clearly the Bayesian has the more natural and powerful account. Bayesians are able to model many of our natural methodological principles. Furthermore, Bayesian appeals to the Dutch Book and representation theorem arguments aim to capture some of our natural

---

[41] See Fitelson and Hawthorne (2010) section 1.3.2.
[42] Ibid., section 1.3.3

judgments about rationality. The overall Bayesian canon is a powerful framework for modeling induction. Yet, as I've pointed out, the arguments designed to motivate Bayesianism are compatible with an explanationist view. In fact, I take them to vindicate the correctness of older, explanationist principles. In the next section I turn more explicitly to the compatibility of Bayesianism and explanationism by examining van Fraassen's argument that the views are incompatible.

7.2 Are Bayesianism and IBE compatible?

Bayesianism provides a relatively new and powerful formal framework for analyzing inductive inference. Yet the mathematical theory of probability is purely a formal structure, lacking any content normally associated with inductive inference. Inductive inference normally proceeds in terms of law, causation, and explanation. Yet the Kolmogorov axioms have nothing to say about the role of laws, causation, or explanation. Perhaps, in virtue of the difference in content between Bayesianism and explanationism, the two views are compatible. Whereas explanationists hold evidence confirms a theory to the extent it provides an explanatory contribution, the Bayesian holds evidence confirms by raising a theory's probability. It's not obvious that these two theories cannot be coordinated. If this is possible then Bayesians can bring on board the concepts of law, cause, and explanation, and explanationist can appeal to the powerful mathematical theory of probability. The result may be a strengthening of both views.

The purpose of this section is to evaluate this suggestion. After presenting van Fraassen's incompatibility argument, I turn to the development of the heuristic view. This view holds that inference to the best explanation (IBE) is a way of realizing Bayesian inference. On this view Bayesianism provides the correct normative theory of inductive inference but explanationist virtues aid subjects in implementing Bayesian inferences. On one interpretation of the heuristic view, explanatory considerations are aids to realize Bayesian reasoning but they are dispensable. On this weak heuristic view, explanatory considerations are crutches for those who are not smart enough to do probability theory on the fly.[43] On another interpretation of the heuristic view, explanatory considerations are aids to realizing Bayesian reasoning but they are also much more than an aid: explanatory considerations are *required*

---

[43] Lipton (2004, 120).

for inductive confirmation. I argue for this stronger view. On this view, Bayesianism and explanationism are compatible because explanatory considerations are required for good (i.e., induction-friendly) probability functions.

7.2.1 Van Fraassen's incompatibility argument

Bas van Fraassen, in *Laws and Symmetry*,[44] presents an argument that IBE is incompatible with Bayesianism. Van Fraassen's incompatibility argument begins with the claim that as a rule of inference IBE must be formulated in terms of probability. The rule to infer the best of an available set of hypotheses should connect the explanatory merits of a theory with its probability. A theory whose explanatory merits are high should have a high probability and a theory whose explanatory merits are low should have a low probability. This suggests that IBE be given as a probabilistic rule for induction. But van Fraassen's argues that to the extent that probabilistic IBE differs from Bayes's theorem, it is incoherent. For, either probabilistic IBE just is Bayes's theorem or it is Bayes's theorem plus some extra weighing factor which gives a probabilistic boost for explanatory hypothesis. In the first case, IBE is trivial. In the second case, IBE is incoherent. Van Fraassen thinks that probabilistic IBE is not trivial in that it ought to give an extra boost to good explanations. He roots this suggestion in a remark Fred Dretske makes about the special role of laws in inductive confirmation. Dretske writes:

> Laws are the sort of thing that can become well established prior to an exhaustive enumeration of the instances to which they apply. This, of course, is what gives laws their predictive utility. Our confidence in them increases at a much more rapid rate than does the ratio of favorable examined cases to total number of cases. Hence, we reach the point of confidently using them to project the outcome of unexamined situations while there is still a substantial number of unexamined situations to project.[45]

Van Fraassen suggests we understand Dretske's idea as a probabilistic rule that gives good explanations an extra probabilistic boost. Whereas Bayes's theorem is

$$Pr(h \mid e) = \frac{Pr(e \mid h)Pr(h)}{Pr(e)},$$

---

[44] van Fraassen (1989).
[45] Dretske (1977, 256).

IBE would specify an additional factor $f(h)$ would gives a positive quantity to good explanations. Thus, probabilistic IBE would be

$$Pr(h \mid e) = \frac{Pr(e \mid h)Pr(h) \times f(h)}{Pr(e)}.^{46}$$

Van Fraassen then presents a diachronic Dutch Book argument that probabilistic IBE leads to incoherence. He argues that adopting any update rule other than Bayes's theorem leaves one in a position of regarding a series of bets as fair even though they guarantee loss. This argument can be depragmatized along similar lines as Christensen suggests. The point would be that a rational agent is subject to legitimate criticism if she sanctions a series of bets as fair when it is a priori that they will lead to overall loss.

Van Fraassen's argument that probabilistic IBE is incoherent has generated a number of responses. Igor Douven has recently argued that incoherence is not necessarily a strike against probabilistic IBE since an advocate of IBE may have other cognitive goals than avoiding diachronic incoherence.[47] For example, a person may be interested in being in a better position to assert the truth. Douven convincingly shows that probabilistic IBE outperforms Bayesian conditionalization with respect to being in a position to assert the truth. Another response, though, denies that there is an incompatibility between IBE and Bayesianism by arguing that explanatory considerations do not require adding some factor—$f(h)$—to Bayes's theorem. Rather, explanatory considerations are reflected in the probability function itself. In the following I examine this suggestion. The most popular version of this approach—known as the heuristic view—claims that explanatory considerations just help one to realize ideal Bayesian reasoning.

7.2.2 The Heuristic view

Van Fraassen's incompatibility argument assumes that probabilistic IBE requires that explanatory hypotheses are given an extra boost of probability. But there are good reasons to think that standard explanatory considerations—*simplicity, fit with background evidence,* and *explanatory power*—correlate with the prior probability and likelihoods of hypotheses. In fact, it is these considerations that those sympathetic to IBE appeal to in response to van Fraassen's incompatibility argument. This

---

[46] This follows Douven's formulation. See Douven (2013).
[47] Douven (2013).

response argues that far from being incompatible with Bayesianism, IBE is complementary with it. As Peter Lipton suggests, "Bayesian conditionalization can indeed be an engine of inference, but it is run in part on explanationist tracks."[48] In the following I examine the nature and motivation for this view.

The heuristic view is developed by Okasha (2000); McGrew (2003); Lipton (2004). I restrict my discussion primarily to Lipton's development of the view. What exactly is the heuristic view? Lipton delineates four views on the relationship between Bayesianism and explanationism in response to the objection that Bayesianism provides the correct descriptive and normative account of induction.[49] One response is that Bayesianism is not a correct normative theory.[50] This response considers standard problems afflicting Bayesianism and argues that such problems undermine the substance of the view. A second response is that while Bayesianism is a corrective normative view, it is not a correct descriptive view. A third response argues that the views are compatible because Bayesianism is just logic for degrees of belief, and logic doesn't conflict with any substantive epistemological theory. On this response Bayesianism is a logic for degrees of belief just as deductive logic is a logic for full belief. If, for instance, a proposition is a deductive consequence of a set of premises logic does not require that you accept the consequence even if you already accept the set of premises. One may subsequently reject one of the premises. Similarly, on this third response, Bayesianism doesn't imply a dynamics to belief since if one learns that e and sees that updating by Bayes's theorem leads one to have an unacceptable high posterior probability then one can change one's priors to restore probabilistic consistency. Thus, on this third view, induction is driven by explanation but one need not flout any theorem of the probability calculus.[51]

Lipton's preferred response goes beyond the third view in suggesting that Bayesianism and explanationism are complementary because explanatory considerations "play an important role in the actual mechanism by which inquirers 'realize' Bayesian reasoning."[52] On Lipton's account Bayesianism provides the correct normative and descriptive account of inductive practice. But explanatory considerations

---

[48] Lipton (2004, 107).
[49] Ibid., 104.
[50] See, for instance, Kelly and Glymour (2004).
[51] Lipton (2004, 106).
[52] Ibid., 107.

play a crucial role in helping us meet Bayesian constraints. Lipton explains:

> Bayes's theorem provides a constraint on the rational distribution of degrees of belief, but this is compatible with the view that explanatory considerations play a crucial role in the evolution of those beliefs, and indeed a crucial role in the mechanism by which we attempt, with considerable but not complete success, to meet that constraint.[53]

Lipton's idea is that even though we are not good at abstract probabilistic reasoning, as shown by the work of Tversky and Kahneman,[54] we use explanationist reasoning to help us respect the constraints of Bayes's theorem.[55] Lipton explicitly roots talk of 'methods and heuristics' in Tversky and Kahneman's work. They write, "people rely on a limited number of heuristic principles which reduce the complex tasks of assessing probabilities and predicting values to simpler judgmental operations. In general, these heuristics are quite useful, but sometimes they lead to severe and systematic errors."[56] While Tversky and Kahneman seem to suggest that we would do better epistemically if we didn't have to reply on these heuristics, Lipton seems more optimistic about the role of explanatory considerations as a heuristic for realizing ideal Bayesian constraints. Lipton explains:

> We are not good at probabilistic reasoning, so we use other methods or heuristics. With this I agree, only where Kahneman and Tversky take these heuristics to replace Bayesian reasoning, I am suggesting that it may be possible to see at least one heuristic, Inference to the Best Explanation, in part as a way of helping us to respect the constraints of Bayes's theorem, in spite of our low aptitude for abstract probabilistic thought.[57]

It is unclear from Lipton's position whether explanatory considerations are indispensable for inductive confirmation. On one reading, explanationist reasoning is like the representativeness heuristic Tverksy

---

[53] Ibid., 1124.
[54] See Tversky, Slovic and Kahneman (1982).
[55] Lipton (2004, 112).
[56] Tversky and Kahneman (1974, 112).
[57] Lipton (2004, 112).

172 *Reason and Explanation*

and Kahneman discuss. This is a method that people use to determine the likelihood that an instance, *a*, is a member of a general class, *F*. The representativeness heuristic assigns a probability that *a is F* to the extent that *a* shares salient characteristics with *F*. But as Tversky and Kahneman argue this leads to probabilistic errors, such as the base rate fallacy.[58] One could read Lipton has suggesting that explanationist reasoning is like the representative heuristic. It works in some cases and not others, but on the whole it'd be better if we reasoned in a Bayesian way.

Another interpretation of Lipton's heuristic position is that explanationist reasoning is not like the representativeness heuristic; for the latter is dispensable but explanationist reasoning is required for induction. Whether or not this is Lipton's actual position, this is the view I argue for.[59] Before I turn to the argument for this view, let us, following Lipton, consider four areas in which explanatory considerations help inquirers realize Bayesian reasoning. First, explanatory considerations can help inquirers determine the likelihood—Pr(e|h)—which helps transition from a prior to a posterior. This may be done by considering how well *h* would explain *e*.[60] The value of Pr(e|h) is directly proportional to how well *h* explains *e*. As we saw above, Newton's theory offered no explanation of the bending of light in a strong gravitational field; hence P(e|Newton's theory) is low. But the relevant likelihood for general relativity is high since it explains the phenomenon. Second, explanatory considerations can help inquirers determine prior probabilities.[61] One obvious suggestion is that considerations of simplicity and fit with background evidence are primary determinants of a prior. Another suggestion is that considerations of the explanatory power of a hypothesis should be reflected in the prior of a hypothesis. Third, they can help determine which data are relevant to the hypothesis under investigation. Lipton observes that Bayes's theorem does not indicate which evidence to use for conditionalization and that explanatory considerations can help to determine this. Lipton suggests that "we sometimes come to see that a datum is epistemically relevant to a

---

[58] For details see Tversky and Kahneman (1974).

[59] See Lipton (2005) for further clarification. He does think that IBE has normative force but he does not argue that inductive confirmation *requires* explanatory considerations.

[60] Lipton (2004, 114–115).

[61] Lipton (2004, 115–116).

hypothesis precisely by seeing that the hypothesis would explain it."[62] Finally, explanatory considerations can play a role in the judgment of which hypotheses promise to be fertile. Bayes's theorem has nothing to say about the genesis of hypotheses. Lipton observes that scientists are interested in "fertile hypotheses with high content."[63] Explanationists, thus, can offer to the Bayesian a way of understanding the context of discovery that aims for theories with some well-studied Bayesian virtues. This latter consideration shows that explanationism captures an aspect of inferential practice where Bayesianism is silent.[64]

These explanationist considerations are relevant to Bayesian reasoning. As Timothy McGrew puts it:

> Attention to our pre-theoretical notions of loveliness may at times be a surer guide to a theory's probabilistic merits and the structure of our reasoning than purely algebraic manipulations even in the hands of an acknowledged master.[65]

Both Lipton and McGrew suggest that explanatory reasoning has a natural fit with Bayesian reasoning. Okasha, though, poses the question of whether the fact that Bayesianism can be retrofitted to align with explanationist reasoning is deeply significant.[66] Okasha asks whether Bayesians are explaining the correctness of old methodological views or whether they are just representing those rules by adding probabilistic constraints. This question gets at the essence of a problem with the weak heuristic view. It's unclear just why a Bayesian should be moved by the explanationist retrofitting move. In the following, I turn to argue that the Bayesian ought to bring on board explanatory considerations as constraints on a Pr-function because explanatory considerations are required for inductive confirmation.[67]

---

[62] Ibid., 116.
[63] Ibid.
[64] Ibid., 117.
[65] McGrew (2003, 564–565).
[66] Okasha (2000, 706).
[67] A recent paper (Henderson, forthcoming) argues for a new compatibilist response which differs from the constraint-based compatibilism I am urging. Henderson argues for an emergent compatibilism according to which IBE and Bayesianism track the same epistemic considerations. Henderson's view makes use of a 'natural prior' to get inductive confirmation. On my view this 'natural prior' must come from explanatory considerations. In contrast to Henderson's view, I see constraint-based compatibilism as itself compatible with

7.3 Bayesian explanationism

We've seen in Lipton's remarks how explanatory considerations are relevant for determining a Pr-function: they help determine the prior, the likelihood, the relevance of evidence to a hypothesis, and the formulation of new hypotheses. There is even stronger reason to think that explanatory considerations are relevant for determining a Pr-function: they are required to avoid inductive skepticism. We noted above Dretske's remark that our confidence in laws increases at a greater rate than the ratio of favored cases to all cases. We can make this clearer by considering a specific case. Suppose I have two coins in my pocket. One has a perfect bias for heads (i.e., a two-headed coin) and the other is fair. I select one at random and will flip it ten times. The first seven flips result in all heads. Consider two hypotheses. H1 states that the fair coin is selected and yet all its tosses will come up heads. H1 is a strange hypothesis but nothing in the Bayesian machinery prevents odd hypotheses. H2 is a more straightforward hypothesis which states that the biased coin is selected. Which hypothesis has greater confirmation after observing seven heads? Clearly, H2. Why? Because H2 explains the evidence, whereas H1 merely entails the evidence. H1 leaves the positive run of seven heads entirely mysterious.[68]

The judgment that the explanatory virtue of H2 is the crucial factor in its confirmation is compatible with Bayesian updating. We start by assigning priors to the two hypotheses. The coin to be selected is either fair or biased. So, $\Pr(C_F) = \Pr(C_B) = .5$. H2, the hypothesis that the biased coin is selected just is, C_B. H1 = C_F & heads results on every flip. Let D_7 be the observational data that the initial seven flips result in all heads. $\Pr(D_7 \mid H1) = \Pr(D_7 \mid H2) = 1$. Using the odds form of Bayes's theorem, we can compare the confirmation D_7 offers to H1 and H2 by the following:

$$\frac{\Pr(H_1 \mid D_7)}{\Pr(H_2 \mid D_7)} = \frac{\Pr(H_1)}{\Pr(H_2)} \times \frac{\Pr(D_7 \mid H_1)}{\Pr(D_7 \mid H_2)}$$

---

her emergent compatibilism because explanatory constraints are necessary for a natural prior.

[68] The puzzle here is related to grue paradox. The hypothesis that all emeralds are green explains the evidence, whereas the hypothesis that all emeralds are grue entails the evidence but does not explain it. Thanks to Branden Fitelson for pointing out this parallel.

Since the last ratio is 1, the confirmation turns on the first ratio, viz. $\frac{Pr(H_1)}{Pr(H_2)}$. The $Pr(H_2) = .5$. And the $Pr(H_1) = .5 \times \frac{1}{2}^{10}$. Clearly, D_7 favors H2 over H1.

The point of this case is to show that explanatory reasoning is compatible with Bayesian updating. In the above case, the assignments of likelihoods track non-epistemic, objective chances. These chances are explanatory and also provide the gears that turn the Bayesian machinery. This provides a simple illustration of the compatibilist point that we should not be surprised to see a concurrence between IBE and Bayesianism.

There is another feature to this example that is worthy of note. Suppose we just consider H1, the hypothesis that the fair coin will result in heads on every flip. How confident are we that having observed an initial run of seven consecutive heads the next flip will be heads? Given that H1 is the fair coin hypothesis the probability that the next flip will be heads is unaffected by previous successes. In this case a track record of success does *nothing* to change our confidence in the unexamined cases. The probability of unexamined cases remains precisely what it was at the outset. If we get to the penultimate flip and observe it is an head, our confidence in H1 will have increased from $\frac{1}{2}^{10}$ to $\frac{1}{2}$, but, while this is a significant change to its probability, it is simply a change that tracks the ratio of favorable cases to all cases. It is a change we get by eliminating counterexamples and it does nothing to change the probability of the unexamined case.

The situation is drastically different when an explanatory hypothesis is a live option. For the explanatory hypothesis can *explain* the data in such a way that it changes the probability of the unexamined cases. In the above case, as one observes more and more heads our confidence in the biased coin hypothesis significantly increases and the probability that the unexamined cases are heads also significantly increases.

Mike Huemer develops an argument that generalizes this point.[69] He makes use of the following example.[70]

> A physical process X has been discovered, the laws governing which are as yet unknown, except that the process must produce exactly one of two outcomes, A or B, on every occasion. No relevant further information is known about X, A, or B. We plan an experiment in

---
[69] Huemer (2009).
[70] The following paragraphs rely heavily on Huemer's discussion.

which X will occur n times, and we will observe on each occasion whether A or B results.[71]

Let A_i = [Outcome A occurs on the ith trial],
U_i = [Outcome A occurs on all of the first ith trials].
Huemer then considers two positions for large values of i.

Inductivism: $\Pr(A_{i+1} \mid U_i) > \Pr(A_{i+1})$
Skepticism: $\Pr(A_{i+1} \mid U_i) = \Pr(A_{i+1})$

The argument I gave above with the coin-flipping case suggested that inductivism is true only if there are explanatory considerations in the background. For if the coin to be flipped is fair then skepticism is true. The chance that the next flip is favorable for heads is unaffected by what has come before. What we want to show in general is that an Pr-function that supports induction is rationally preferable to one that supports skepticism.

The argument centers around two different ways to understand the principle of indifference. According to the bare bones principle one is to distribute probabilities among hypotheses in accord with how much reason one has to believe one hypothesis over another. When one has no reason for believing any one among a set of rival hypotheses one is to distribute the probabilities evenly. Where $H_1, H_2, \ldots, H_n$ are rival hypotheses and one has no reason to think any one is more likely than another then, for each H_i, H_j $\Pr(H_i) = \Pr(H_j)$. The principle of indifference counsels a flat probability distribution over a set of hypotheses one lacks any distinguishing information about.

The problem with the bare bones principle of indifference is that it is inconsistent. We can describe various hypotheses using different parameters and the principle of indifference will, in some cases, imply that we assign the same hypothesis different probabilities. Consider the following example from Richard Fumerton:[72]

> Sue has taken a trip of 100 miles in her car. The trip took between 1 and 2 hours, and thus, Sue's average speed was between 50 and 100 miles per hour. Given only this information, what is the probability that the trip took between 1 hour and $1\frac{1}{2}$ hours?

---

[71] Huemer (2009, 347).
[72] Fumerton (1995, 215). Huemer also uses this example Huemer (2009, 349).

On one solution we give a flat probability distribution over times in which case the probability is $\frac{1}{2}$. Yet another solution gives a flat probability distribution over speeds. Thus her journey was between 60 and 90 minutes if and only if she traveled between $66\frac{2}{3}$ mph and 100mph. That range is $\frac{2}{3}$ of the range from 50 mph to 100 mph. So, using the principle of indifference the relevant probability is $\frac{2}{3}$.

To avoid these inconsistencies we need a more fine-grained way of understanding the principle of indifference. Huemer observes that there are two ways to interpret the principle of indifference. The first way favors a flat probability distribution over "each possible way of distributing properties to individuals."[73] In Huemer's example about the physical process X, this amounts to assigning each possible sequences of A and B the same probability. In i trails, there will be 2^i possible ways of distributing A and B. The probability of each sequence is $\left(\frac{1}{2}\right)^i$. But, as Huemer observes, this application of the principle of indifference implies **Skepticism**: $P(A_{i+1} \mid U_i) = P(A_{i+1})$. The reason is that each sequence of outcomes is treated as equiprobable. Past success doesn't favor projecting into the future.[74]

Huemer observes, though, that there is an alternative to this "fair coin" interpretation of the principle of indifference. The alternative assigns probabilities to possible *proportions* of As in the sequence. This Laplacean distribution favors a flat distribution over proportions of As in a sequence of i instances of process X. The proportion of As in i trials is either 0/i or 1/i or ...i/i. Consider, for example, two trials of process X. This can result in the following sequences: <A, A>, <A, B>, <B A>, <B, B>. The 'fair coin' interpretation treats each of these sequences as distinct events. Thus the probability of any sequence in two trials of process X is 1/4. But the 'proportion' interpretation does not distinguish the *order* of the events. Thus the middle two sequences are treated as a single event of getting one A. In general, on the 'proportion' interpretation each possibility of i runs of sequence X has a probability of 1/i+1.

Huemer notes that this interpretation of the principle of indifference yields **Inductivism**: $\Pr(A_{i+1} \mid U_i) > \Pr(A_{i+1})$. He explains: "after i cases of

---

[73] Huemer (2009, 351).
[74] As Huemer explains (2009, 351): $\Pr(A_{i+1}) = .5$ since A_{i+1} is one of two possible results. $\Pr(U_i) = \frac{1}{2}^i$, just like the fair coin setup. $\Pr(U_i \& A_{i+1}) = \frac{1}{2}^{i+1}$. So, $\Pr(A_{i+1} \mid U_i) = \frac{\Pr(U_i \& A_{i+1})}{\Pr(U_i)} = \frac{\frac{1}{2}^{i+1}}{\frac{1}{2}^i} = \frac{1}{2}$.

A have been observed, with no Bs, the probability of the next observed case being A as well is given by

$$\Pr(A_{i+1} \mid U_i) = \frac{\Pr(U_i \& A_{i+1})}{\Pr(U_i)} = \frac{\Pr(U_{i+1})}{\Pr(U_i)} = \frac{1/(i+2)}{1/(i+1)} = \frac{i+1}{i+2}.\text{"75}$$

To illustrate the non-skeptical character of the proportion interpretation consider a specific case. Let H_8 be the hypothesis that an A occurs on the eighth run of process X and U_7 the hypothesis that As occurred on the previous seven runs. On the proportion interpretation the $\Pr(U_7) = \frac{1}{8}$ and the $\Pr(H_8 \mid U_7) = \frac{H8 \& U7}{U7} = \frac{U8}{U7} = \frac{1/9}{1/8} = \frac{8}{9}$. In this case the observation of past success significantly confirms that the next case will resemble past cases.

Let us call the first interpretation of the principle of indifference the *sequence* interpretation and the second the *proportion* interpretation. Is there any reason to prefer one interpretation over the other? The two interpretations are not unrelated. For each proportion of As among Bs, there are different sequences. If process X runs three times then there are three different sequences in which one A occurs: ABB, BAB, and BBA. The proportion interpretation is naturally associated with there being an objective chance that process X will produce a specific proportion of As in i runs. The sequence interpretation, however, requires a more fine-grained look at sequences of ordered n-tuples. If process X is carried out n times then there will be 2^n number of ordered n-tuples. A flat probability distribution over these orders pairs yields skepticism because each ordered n-tuple is treated as the same. Thus having a sequence of As up to n, there are two equiprobable ways to extend this sequence at stage $n+1$, viz where the sequence continues to yield A at $n+1$ or the sequence diverges at $n+1$ to throw up ¬A.

However, if we think that there is a physical process that yields a non-epistemic, objective chance that there will be n As among all cases then we shouldn't think that the ordered n-tuple analysis is the right interpretation of the principle of indifference. Rather we should go with the proportion interpretation. This is because the relevant non-epistemic, objective chance is *explanatory* with respect to the proportions but not the sequences. If a process has a propensity to generate As over Bs then we should expect that the proportion of As to Bs will approximate whatever the propensity is. However, this proportion can be realized by many

---

[75] Huemer (2009, 351).

different ordered n-tuples. The propensity of process X explains the proportion without explaining the particular ordered n-tuple. This captures the observation that some particular events—for example, the particular ordered n-tuple—do not have contrastive explanations, for example, an explanation for this ordered n-tuple over another. Even so, our explanation for that event appeals to the explanatory consideration of the propensity of the process to yield a specific result.

This defense of the *proportion* principle of indifference applies only when we think that there is a non-epistemic, objective chance which explains distribution of As over total cases. If we think that there is no relevant objective chance then we should be skeptical that any particular sequence projects in the future. In such a case, we should prefer the *sequence* principle of indifference. Explanatory considerations, thus, figure centrally in a Bayesian explanationism.

7.4 Explaining or representing?

The explanatory Bayesian view I have offered is stronger than Lipton's heuristic view in that explanatory considerations—specifically objective chances—are required for non-skeptical inductive inferences. It is worth recognizing that normally epistemic subjects do not reason directly about probabilities. In this connection explanatory connections enable an epistemic agent to grasp the probabilistic structure of a situation. Timothy McGrew puts this point thus:[76]

> At a carnival poker booth I espy a genial looking fellow willing to play all comers at small stakes. The first hand he deals gives him four aces and a king, the second a royal flush, and indeed he never seems to come up with less than a full house any time the cards are in his hands. Half an hour older and forty dollars wiser, I strongly suspect that I have encountered a card sharp. I have made no attempt to compute the odds against his obtaining those particular hands on chance; I may not even know how to do the relevant calculation. Nor do I have any clear sense of the probability of his getting just those hands given that he is a sharp. For neither P(E|H) nor P(E) am I in a

---

[76] The issue with the two different interpretations goes back (at least) to Carnap under the heading of "Structure descriptions vs State descriptions." For a good discussion of these issues see Fitelson 2005. Carnap proposed, though under different names, the 'proportion' interpretation in response to the observation that the 'sequence' interpretation does not allow for learning from experience.

position to estimate a value within, say, three orders of magnitude; the best I can say in non-comparative terms is that each of them is rather low. But I know past reasonable doubt that the explanatory power of my hypothesis is very great.[77]

McGrew does not explicitly say whether explanatory considerations are required for this inference. On my view, they are required because we need explanatory appeal to objective chances to make sense of this as a rational inference. The fact that explanatory considerations are required provides a partial answer to Okasha's question about whether Bayesianism, at least on the heuristic view, is just representing IBE or explaining the goodness of IBE. He writes:

> As for whether IBE's rational credentials are wholly derivative, the issue here is subtle. IBE belongs to an old tradition of trying to describe the scientific method in informal or semi-formal terms, a tradition that includes Descartes, Newton, Mill, Whewell, Herschel and Popper among its ancestors. Writers in the Bayesian tradition have often tried to produce probabilistic reconstructions of the various methodological strategies that the first tradition has uncovered. A fundamental, and unresolved question is whether the Bayesians are explaining, or just representing these strategies. Those who say "representing" think that the Bayesian apparatus is "just a kind of tally device used to represent a more fundamental sort of reasoning, whose essence does not lie in the assignment of little numbers to propositions in accord with the probability axioms", in the words of Earman (1992, p. 59); those who say "explaining" deny that there is a more fundamental sort of inductive reasoning.[78]

On the view I have defended IBE's rational credentials are not wholly derivative. The goodness of explanatory features is a constraint on proper probability functions. On my view, inductive inferences are justified only if there are explanatory appeals to objective chances in the background. Apart from this, Bayesian amounts to a sophisticated device to track the elimination of counterexamples and subsequent renormalization of one's probability space. One's confidence tracks simply the ratio of favorable cases to total number of cases.

---

[77] McGrew (2003, 560).
[78] Okasha (2000, 706).

Finally, this Bayesian explanationist view gives informative constraints on probability functions. A probability function is epistemically good to the extent that it is simple, explanatory, and conservative. There are many details to this view that need to be worked out more carefully, but, in line with the overall view of this book, there are no foundationally a priori correct ways to develop an account of simplicity, power, conservativeness, or a metric to weigh these various values. We are always and everywhere in the business of seeking better explanations. A probability function should reflect this. Even without an appeal to informative a priori accounts of the virtues, we can still utilize explanatory information to constrain Pr functions. As Huemer observes there are relations of explanatory priority and one's probability function should respect explanatory priority relations.[79] If one parameter depends on another parameter then the principle of indifference should be applied to the latter. If there are multiple fundamental explanatory parameters then probability should be distributed that favors simple, conservative, and powerful hypotheses. To the extent that there are incompatible yet equally virtuous explanatory hypotheses, we should withhold judgment. This fits within the overall explanationist account I've defended: one has a justified belief only if it is part of a good explanatory system which beats relevant competitors.

---

[79] Huemer (2009, 351–357).

Bibliography

Achinstein, P. (2001). *The Book of Evidence*, Oxford University Press.
Alston, W. (1980). Level-confusions in epistemology, *Midwest Studies in Philosophy* 5(1): 135–150.
Alston, W. (1983). What's wrong with immediate knowledge? *Synthese* 55 (73–95).
Alston, W. (1986). Epistemic circularity, *Philosophy and Phenomenological Research* 47: 1–30.
Alston, W. (1993). *The Reliability of Sense Perception*, Cornell University Press.
Baker, A. (2011). Simplicity, in E. N. Zalta (ed.), *The Stanford Encyclopedia of Philosophy*, summer 2011 edn.
Beebe, J. (2008). Bonjour's arguments against skepticism about the a priori, *Philosophical Studies* 137: 243–267.
Beebe, J. (2011). A priori skepticism, *Philosophy and Phenomenological Research* 83(3): 583–602.
Bergmann, M. (2004a). Epistemic circularity: malignant and benign, *Philosophy and Phenomenological Research* 69(3): 709–727.
Bergmann, M. (2004b). What's not wrong with foundationalism, *Philosophy and Phenomenological Research* 68: 161–165.
Bergmann, M. (2006a). Bonjour's dilemma, *Philosophical Studies* 131: 679–693.
Bergmann, M. (2006b). *Justification without Awareness*, Oxford University Press.
Boghossian, P. (2001). Inference and insight, *Philosophy and Phenomenological Research* 63(3): 633–640.
BonJour, L. (1978). Can empirical knowledge have a foundation? *American Philosophical Quarterly* 15(1): 1–13.
BonJour, L. (1985). *The Structure of Empirical Knowledge*, Harvard University Press.
BonJour, L. (1997). Haack on experience and justification, *Synthese* 112: 13–23.
BonJour, L. (1998). *In Defense of Pure Reason*, Cambridge University Press.
BonJour, L. (1999). Foundationalism and the external world, *Philosophical Perspectives* 13: 229–249.
BonJour, L. (2000). Critical study of Evan Fales, A Defense of the Given, *Nous* 43(3): 468–480.
BonJour, L. (2001a). Precis of in defense of pure reason, *Philosophy and Phenomenological Research* 63(3): 625–631.
BonJour, L. (2001b). Replies, *Philosophy and Phenomenological Research* 63(3): 673–698.
BonJour, L. (2001c). Replies to Pollock and Plantinga, in M. R. DePaul (ed.), *Resurrecting Old-Fashion Foundationalism*, Rowman and Littlefield.
BonJour, L. (2001d). Toward a defense of empirical foundationalism, in M. R. DePaul (ed.), *Resurrecting Old-Fashion Foundationalism*, Rowman and Littlefield.
BonJour, L. (2004). C.I. Lewis on the given and its interpretation, *Midwest Studies in Philosophy* 28: 195–208.
BonJour, L. (2006). Replies, *Philosophical Studies* 131: 743–759.

BonJour, L. and Sosa, E. (2003). *Epistemic Justification: Internalism vs. Externalism, Foundations vs. Virtues*, Blackwell.
Brewer, W. and Lambert, B. (2001). The theory-ladenness of observation and the theory-laddenness of the rest of the scientific process, *Philosophy of Science* **68**: S176–S186.
Bromberger, S. (1966). Why-questions, in J. Colodny (ed.), *Mind and Cosmos*, University of Pittsburgh Press.
Carnap, R. (1950). *Logical Foundations of Probability*, University of Chicago Press.
Chalmers, A. (2013). *What Is This Thing Called Science?* 4th edn, Hackett.
Chalmers, D. (2010). *The Character of Consciousness*, Oxford University Press.
Chisholm, R. (1942). The problem of the speckled hen, *Mind* **51**: 368–373.
Chisholm, R. (1977). *The Theory of Knowledge*, 2nd edn, Prentice Hall.
Christensen, D. (1994). Conservatism in epistemology, *Nous* **28**: 69–89.
Christensen, D. (2000). Diachronic coherence versus epistemic impartiality, *The Philosophical Review* **109**: 349–371.
Christensen, D. (2004). *Putting Logic in Its Place*, Oxford University Press.
Clark, M. (1963). Knowledge and grounds: a comment on Mr. Gettier's paper, *Analysis* **24**: 46–48.
Cohen, S. (1984). Justification and truth, *Philosophical Studies* **46**: 279–295.
Conee, E. and Feldman, R. (2004). *Evidentialism: Essays in Epistemology*, Oxford University Press.
Daniels, N. (2008). Reflective equilibrium, *The Stanford Encyclopedia of Philosophy* Fall 2008.
Daniels, N. (ed.) (1996). *Justice and Justification: Reflective Equilibrium in Theory and Practice*, Cambridge University Press.
David, M. (2007). "Truth as the primary epistemic goal" in Matthias Steup and Ernest Sosa (eds), *Contemporary Debates in Epistemology*, Blackwell.
Davidson, D. (1986). *Truth and Interpretation: Perspectives on the Philosophy of Donald Davidson*, Blackwell.
Douven, I. (2013). Inference to the best explanation, dutch books, and inaccuracy minimisation, *Philosophical Quarterly* **63**(252): 428–444.
Dretske, F. (1970). Epistemic operators, *The Journal of Philosophy* **67**: 1007–1023.
Dretske, F. (1977). Laws of nature, *Philosophy of Science* **44**(2): 248–268.
Earman, J. (1992). *Bayes or Bust?* MIT Press.
Feldman, E. C. R. (2008). *Epistemology: New Essays*, Oxford University Press, chapter Evidence.
Feldman, R. and Conee, E. (2003). Evidence in Quentin Smith (ed.), *Epistemology: New Essays*, Oxford University Press.
Field, H. (1996). The a prioricity of logic, *Proceedings of the Aristotelian Society* **96**: 359–379.
Fitelson, B. (2001). A bayesian account of independent evidence with applications, *Philosophy of Science* **68**(3): 123–140.
Fitelson, B. (2005). Inductive logic, in J. Pfeifer and S. Sarkar (eds.), *Philosophy of Science: An Encyclopedia*, Routledge, pp. 384–394.
Fitelson, B. and Hawthorne, J. (2010). The wason task(s) and the paradox of confirmation, *Philosophical Perspectives* **24**: 207–241.
Foley, R. (1983). Epistemic conservatism, *Philosophical Studies* **43**: 165–182.
Friedman, M. (1999). *Reconsidering Logical Positivism*, Cambridge University Press.

Bibliography

Fumerton, R. (1995). *Metaepistemology and Skepticism*, Rowman and Littlefield.
Fumerton, R. (2005). Speckled hens and objects of acquaintance, *Philosophical Perspectives* **19**: 121–138.
Fumerton, R. (2008). Epistemic conservatism: theft or honest toil? in T. S. Gendler and J. Hawthorne (eds), *Oxford Studies in Epistemology*, Vol. 2, Oxford University Press, pp. 63–86.
Fumerton, R. and Foley, R. (1985). Davidson's theism, *Philosophical Studies* **48**: 83–89.
Garrett, D. (1997). *Cognition and Commitment in Hume's Philosophy*, Oxford University Press.
Gendler, T. S. (2001). Empiricism, rationalism, and limits of justification, *Philosophy and Phenomenological Research* **63**: 641–648.
Gertler, B. (2001). Introspecting phenomenal states, *Philosophy and Phenomenological Research* **63**: 305–328.
Gertler, B. (2011). *Self-Knowledge*, Routledge.
Gettier, E. (1963). Is justified true belief knowledge, *Analysis* **23**(6): 121–123.
Goldman, A. (1979a). What is justified belief in G. Pappas (ed.), *Justification and Knowledge*, pp. 1–23.
Goldman, A. (1979b). Varieties of cognitive appraisal, *Nous* **13**: 23–38.
Goldman, A. (1980). The internalist conception of justification, *Midwest Studies in Philosophy* **5**: 27–52.
Goldman, A. (2011). Toward a synthesis of reliabilism and evidentialism? in Trent Dougherty (ed.), *Evidentialism and Its Discontents*, Oxford University Press, pp. 254–280.
Good, I. (1960). The paradox of confirmation, *The British Journal for the Philosophy of Science* **11**(42): 145–149.
Goodman, N. (1952). Sense and certainty, *Philosophical Review* **61**(2): 160–167.
Goodman, N. (1965). *Fact, Fiction, and Forecast*, Bobbs-Merrill.
Goodman, N. (1979). *Ways of Worldmaking*, Harvard University Press.
Grice, H. (2001). Logic and conversation in A.P. Martinich (ed.), *The Philosophy of Language*, Oxford University Press, pp. 165–175.
Haack, S. (1993). *Evidence and Inquiry*. Blackwell.
Harman, G. (1965). Inference to the best explanation, *Philosophical Review* **74** (88–95).
Harman, G. (1973). *Thought*, Princeton.
Harman, G. (1986). *Change in View: Principles of Reasoning*, MIT Press.
Harman, G. (1995). Rationality, in E.E. Smith and D.N. Osherson (eds), *Thinking: Invitation to Cognitive Science*, MIT Press.
Harman, G. (1999). *Reasoning, Meaning, and Mind*, Oxford University Press.
Harman, G. (2001). General foundations versus rational insight, *Philosophy and Phenomenological Research* **63**(3): 657–663.
Harman, G. and Sherman, B. (2004). Knowledge, assumptions, and lotteries, *Philosophical Issues* **14**: 492–500.
Hempel, C. G. (1945). Studies in the logic of confirmation (i.), *Mind* **213**: 1–26.
Hempel, C. G. (1966). *Philosopy of Natural Science*, Prentice-Hall.
Hempel, C. G. (1965). *Aspects of Scientific Explanation and Other Essays in the Philosophy of Science*, The Free Press.
Hempel, C. G. and Oppenheim, P. (1948). Studies in the logic of explanation, *Philosophy of Science* **15**(2): 135–175.

Henderson, L. (forthcoming). Bayesianism and inference to the best explanation, *British Journal for the Philosophy of Science*.

Howard-Snyder, D. (2005). Foundationalism and arbitrariness, *Pacific Philosophical Quarterly* 86: 18–24.

Howard-Snyder, D. and Coffman, E. (2006). Three arguments against foundationalism: arbitrariness, epistemic regress, and existential support, *Canadian Journal of Philosophy* 36: 535–564.

Howson, C. and Urbach, P. (1993). *Scientific Reasoning: The Bayesian Approach*, 2nd edn, Open Court.

Huemer, M. (2001). *Skepticism and the Veil of Perception*, Rowman and Littlefield.

Huemer, M. (2003). Arbitrary foundations? *Philosophical Forum* 34: 141–152.

Huemer, M. (2009). Explanationist aid for the theory of inductive logic, *British Journal for the Philosophy of Science* 60: 345–375.

Huemer, M. (2011). Does probability theory refute coherentism? *Journal of Philosophy* 108: 463–472.

Hume, D. (2007). *An Enquiry Concerning Human Understanding*, Oxford University Press.

Hylton, P. (2007). *Quine*, Routledge.

Jackson, F. (1982). Epiphenomenal qualia, *Philosophical Quarterly* 32: 127–136.

Jenkins, C. (2008). Romeo, René, and the reasons why: what explanation is, *Proceedings of the Aristotelian Society* 58(1): 61–84.

Joyce, J. (1998). A non-pragmatic vindication of probabilism, *Philosophy of Science* 65: 575–603.

Joyce, J. (2009). Accuracy and coherence: prospects for an alethic epistemology of partial belief, in F. Huber and C. Shmidt-Petri (eds), *Degrees of Belief*, Springer, pp. 263–300.

Kahneman, D. Slovic, P. and Tversky, A. (1982). *Judgment under Uncertainty: Heuristics and Biases*, Cambridge University Press.

Kaplan, M. (1996). *Decision Theory as Philosophy*, Cambridge University Press.

Kelly, K. and Glymour, C. (2004). Why probability does not capture the logic of scientific justification, in C. Hitchcock (ed.), *Contemporary Debates in Philosophy of Science*, Blackwell, pp. 94–114.

Klein, P. (1999). Human knowledge and the infinite regress of reasons, *Philosophical Perspectives* 13: 297–325.

Klein, P. (2000). The failures of dogmatism and the new pyrrhonism, *Acta Analytica* 15: 7–24.

Klein, P. (2004). What is wrong with foundationalism is that it cannot solve the epistemic regress problem, *Philosophy and Phenomenological Research* 68: 166–171.

Kvanvig, J. (1989). Conservatism and its virtues, *Synthese* 79: 143–163.

Kvanvig, J. (1995a). Coherentism: misconstrual and misapprehension, *Southwest Philosophy Review* 11: 159–168.

Kvanvig, J. (1995b). Coherentists' distractions, *Philosophical Topics* 23: 257–275.

Kvanvig, J. (2003). *The Value of Knowledge and the Pursuit of Understanding*, Cambridge University Press.

Kvanvig, J. (2008). Coherentist theories of epistemic justification, *The Stanford Encyclopedia of Philosophy*. Fall 2008 Edition.

Kvanvig, J. and Riggs, W. (1992). Can a coherence theory appeal to appearance states? *Philosophical Studies* 67: 197–217.

Laudan, L. (1984). *Science and Values*, Univeristy of California Press.
Lehrer, K. (1974). *Knowledge*, Oxford University Press.
Lehrer, K. (2000). *Theory of Knowledge*, Westview.
Lewis, C. (1946). *An Analysis of Knowledge and Valuations*, Open Court.
Lewis, D. (1982). Logic for equivocators, *Nous* 16(3): 431–441.
Lipton, P. (2004). *Inference to the Best Explanation*, Routledge.
Lipton, P. (2005). Author's response, *Metascience* 14: 331–361.
Lycan, W. (1988). *Judgment and Justification*, Cambridge University Press.
Lycan, W. (1996). Plantinga and coherentisms in Jonathan Kvanvig (ed.), *Warrant in Contemporary Epistemology*, Rowman and Littlefield.
Lycan, W. (2002). Explanation and epistemology in Paul Moser (ed.), *The Oxford Handbook of Epistemology*, Oxford University Press.
Lycan, W. (2012). Explanationist rebuttals (coherentism defended again), *The Southern Journal of Philosophy* 50(1): 5–20.
Mackie, J. (1974). *The Cement of the Universe: A Study of Causation*, Oxford University Press.
Maddy, P. (2007). *Second Philosophy: A Naturalistic Method*, Oxford University Press.
Martin Curd, Cover, J. and Pincock, C. (2013). *Philosophy of Science: The Central Issues*, 2nd edn, Norton.
McCain, K. (2008). The virtues of epistemic conservatism, *Synthese* 164: 185–299.
McCain, K. (2014). *Evidentialism and Epistemic Justification*, Routledge.
McGrath, M. (2007). Memory and epistemic conservatism, *Synthese* 157: 1–24.
McGrew, T. (2003). Confirmation, heuristics, and explanatory reasoning, *British Journal for the Philosophy of Science* 54: 553–567.
Meacham, C. and Weisberg, J. (2011). Representation theorems and the foundations of decision theory, *Australasian Journal of Philosophy* 89(5): 641–663.
Mink, L. (1966). The autonomy of historical understanding, *History and Theory* 5: 24–47.
Nozick, R. (1981). *Philosophical Explanations*, Belknap Press.
Okasha, S. (2000). Van fraassen's critique of inference to the best explanation, *Studies in History and Philosophy of Science* 31(4): 691–700.
Olsson, E. (2005). *Against Coherence: Truth, Probability, and Justification*, Oxford University Press.
Owen, D. (1999). *Hume's Reason*, Oxford University Press.
Plantinga, A. (1993a). *Warrant and Proper Function*, Oxford University Press.
Plantinga, A. (1993b). *Warrant: The Current Debate*, Oxford University Press.
Popper, K. (1959). The propensity interpretation of probability, *British Journal for the Philosophy of Science* 10: 25–42.
Poston, T. (2012a). Basic reasons and first philosophy, *The Southern Journal of Philosophy* 50(1): 75–93.
Poston, T. (2012b). Is there an 'i' in epistemology? *Dialectica* 66(4): 517–541.
Poston, T. (2013a). Bonjour and the myth of the given, *Res Philosophica* 90(2): 185–201.
Poston, T. (2013b). Is a priori justification indispensible? *Episteme* 10(3): 317–331.
Poston, T. (2014). Direct phenomenal beliefs, cognitive significance, and the specious present, *Philosophical Studies* 168: 483–489.

Priest, G. (1985–1986). Contradiction, belief and rationality, *Proceedings of the Aristotelian Society* **86**: 99–116.
Priest, G. (1998). What is so bad about contradictions? *Journal of Philosophy* **95**(8): 410–426.
Quine, W. (1953). Two dogmas of empiricism, in *From a Logical Point of View*, Harvard University Press, Cambridge, MA. pp. 27–46.
Quine, W. (1960). *Word and Object*, MIT Press.
Quine, W. (1990). *In Pursuit of Truth*, Harvard University Press.
Quine, W. and Ullian, J. (1970). *The Web of Belief*, Random House.
Rawls, J. (1999). *A Theory of Justice*, Belknap Press.
Rescher, N. (1973). *The Coherence Theory of Truth*, Oxford University Press.
Roche, W. (2012). Witness agreement and the truth-conduciveness of coherentist justification, *Southern Journal of Philosophy* **50**(1): 151–169.
Roland, J. (2009). On naturalizing the epistemology of mathematics, *Pacific Philosophical Quarterly* **90**: 63–97.
Russell, B. (1948). *Human Knowledge*, Simon and Schuster.
Russell, B. (1993). *Our Knowledge of the External World*, Routledge.
Salmon, W. (1989). *Four Decades of Scientific Explanation*, University of Pittsburgh Press.
Salmon, W. (1998). *Causality and Explanation*, Oxford University Press.
Scheffler, I. (1967). *Science and Subjectivity*, Bobbs-Merrill.
Sellars, W. (1963). Empiricism and the philosophy of mind, in *Science, Perception and Reality*, Routledge & Kegan Paul, pp. 127–196.
Sklar, L. (1975). Methodological conservatism, *The Philosophical Review* **84**: 374–400.
Sosa, E. (1991). *Knowledge in Perspective*, Cambridge University Press.
Sosa, E. (2009). *Apt Belief and Reflective Knowledge, Volume 1: Reflective Knowledge*, Oxford University Press.
Striven, M. (1959). Explanation and prediction in evolutionary theory, *Science* **130**(3374): 477–482.
Thagard, P. (2000). *Coherence in Thought and Action*, MIT Press.
Tucker, C. (ed.) (2013). *Seemings and Justification*, Oxford University Press.
Tversky, A. and Kahneman, D. (1974). Judgment under uncertainty: heuristics and biases, *Science* **185**(4157): 1124–1131.
Tversky, A., Slovic, P. and Kahneman, D. (1982). *Judgment under Uncertainty: Heuristics and Biases*, Cambridge University Press.
Vahid, H. (2004). Varieties of epistemic conservatism, *Synthese* **141**: 97–122.
van Cleve, J. (2011). Can coherence generate warrant ex nihilo? *Philosophy and Phenomenological Research* **82**: 337–380.
van Fraassen, B. C. (1989). *Laws and Symmetry*, Oxford University Press.
Vogel, J. (1990). Cartesian skepticism and inference to the best explanation, *The Journal of Philosophy* **87**(11): 658–666.
Vogel, J. (1992). Sklar on methodological conservatism, *Philosophy and Phenomenological Research* **52**: 125–131.
von Mises, R. (1957). *Probability, Statistics, and Truth*, Allen.
Weisberg, J. (2009). Locating IBE in the bayesian framework, *Synthese* **167**: 125–143.
Wheeler, G. (2012). Explaining the limits of Olsson's impossibility results, *The Southern Journal of Philosophy* **50**(1): 136–150.

White, R. (2007). Epistemic subjectivism, *Episteme* **4**: 115–129.
Williamson, T. (2000). *Knowledge and its limits*, Oxford University Press.
Wittgenstein, L. (1969). *On Certainty*, Harper and Row.
Wright, C. (2011). Frictional coherentism, *Philosophical Studies* **153**: 29–41.

Index

acquaintance theory, 51–2
Alston, William, 2, 5, 7, 22, 65, 111
alternative systems objection, 8, 10–12, 62
analytic statements, 3–4
animal knowledge, 76
anti-coherence objection, 139–45
anti-conservative probability argument, 20–7
anti-explanationists, 104–6
anti-infinitism, 48
appearances, 57–8, 76, 106, 113, 115, 120–1
a priori
  analysis, 83
  basic *a priori* beliefs, 135
  justification, 15, 86–7, 130–1, 141, 145
  knowledge, 15, 139
  truths, 133–6
arbitrariness, 13, 46–8, 56–8
argumentation, 13
Aristotle, 1, 82–3, 103, 147–8
arithmetic inference, 107–8
Armstrong, D.M., 5
assertions, warranted, 28–30
assumptions, 22, 132, 151
asymmetry, prediction-explanation, 103–6
autobiographical epistemology, 30–4
awareness, 117, 119, 145–8

background beliefs, 16, 18, 41, 45
background conditions, 61
background knowledge, 150–1
basic *a priori* beliefs, 135
basic reasons
  dilemma, 13, 45–9
  nature of, 49–52
Bayesianism, 7, 15–16, 36, 149–81
  arguments for, 154–61
  Bayesian explanationism, 174–9

deductivism and, 166–7
examples of Bayesian unification, 161–6
explanatory, 150
heuristic view, 167–73, 179–80
inference to the best explanation (IBE) and, 167–73
introduction to, 151–3
Bayes's theorem, 151–3, 161–2, 169, 171, 174
beliefs, 5
  about past, 131
  background, 16, 18, 41, 45
  content of, 4
  de se, 11–12
  empirical, 111–13
  false, 20
  higher-order, 105
  immanent, 131, 133
  justification of, 1–13, 20, 59, 141–2
  justified, 45, 66–7, 140–1
  mere, 21, 23
  non-observational, 132
  observation-transcendent, 131–3
  perceptual, 58–9, 141
  phenomenal, 14–15, 121, 124–7
  a priori, 135
  relation between, 8
  revision of, 2–3, 52–3
  sensory, 62
Bergmann, Michael, 64–8, 119, 140–1
Berker, Selim, 60, 61
bet defectiveness, 155–6
Boghossian, P., 138
BonJour, Laurence, 10, 52
  anti-coherence objection of, 139–45
  anti-foundationalist argument and, 111–12
  basic reasons dilemma and, 48–9
  defense of coherentism by, 5–6
  doctrine of the given and, 49–50
  Doxastic Presumption and, 145

epistemic internalism and, 110
on epistemic justification, 23, 41
indispensibility arguments of, 129–39
on the input objection, 8, 43
internalistic foundationalism and, 110–11
myth of the given and, 14–15, 110–28
new foundationalism of, 115–21
nonconceptualism of, 116–21
observation-transcendent inference and, 131–3
a priori truths and, 133–6
on rational insight, 135–6
rationalist position of, 129–30
on reality, 85
on reasoning, 136–9
Sellarsian dilemma and, 112–21
weak foundationalism and, 62–3
brute force proofs, 78–9

Carnap, R., 3, 7, 26
Carroll paradox, 59
causal theory of explanation, 71–2
causation, 57, 60–1, 75
CF-evidentialism, 93–4, 96–101, 107
Chalmers, Alan, 150
Chalmers, David, 15, 110–11, 121–7
Chisholm, Roderick, 20, 102, 118
Christensen, David, 19, 28, 30–4, 36, 37, 155–9, 169
circularity, 13, 22, 48–9, 56, 58, 64–8, 140–2
claims
justification of, 1–2
a priori, 133–6
Clark, Michael, 72
cognition, 14, 74–6, 132–3
cognitive development, 76
cognitive efficiency, 18
cognitive states, 114
coherence
awareness and, 145–8
circularity and, 140–2
explanatory, 13, 14, 63
objections to, 139–45
presupposition and, 142–5

probablistic measures of, 7
as relation between beliefs, 8
coherence view, 37–8
coherentism
explanatory, 13, 14, 63, 69–109, 129–30, 142
history of, 2–7
neglect of, 1–2
objections to, 8–13
common sense, 16
community relational concept, 122
compatibilism, 15–16, 173
complexity, 85
conditionalization, 153
Conee, Earl, 70, 91–5
confirmation, 150–1, 162–6
confirmational independence, 163
conservatism, 6, 13, 18–44, 62
anti-conservative probability argument and, 20–7
arguments for, 38–44
autobiographical epistemology and, 30–4
benefits of, 18–19
conservative justification and, 28–30
conversion objections, 36–8
counterexamples, 31–2, 37
criticism of, 19–20
extra boost objection, 34–6
perspectival character of justification and, 38–44
conservative justification, 28–30, 35, 94–5
conservativeness, 14
constraint-based compatibilism, 173
contradictions, 143–4
conversation, 28
conversion objections, 13, 36–8
Cooperative Principle, 28–9
correspondence theory of truth, 2
counterbalanced evidence, 21
Cover, J. A., 160
Curd, Martin, 160–1

Davidson, Donald, 8, 10, 20
deductivism, 53–5, 103, 141, 166–7
Descartes, René, 1, 100, 126–7

Index

de se beliefs, 11–12
dialetheism, 143–4
difference measure, 152
direct ampliative inference, 50–2, 58
'distinct existence' argument, 5
diverse evidence, 162–4
D-N model of explanation, 71
downloader case, 32–3
doxastic justification, 95
doxastic presumption, 145
Dretske, Fred, 28–9, 168
Dutch Book arguments, 154–7, 169

easy knowledge, 19
Eddington, Arthur, 161–2
Einstein, Albert, 83, 161–2
elegance, 83
empirical beliefs, 111–13
empirical knowledge, 5–6
empiricism, 3–4, 7, 129
empty symmetrical evidence, 21–3, 26–7, 37, 39, 41, 43, 45, 56, 94
epistemic circularity, 64–8, 140–2
epistemic coherentism, *see* coherentism
epistemic conservatism, *see* conservatism
epistemic improvement, 2–3
epistemic internalism, 110
epistemic justification, 23–4, 27, 41, 80, 86
  doxastic justification, 95
epistemic normativity, 16
epistemic principles, 79–80
epistemic rights, 42
epistemological primitiveness, 79–80
epistemology, 4–6, 13, 26, 72
  autobiographical, 30–4
evidence
  counterbalanced, 21
  diverse, 162–4
  empty symmetrical, 21–3, 26–7, 37, 39, 41, 43, 45, 94
  evaluation of, using Bayes's theorem, 152–3
  forgotten, 97–8
  independent, 163

positive symmetrical evidence, 32, 37, 94
prior probability of the, 151
evidential interpretation of probability, 26–7
evidentialism, 92–101, 107
evil demon problem, 99–100
evolutionary theory, 71
Ex-J, 85–109
  doxastic justification and, 95
  evidentialism and, 92–4
  Ex-J', 89–90
  Ex-J", 90
  mentalism and, 91–2
  propositional justification and, 95
  putative counterexamples, 102–9
  statistical syllogism and, 108–9
  supportive cases, 96–102
experience, 4, 5, 9–10, 40, 93–4, 116–17, 119–21, 147–8
experiential statements, 3, 4
explanandum, 87
explanans, 87
explanation, 14, 16, 69–109
  causal theory of, 71–2
  D-N model of, 71
  historical, 72
  Inductive-Statistical model of, 71
  mathematical, 72, 77–9
  primitiveness of, 73–80
  virtues of, 80–5
explanationism, 15–17, 64, 80, 85–109, 142, 146–8
  Baynesian, 149–81, 150
  noncontradiction and, 140, 144–5
explanatory coherentism, 13, 14, 63, 69–109, 129–30, 142
explanatory considerations, 55, 179–80
explanatory inference, 69
explanatory knowledge, 103–4
explanatory power, 14, 82
explanatory theories, 100–1
explication, 7
externalism, 4–5, 41–2, 67, 101, 145–6
extra boost objection, 13, 34–6

false beliefs, 20
false expectations, 28
falsehoods, 25, 27
false propositions, 24
Feldman, Richard, 70, 91–5, 147
first-order logic, 140
first philosophy, 45, 49–56, 57
Firth, Roderick, 62
Fitelson, Branden, 163, 164, 165, 166, 174
Foley, Richard, 19, 36
forgotten evidence, 19, 97–8
foundationalism, 5–7, 46, 47, 50
 Bergmann on, 64–8
 internalistic, 14–15, 110–11
 new, 115
 regress argument for, 52
 special, 62–3
 theory of inference, 52
 theory of justification, 52
 weak, 62–4
foundations view, 37–8
foundherentism, 63
framework view of reasons, 45, 56–64, 141
Frege, Gottlob, 24
Friedman, Michael, 3
fruitfulness, 81–2
Fumerton, Richard, 55–6, 146

Gaussian proof, 77
general foundationalism, *see* conservatism
Gettier, Edmund, 4–5, 12
Gettier problem, 72–3
given, doctrine of the, 112–15
 apprehension of the given, 113–15, 119
 myth of the given and, 14–15, 110–28
Glymour, Clark, 160
Goldbach's conjecture, 30
Goldman, Alvin, 40, 106–8
Good, I.J., 165
Goodman, Nelson, 6, 26, 53, 62, 130
Grice, H., 28
grue paradox, 174

Harman, Gilbert, 6, 22, 23, 37–8, 62, 69, 77, 79–80, 108, 134
Hawthorne, J., 165, 166
Hempel, C. G., 24–5, 70, 71, 103, 150–1, 162–3, 164–5
higher-order beliefs, 105
hinge propositions, 22
historical explanation, 72
holism, 2, 3, 6, 7
Howson, C., 163
Huemer, Mike, 175–6, 177, 181
Hume, David, 54–5, 104
hypothesis
 confirmation of, 162–6
 explanatory power of, 82
 likelihood of the, 151
 posterior probability of the, 151

IBE, *see* inference to the best explanation (IBE)
idealism, 2
identification problem, 80
immanent beliefs, 131, 133
impossibility result, 7
incompatibility argument, 167, 168–9
independent evidence, 163
indifference, 176–9
indispensibility arguments, 15, 87, 129–39
individual relational concept, 122
induction, 18, 22, 50–1, 54–5, 105, 141, 170, 176–8
inductive inference, 108, 121, 150, 154, 160, 167, 179
Inductive-Statistical model of explanation, 71
inference, 17, 50–8, 69–70, 107–9, 127, 150–1, 179–80
 inductive, 108, 121, 150, 154, 160, 167, 179
 observation-transcendent, 131–3
inference to the best explanation (IBE), 167–73, 180
informational states, 151
informed preference, 159
input objection, 8–10
intellectual skills, 59–60
internalism, 121

internalistic foundationalism, 14–15, 110–11
intrinsic value justification, 84–5
intuition, 19, 61, 136, 137
INUS conditions, 57–8
isolation objection, 8
"I think," 126–7

Jackson, Frank, 122
Jenkins, Carrie, 73
justification
  of beliefs, 1–13, 20, 59, 141–2
  Chisholm's theory of, 102
  coherence view of, 142–5
  conservative, 28–30, 35, 94–5
  epistemic, 23–4, 27, 41, 80, 86
  explanationist theory of, 85–109
  of knowledge, 111–12
  nonconceptualism and, 118–21
  non-experiential, 134
  noninferential, 45, 46, 50, 52, 56, 62–6
  perspectival character of, 38–44
  a priori, 15, 86–7, 130–1, 141, 145
  probability and, 27
  propositional, 85–109, 149
  reliability theory of, 40
justified beliefs, 45, 66–7, 140–1
justified commitments, 13
justified necessary falsehoods, 25, 27

Kahneman, D., 171–2
Kaplan, Mark, 158–9
Kelly, Kevin, 160
Keynesian strategy, 55–6
Klein, Peter, 47
knowledge, 4–5
  animal, 76
  background, 150–1
  cognition and, 74–6
  easy, 19
  empirical, 5–6
  explanatory, 103–4
  Gettier problem and, 72–3
  justification of, 111–12
  nature of, 72
  a priori, 15, 139

propositional, 103–4
quiz-show, 98–9
knowledge-first approaches, 16–17
Kolmogorov axioms, 152, 153, 154, 167
Kvanvig, Jonathan, 19, 57–8

Lehrer, Keith, 6, 58–9, 73, 103–5
Lerher, Keith, 40
Lewis, C.I., 63, 112–15
Lewis, David, 144
Lipton, Peter, 53, 170–3, 174
logic, 140
logical empiricism, 3–4, 7
logical paradoxes, 143–4
Lycan, William, 6, 29, 53–4, 70, 108–9, 146

Mackie, J. L., 57, 60
mathematical explanations, 72
mathematical proofs, 77–9
mathematics, 87, 130
McCaine, Kevin, 89, 91, 95
McGrew, Timothy, 170, 173, 179–80
memorial states, 93
memory, 19, 22, 29, 43, 67, 93, 97–9, 106, 114, 141
mentalism, 91–2, 107
mentalist evidentialism, 16
mental states, 93
mere beliefs, 21, 23
metaphysical analysis, 74–6, 79–80
metaphysical assumptions, 16
mind-body dualism, 2
Mink, Louis, 72
moderate empiricism, 129
modus ponens, 79–80, 131

naturalism, 129, 130
Neurath, Otto, 2–3, 133
new evil demon problem, 99–100
new foundationalism, 115
Newton, Isaac, 83, 161–2, 163
Nicod's condition, 165
no-false lemmas, 72
noncognitive states, 114
nonconceptualism, 116–21

noncontradiction, 140, 142–5
non-experiential justification, 134
noninferential justification, 45, 46, 50, 52, 56, 62–6
non-observational beliefs, 132
non-observational properties, 51
normative theory, 170
Nozick, R., 53

observational beliefs, 132
observational properties, 51
observation-transcendent inference, 131–3
Okasha, S., 170, 180
ontological simplicity, 83
Oppenheim, P., 70, 71

parade argument, 133–6
parsimony, 83
particularism, 19
past, beliefs about, 131
Pastin, Mark, 5, 7
peer case, 33
peer disagreement, 19
perception, 17, 19, 141, 142
perceptual beliefs, 58–9, 141
perceptual states, 93
perspective, 39–44
phenomenal beliefs, 14–15, 121, 124–7
phenomenal concept strategy, 121–7
Pincock, Christopher, 160
Plantinga, Alvin, 8–9, 135, 136, 137
plausiblity, 53, 55, 56, 152
Popper, Karl, 150
positive symmetrical evidence, 32, 37, 94
posterior probability of the hypothesis, 151
pragmatism, 42–3
prediction, 152
prediction-explanation asymmetry, 103–6
predictions, surprising, 161–2
preference consistency, 157–8, 159
premise circularity, 140
preservative memory, 106–7
presupposition, 142–5

Pr-function, 150, 173, 174, 181
Priest, Graham, 143–4
primitive relation, explanation as, 73–80
prior probability, 151
probabilism, 153, 155–9
probability, 23–7, 55, 56, 63, 101, 149, 150, 176–7
  functions, 180–1
  logical interpretation of, 153
  mathematical theory of, 153, 154, 167
  objective approach to, 153
  personalist approach to, 153
  prior, 151
proportion principle, 179
propositional justification, 85–109, 95, 149
propositional knowledge, 103–4
propositions, 49–50, 69–70, 87
  false, 24
proprioceptive awareness, 12
prudential rights, 42, 43
putative *a priori* truths, 133–6
pyramid metaphor, 3

qualitative parsimony, 83
quantitative parsimony, 83
Quine, W.V.O., 3–4, 6, 7, 53, 129, 130
Quinean thesis, 86–7
quiz-show knowledge, 98–9

radical empiricism, 129
radical skepticism, 18, 64, 65
rational insight, 135–8
rationalism, 129–30, 138–9, 141, 142
raven paradox, 164–6
Rawls, John, 53
reality, 85
  vs. appearance, 76, 106
reasoning, 136–9
  circular, 48–9, 56, 58, 64–8, 140–2
  deductive, 141
  explanatory, 172–3, 175
  inductive, 141
reasons, 13
  basic, 49–52
  basic reasons dilemma, 45–9

first philosophy and, 49–56
framework view of, 45, 56–64, 141
perception as source of, 19
reference class problem, 24–5
regress argument, 52, 56–7
reliabilism, 101
representation accuracy, 158
representation theorem, 157–9
Rescher, Nicholas, 62
Riemann hypothesis, 25
Russell, Bertrand, 16, 51, 62

Salmon, Wesley, 71
sanctioning, 155–6
Scheffler, Israel, 62
Schlick, Moritz, 3
scientific investigation, 21–2
"seeing the fit," 120
self-apprehending, 113
self-knowledge, 17
Sellars, Wilfrid, 3, 4, 6, 53, 111, 132–3
Sellarsian dilemma, 14–15, 46–8, 110, 112–21
sense experience, 4
sensory beliefs, 62
simple agent probabilism, 156
simplicity, 14, 82–5
skepticism, 18, 39, 64, 65, 69, 84, 100, 176, 177
Sklar, Lawrence, 19, 27
Socrates, 1
Sosa, Ernest, 10–11, 42, 116
special foundationalism, 62–3
statistical syllogism, 108–9
Striven, Michael, 71
supervenience, 91–2
surprise, 152
surprising predictions, 161–2
symmetrical evidence, 21–3, 26–7, 32, 37, 39, 41, 43, 45, 56, 94

syntactic simplicity, 83
synthetic statements, 3–4

tacking paradox, 87–8
testability, 81
testimony, 17
Thagard, Paul, 7
theoretical statements, 3
theory choice, 80–5
true belief, 4–5
truth, 2
  goal, 13, 20, 34, 41
  a priori, 133–6
  truth connection objection, 8, 10
Tverksy, A., 171–2

unification, Bayesian, 161–6
unification argument, 159–61
Urbach, P., 25, 163

Vahid, Hamid, 19
van Cleve, James, 63
van Fraassen, B. C., 167, 168–9
Vienna Circle, 3
virtue reliabilism, 42
Vogel, Jonathan, 69

warranted assertions, 28–30
weak foundationalism, 62–4
Wiles, Andrew, 30
Williamson, Timothy, 69–70, 72–3
witnesses, 63
Wittgensetin, L., 21–2
Wright, Crispin, 22

Zebra Case, 28–9